Ginseng Tango

Cheryl Pallant

ISBN: 978-1-945917-14-1

Printed in the United States of America

Sections of *Ginseng Tango* have previously been published in *Ducts.org*, *North Dakota Quarterly*, and *Shaman's Drum*

Cover Design: Robert Smith

Also by Cheryl Pallant:
Her Body Listening
Continental Drifts
Morphs
Into Stillness
Uncommon Grammar Cloth
Contact Improvisation: An Introduction to a Vitalizing Dance Form
Declaration of Independence
The Phrase
Poetry by Chocolate
Spontaneities

"Making other books jealous since 2004"

Big Table Publishing Company
Boston, MA
www.bigtablepublishing.com

To all whose lives have been upended by calamity,
know darkness too well, and welcome the arrival of light.

"To be fully alive, fully human, and completely awake is to be continually thrown out of the nest."
— Pema Chödrön

Prologue

I biked to her house. Something was up. She wasn't returning my calls and my husband was increasingly irritated with me, complaining about trivialities like crumbs left on the kitchen counter, a parking spot not taken, a hair in the sink. These signs and a dull ache in my belly pointed to something more than a friendship between them.

She greeted me on her front porch without her usual warm hug. I refused to sit down or accept her offer of a cup of tea. I stood. I wanted answers. Soon enough, she confessed to their affair. I got back on my bike. It was dusk. There were probably cars on the roads, children playing in their yards, a bus stopping at the corner, but my stilled heart muted any nearby sounds. Someone's legs pressed the pedals through the streets. Someone's arms carried her bicycle up the front steps into the house. Someone climbed the stairs to interrupt his reading and ask him the same question: Were they having an affair? He put the book down and offered a denial similar to the one from a few weeks earlier when I asked the same question. No, he said. Only friends. How I exaggerate, am overly sensitive.

That was an end of a marriage. My marriage. He who had been my closest friend for fifteen years closed the door to our affection and to the sun to moon details of two individuals who chose to twine their lives. No more shared meals, walks through the park; no more movies together, concerned phone calls, looking over the shoulder at the other's book, watching the arrival of dusk from the back porch, curling up together in bed. He moved out a few months later, the door shutting to the remnants of a comfortable life. The house filled by a we emptied into a me. The familiar rhythm of the day altered radically.

I lost my husband, but refused to lose my home. With a mortgage and bills for which I was now solely responsible, I had to find a better paying job. Change, I know from my years of Buddhist practice, is inevitable, but some changes deliver a harsher blow and are more unwelcome than others. I had a choice. I could plunge into bitterness or turn my demolished life into an opportunity. I chose the latter and vowed to accept the first job offer that came along. I hadn't anticipated traveling 11,000 miles away from my home in Richmond, Virginia to a university previously unknown to me in a city in S. Korea. Accepting an offer as Visiting Lecturer, I moved to Daegu, S. Korea, a move marking the first time in my life that finances, not my usual motives of love or art guided an important decision.

Though hired to teach English, American culture, and, eventually, dance, I knew much time would be devoted to attempting to fill in huge gaps in my knowledge of this Asian peninsula the size of Indiana. I knew its location on a map, that my television and stereo carried Korean brand names, that American soldiers fought against communism there in the 50's, but that's about as far as my knowledge went. I had no images of its landscape and architecture, no familiarity with its language, people, history, or culture. All of this changed in the year of living in an apartment nestled against a mountain near the Nakdong River.

I'm Here

Two western colleagues and the department chair pick me up from the airport and drive me to my university apartment. The space, much smaller than my house in Richmond, is three *pyeong* large, a dorm-like 350 or so square feet, with kitchen area, desk, wardrobe, bed, and night stand. The floor is heated Korean style, an *ondol,* something to look forward to when the weather cools or I need to dry clothes. The bathroom converts into a shower with the press of a button, a nozzle hanging from the wall near the sink. Through the sliding glass doors near my bed is a view of an angled, red tiled roof and an easily climbable railing for getting to a large flat roof which I anticipate using to extend my small deck.

To tide me over until I buy food, one of my colleagues gives me a bag of staple items: peanut butter, strawberry jam, white bread, the type that sticks to the palate, oranges, and water, not quite the food I might have chosen, but this traveler, weary from a twenty-nine hour trans-Pacific trip, accepts the supplies with gratitude. My other colleague gives me a bag with a lace rimmed pillow and white blanket with pink bows, also not my style but welcome since I packed no bedding. He turns the faucet handle and flips the gas switch to check the hook up status of the utilities before hearing no dial tone for the phone and no signal for the internet. The department chair, almost my height and a foot shorter than my western colleagues, hovers near the doorway. He eyes me curiously but steps no closer as if not to provoke a wild animal who crawled in through the window or, in my case, off the airplane.

"Call if you need something," I hear as the door closes between us.

3

I place a paper with everyone's cell phone numbers beside the unconnected land line and sprawl out on the bed, arms and legs reaching toward the mattress edge. I'm glad to finally be flat and free of shifting elbows of fellow restless airline passengers.

This is my new space: neutral, empty, unfamiliar. I hesitate to use the word "home" which I associate as crumbled beyond repair. I don't know how long I'll live here nor what my future holds. No t-shirt drapes over a chair. No photo of a friend, brother, or parent eyes me from a shelf. Any sign of warmth or domestic welcome is missing from the blank walls and glass covered modular furniture. Hour upon hour of the deadening whoosh of jet engine noise and wind over the Pacific have dulled, like the reverse developing of light sensitive photographs, details of my American life. Stacks of poetry books, a stuffed mouse cat toy, the key to my dance studio, a Moroccan rug, tree-lined sidewalks, the man who was... all fade into a dimming memory. The airline tickets on my suitcases, waving from a breeze entering the open sliding door, dangle confused from their handles as if saying goodbye, hello, goodbye, hello. I have yet to unzip either suitcase and unpack.

It's late, yet my body hasn't registered crossing several time zones and continues to operate on Eastern Standard Time. I walk to the porch door, then return to my supine position on the bed, unconvinced by the options of eating, sleeping, or taking a walk in the dark. What awaits me beyond my apartment? What plants and people? What meetings and challenges? I try to sleep, my eyes closing, then opening to shadows and outlines of the wardrobe and table. I braid my fingers, a loose clasp, and settle them protectively atop my raw heart.

Classes begin in two days. My body clock must reset quickly to handle wherever it is I've landed. Then there's the small matter of the language, a considerable gap really, given my Korean speaking skills amount to an unfortunate nil, nada, zero.

Shopping Opportunities & Pottery

The problem with using the phrase "*Ol ma yeo*" (How much?) is that the vendor selling the cucumbers, lotus roots, eggplants, and green onions you want to add to your instant noodles will tell you the price in Korean which presumes you know the numbers. I show the woman squatting on the sidewalk surrounded by plastic bins of her garden's bounty that I want one eggplant by raising one finger, what seems to me a universal sign for one. She grabs three. Either she thinks I'm pointing to the clouds or eggplants come in one group of three. Cucumbers follow the same rule. One equals three, enough to last a few weeks.

When I ask "*Ol ma yeo*," she makes a sound that every passerby but me understands. I didn't bring paper for her to write down the cost. I pull out ten thousand *won*, about $8, from my pocket and trust her not to take advantage of my ignorance. She dips a hand into an apron and counts change for me.

Numbers come in two systems, Korean and Chinese. Korean numbers are used with hours, months, age, and general counting while minutes, money, and floor numbers use Chinese. If I'm to buy lotus roots or a juicer and not get ripped off, I better learn the system.

Korean numbers are pronounced as follows:

1	il	20	i ship
2	i (ee)	21	i ship il
3	sam	30	sam ship
4	sa	40	sa ship
5	o	50	o ship
6	yuk	60	yuk ship
7	chil	70	chil ship
8	pal	80	pal ship
9	gu	90	gu ship
10	ship	100	baek
11	ship il	1000	cheon
12	ship i		

I put out my hand to receive change for my vegetables. To be polite and demonstrate respect, when extending my hand, I'm told to place my opposite hand beneath the forearm or elbow as if to support the arm. The woman gives me a small stack of *won* which, counted later in my apartment, comes to *cheon ship o*, 8500 *won*. My purchase amounted to about $1.30. I lean back on my kitchen table chair and prop up my legs in the success of my first excursion.

Other, more accessible shopping opportunities require no foreign language acquisition or money exchange. One exists diagonally across the hall from my apartment door.

Each day a stack of items collects on the window sill and floor near the laundry room. A much larger stack awaits downstairs. The hodgepodge of goods near my room has so far turned up a Jane Austen video, Christmas lights, Australian made men's shorts and shirts, oven mitt (grabbed), small unopened packets of gourmet coffee (grabbed, tasted, poured down the drain), exercise equipment (place feet on pads for going up and down and side to side), computer discs, and a Hello Kitty pillow. So far, every item disappears, claimed by someone in the building.

Downstairs, bins marked metal, bottles, cardboard and paper, plastic, food waste, and trash separate recyclables from rubbish. There my gleaning turns up greater success. In one day, I snatch a Teflon pot, a spaghetti strainer, a rug for outside my bathroom, towels that match the ones bought at Emart, a cotton quilted handbag, and an unopened package of paper towels. I leave the speakers, book shelf, the 64 oz Skippy peanut butter jar, videos in Japanese, a laundry basket, sweat shirts, dish washing soap, hand cream, and pillow, choosing not to rummage farther than a few inches down each overflowing bin. Not everyone has followed the rule of separating the chaff from the wheat. Food-smeared, sun-baked t-shirts foul an otherwise perfectly gleanable item.

When I first moved to Richmond, a trash can outside my apartment regularly turned up clothes, all with price tags securely in place. None of the clothes fit me but a few made handy gifts for friends. I explain the Richmond bounty as a shoplifter or shopaholic aiming for reform. Here at International House, my apartment building, faculty moving out toss what they're unwilling to transport home, and those moving in pitch the unwanted leftovers of previous tenants. My eyes are keen for a moped.

A few days later, my student Minji offers to take me to the grocery store. She waits for me in the hall after the first day of class and flashes a smile. She explains that she knocked on my office door a few times and got no answer. "If you need help," she says, "tell me. Anytime, I ready." Help? Already I've sliced up a small orange sphere, thinking it a type of tomato. I added it to my salad sprinkled with soy sauce, not my preferred dressing of olive oil and balsamic vinegar, items which, if available, I have yet to locate. The tomato greatly disappointed, given its true identity as a persimmon, a sweet untomatoey fruit that never passed my lips before.

I'm grateful for her offer, saving me from worse gustatory mishaps. She parks her subcompact car in the garage for my first jaunt into supermarket haven, and I grab a cart. In gleeful anticipation of filling it with preferably recognizable, at least categorizable food, along with instructions for preparing, I sprint across the garage with the cart, leaping by pressing down on the handle, my feet and the rest of me aloft, sailing above the concrete to the store door.

"Professor!" Minji gasps. She looks around uneasily to see who may have witnessed me. "You behave like child!"

I suppose. Some opportunities, be it lotus roots, an oven mitt, or a car ride, are worth grabbing when presented. I couldn't refuse the enticement of a cart ride that promised kinetic expression and liberation. I welcomed my impromptu burst, in short supply of late, which connects to a reanimating energy.

"Where do you live," I ask, trying to initiate a tame conversation during our ride back to my apartment, our conversation as straightforward and precise as the lines on the road.

"Near, Professor."

"How do you like school?"

"I like, Professor."

The singsong quality of her pronunciation—she says Pra-fes-SAH, accent on the last syllable—and her repeated use of it lead me to wonder if she's trying to repair her broken notion about me and my recent unprofessorial conduct. I didn't yet recognize it as a sign of respect nor did I realize her enthusiasm as a mask to loneliness.

Should I find my finances running short, my western colleagues tell me over dinner a day later about a way to earn extra money: teach English to "privates." Privates are individuals who approach you on the street or in your office and ask you to tutor them in English. It may be a business person, housewife, or student needing additional help. You typically meet them in a public space and talk about, well, anything. They value your ability to converse easily in English and they get practice with a native speaker. Pay for this is anywhere from $40-$60 an hour and often includes a meal. Two of my colleagues admit to doing this. A judge wanting to improve his language skills and on his way to the U.S. arranged to meet regularly with one of them.

There's a caveat to this money-making opportunity: it's illegal. The lawful way to teach English is via *hagwons*, official language schools, which are closely monitored by the government. Privates get paid in cash and avoid paying taxes, a frownable, possibly jailable offense. Additionally, we professors have signed a contract that says we won't simultaneously work elsewhere. My ability to speak English and share it with others is a commodity as valuable as gold or oil, to be watched, traded, and regulated.

"Don't tell us if you start tutoring," says one colleague after closing, then locking his office door. "But if you do and have questions, come see one of us and refer to it as 'taking a pottery class.' That's our code."

One professor made an additional $80k. He bought a pager for clients to buzz him between classes. Eventually he stopped working at the university to take advantage of his more lucrative job.

I imagine the scenario for me:

I exit Emart, Korea's equivalent of Target, but with flat, slanting escalators that magnetically secure your shopping cart in place as you move between floors. My bag contains a new pair of clear plastic bathroom flipflops, AA batteries for the remote of my air conditioner, a half dozen locally grown apples, and a few cups of instant Japanese *ramen*, noodles, with mushrooms.

"American?" says a man walking beside me. He looks at me, then the street to see who may be watching. Like Minji, he wants to convey the appearance of propriety.

"*Megook*," I confirm, wanting to use one of the few Korean words I've learned. American.

"Long here?"

"Not too."

Here's where he motions for me to follow him. We duck into a side alley near a *karaoke* bar and a McDonald's. Children walk hand in hand with their moms. An elderly man smoking a cigarette while bicycling passes us. Our umbrellas open as drizzle turns to rain. Under our nylon tent, the man flashes a stack of *won*.

"I to learn English better. You teach."

The man wears a fitted black suit, a teal blue silk tie, and smells of cologne, something expensively French. He pulls out his business card, circles his mobile number, his wrist brandishing a gold Rolex.

We talk about which coffee shop to meet.

"Java City?" I suggest.

"Too bright."

"Sleepless in Seattle?"

"Office near. Not good."

"Coffee Myong-ga," I offer, though usually avoid patronizing because its tinted windows block sunlight and I prefer the warmth of the sun's rays wherever possible.

The owner knows him. No.

We finally decide upon a Pakistani restaurant. I imagine the place

9

packed with judges for whom the laws concerning private English classes don't apply. Perhaps a curtain of cardamom and other aromatic spices shields them from suspecting eyes. Or maybe Koreans avoid foreign cuisine with its absence on the menu of *kimchee*, fermented cabbage, an expected, beloved national side dish that accompanies every meal.

He glances at his watch, then bows deeply in respect before he scurries across the street to his parked BMW. I shift my hold on the Emart bag, stretch my fingers, and wonder about the shape and color of my first pot. Should I go for a dainty porcelain tea pot or something sturdier to hold dirt and flowers? How big or colorful can it get before the authorities choose to enforce the law? If we get caught yet my teaching is successful, I imagine my client defending me, able to do so in Korean or fluent English. A powerful friend may come in handy for protection against threats worse than clay.

Twigs and Stones

In a corner of the parking lot hedged by a bamboo grove is a path which leads up the mountain behind my apartment building. A sign in Korean says not to enter, but it's apparent from the wear of the path that everyone ignores the request. Down leads past traditional houses with tile roofs, courtyards with rows of leafy vegetables and rank odors that get me plugging my nose with my fingers, an ancestor's temple with no obvious entry, two new housing complexes built in the last year, and once the trail turns concrete and wide enough for cars, the subway entrance. Locked out, the passkey for the front door mistakenly left behind in my room, I opt to go uphill where crowds of butterflies flutter in greeting.

The mountain is full of pines, deciduous shrubs, and lots of barren, jagged rocks for easy footing. I don't know the length of the trail with its many offshoots and stick to the widest one, preferring the well-traveled, clearly marked path to assure my way back. Periodically the foliage is thin enough to reveal a view of Geunho River, an industrial park, and the 3000 ft. Mount Aspen to the south.

Every several yards stands a cylindrical stack of rocks, about six feet high, a few others in recline covered by green tarps. I finger the rocks, well lodged among others more or less the same size. A few jostle loose, but I push them back into place, securing them against wind, a rambunctious dog, or its owner. These are graves of ancestors, sacred sites, my colleague Daniel explains to me later. Self-exiled from his home in Arizona, he regularly shares stories with me about Daegu and his previous job in Thailand while we sip coffee at a nearby cafe. He, like my other western colleagues, are valuable purveyors of local customs, department policies, and university gossip, sometimes inaccurate and frequently laden with negativity. Ex-pats, I'm learning, left their country with a lengthy list of grievances and an unabated habit of finding fault with their new residence. Lots of eye rolls and vitriol when the topic comes up. I stay mum on the ache of my own back story.

A few hikers pass me coming down. "*An yang haseyo*," we say back and forth. Hello.

I venture up to where the trail curves to an adjacent higher mountain. I'm not that ambitious yet. I didn't bring water, sweat drips in abundance from my forehead, and it's unclear how soon I'll get back into my building. On the way down, I pass a few mountain bikers wearing matching black spandex pants, jackets, and helmets.

Daniel tells me a story about a local wanting to promote these trails to tourists. The man trekked up with his camera to capture the tangle of bushes and trees and shot a picture of a mountain biker which he posted on his website. Unfortunately, the picture showed the biker pedaling close, too close, to one of the grave sites. He was identified by police and arrested. Apparently pedaling and stirring the dirt atop your ancestors is an offense.

My department chair hasn't trekked into the hills behind my

11

apartment in years, yet he provides a twist to the story about the origin of the rock mounds. Years ago, a villager married his childhood sweetheart, birthed four children, and sat at her bedside as she took her last breath. Endless tears and the burden of single parenting weighed upon him. Everyday he bent down in the garden, hour after hour turning the soil, pulling up weeds, and plucking the edibles for a meal. Everyday, too, he cooked for his children, bathed them, taught them to carry wood, count, bow to their elders, and perform an endless series of tasks, too much work for this recent widower. Night after night, he collapsed into his bed roll on the *andol*, dreading the morning. Sunrise after sunrise, he dreaded washing his face and facing the chores alone. To build the energy and wherewithal to raise his children himself, he realized he needed to fortify his health. He added yet another task to his regime: every day he climbed the mountain; every day he picked up stones and placed them in a sack; every day he stacked the stones beneath a stand of pines beside the wild azaleas or on a cliff overlooking the village. Over the years, his muscles and lungs strengthened, assuring him longevity enough to provide food and upkeep for his children for as long as necessary.

For my second trek up the mountain, this time to the peak, an hour of sweat, a prize awaits me. At the top with a few weather-beaten gnarled trees hang a few hula hoops on branches. I slide one off, surprisingly heavy, and insert myself within its ring. I hold it to my hips, then release it to the mercy of momentum, my balance shifting from side to side with vigor to keep it in orbit, gravity working an elliptical path, not a slide down my legs. With numerous circumnavigations achieved, I return the hoop to the branch, and accept the next treasure, a 360 degree view of Daegu, medicinal herb capitol of this country, a ginseng mecca, peaks in every direction, evidence that mountains consume seventy percent of this country.

On the way down, I pass many more rock mounds, several benches, and wood platforms for doing pull-ups. I lift one of the green tarps, prepared to encounter bone fragments, a tooth, or some other human remain. No such thing. Instead, several ants scurry away from browned pine needles, twigs, and woody detritus. I tuck the ends of the tarp back beneath the logs and look around for a photographer. I can't be sure of anything in this foreign land. Given that I'm not selling pottery and meeting a powerful ally, I want to minimize any trouble arising from desecrating a burial site.

Later I learn that grounds keepers, in collaboration with hikers, reduce the fire hazard by gathering nature's detritus which they cover in plastic and carry down the mountain. Families do bury their loved ones in the mountains, considered revered sites where spirits of land and sky can roam unencumbered by the demands, wishes, and mishaps of the living. Within each sizeable mound, a coffin stands upright, the deceased facing a cardinal direction to ensure a satisfying afterlife.

A need for refuge motivates my next ascent. I choose one of the narrow trails winding horizontally along the mountain. My quest is for a tree, not just any tree, but one whose arms branch out far enough to hold my aching heart. When I was a child, an old, knotted apple tree in the woods near the house provided grooved bark and protective branches, a salve to my upsets of school and family. Instead of a tree, I find a family of tall cairns, each standing proudly along a steep incline above a stream. At the bottom of a six feet cairn is a large, flat rock, big enough for sitting cross legged and meditating. I brush it clear of pine needles and scoot to one edge, then the other, my contours fitting to those of the rock.

Black squirrels jump from branch to branch, a few scrambling down the trunk to investigate the intruder. I take a deep breath, then another. Air enters my lungs more easily than in my apartment and office. Among these witnesses, I begin to speak. I whisper to the wind, the stones, the trickle of water, all within ear distance of my heart. My speech is slow with lengthy pauses, the rupture in the center of my chest cracking with the pain of its ragged tears. The swell of pain increases as my words fall away. I do nothing to deflect the pain. I do not cover my heart with my hands as is the ritual each night to help me fall asleep.

13

Now, no story, no justification, no avoidance, no blame. Only feel. Only follow the bellows of my chest, the burn, the rise of tears and their descent on my cheeks. Sensation only. This moment. Only this moment.

Eventually, my unrestrained breath softens and relief arrives, the breeze carrying off the pangs of this wave of affliction. I walk back down to my apartment, my steps lighter, butterflies accompanying me the last several yards to the parking lot.

I welcome levity. I'm about to get it. Sort of.

Korean Mores and Less

Up at 4am, I work for about two hours, eat breakfast, and turn on the television in search of a program in English. Yesterday, I watched BTV, Buddhist television. Practitioners performed their daily prostrations, 108 of them, a sacred Buddhist number, prostrations demonstrating reverence for the Three Refuges: Buddha; *dharma*, the Buddha's teachings; and *sangha*, the community of practitioners. Images of people kneeling to the ground, palms up, were interspersed with images of streams, mountains, birds, flowers, and frogs. Voices chanted in Korean while English subtitles paraded across the bottom of the screen: "I repent for polluting the air, land, and water; I repent for feeling jealous; I repent for treating others unkindly; I repent for segregating good from bad; I prostrate to show compassion to the ailing; I prostrate to show compassion to the depressed; I prostrate to show compassion to the poor; I prostrate with gratitude; I take refuge in the Buddha; I take refuge in the dharma; I take refuge in the sangha; I take refuge in the body; I recognize beauty everywhere; I demonstrate fascination with the universe; Nature is my teacher, mountains are my path, stars and their courtyards are my meditation halls...." Eventually, I turned the channel.

A habit of watching television never took hold at home, but in need of distraction, the remote offers an easy out. At this hour, I imagine viewing a children's show complete with smiling adults and preschoolers in ironed, unsoiled clothes learning the alphabet, colors, and shapes. I stop channel surfing at an image of three animal puppets, a ventriloquist dummy, and a man sitting in a Lazy Boy chair. Great, I think.

Muppets or *Sesame Street* this is not. Within minutes, chain smoking Rocko the Dog lets loose a barrage of curses and slang about sex, surpassing the vulgarities I heard in high school or since. Buttons the Bear is making his daily visit to a medical clinic to donate sperm and get it on with the nurse. Dan the Man tries to convince Buttons about the sacredness of sex, but Buttons will have none of that nonsense and convinces the equally foul-mouthed Bill the Dummy to accompany him. On the couch, Dan scoots beside but barely musters courage to kiss his tight-lipped, frigid girlfriend whose desire heats up later in bed when curled against Buttons. Modesty prevents me from revealing further details about what I heard and witnessed, but after much puppetophilia (puppets having sex) and puppetacide (puppets murdering people) that Dan, a social worker, rationalizes, I gulp down the remainder of my coffee wondering about Korean propriety and the influence of Confucian values. The last few countries I traveled in were Muslim. Kissing in public got you arrested. Censors deleted movie scenes of any adult leaning toward another with lips in a lustful quiver.

A few hours later, after learning that I had been watching *Puppets Who Kill*, a Canadian program, I meet my assistant in my office for the first time. Western professors in my department are assigned an assistant to perform requested tasks, anything from making photocopies to helping me get a cell phone, no foreigner allowed one without the cosigning of a Korean citizen. There's no pay for being an assistant but the position shines on a resume. My assistant is Juno, twenty-four, five feet, eleven inches—tall by Korean standards. He speaks English fluently, wears a navy blue Izod shirt and radiant smile, and leans toward me from his chair at my office table.

"When did you arrive? What do you think of Korea?"

15

"Seven, no, nine days ago." I count with my fingers, then tell him about my difficulty in getting a visa.

I learn he spent two years of high school in Australia where he dyed his hair. "Yellow," he explains, "not blonde," to defend himself against racist classmates threatening to beat him up. "Every day, no friends, only some guy telling me to go back home." He promises to protect me from any assaults, though doesn't expect any.

"Would you describe yourself as happy or depressed," he asks with the polish of a professional interviewer.

"What do you think?" I reply coyly.

"Calm."

"Are you married," he asks, the third time in two days a student has raised the question within minutes of meeting. "You're so fit." As if, I reflect, marriage and fitness are incompatible.

"Unmarried." My legal status hasn't progressed to divorce yet, and any mention of my story prompts tears which I prefer to avoid. I haven't learned the Korean way of refusing to answer a question by changing the subject. Besides, marriage puzzles me. I willingly entered into it years ago, believing it a lasting union between two people, a container for love which, when the goings got rough, generated growth, not an easy slip out the back door. I somehow unwittingly lost my Buddhist footing, forgetting its First Noble Truth that refers to the impermanence of everything, and slipped into believing the fairytale of love everlasting, the embers warm, the horse, chariot, or electric car nightly delivering you into each other's arms.

"What can I do for you?" he says.

"I don't know. Not yet." I wave my hand around the office. "No computer, no books, no pens or paper, no trash can. Full of emptiness," I say.

"I'll do anything you want. Anything. Think of me as your boyfriend."

My mind switches to Buttons the Bear.

Two of my western colleagues married Korean women. I don't

16

know details of their courtships, but one woman was originally his student. I'm looking for posters to hang on my bare walls, plants for my window sill, a stapler, paper clips, tape for my desk, not a young lover.

That afternoon, flipping through one of the English conversation and vocabulary textbooks, *What You Don't Say*, I pause at Lesson 11 and read: "Say: This is my 'friend.' Do not say: This is my 'lover.'" The author explains the difference between friend and lover. Apparently, Juno hasn't read this chapter. He does, however, have a key to my office, a gesture I hope to not regret later. It's hard to gage trust in situations for which you have little to compare. This much I know: a date with me will not be his first task—nor his second. I am hoping he can assist me at an upcoming meeting I dread.

Sign Where

I sign, therefore I am. I'm about to do so again tomorrow to prove my identity, but don't feel hopeful. I'm returning to the Immigration Office without Juno who couldn't cancel a previous commitment. It's my third visit in three weeks, yet another foray into a bureaucratic maze for which I smell the cheese, or in this case, the *kimchi*, walk mirrored hallways, and never locate the door to the administrator who can end my quest.

When the university was considering whether or not to hire me, they asked for several items: CV, two photos, transcript, passport, criminal record, health statement, and copies of my diploma. Within days, diploma copies were scanned and emailed along with my CV, the transcript, ordered for a fee from a company who sends the record of my education, to arrive soon thereafter. Several days later, I received confirmation for all items except the transcript which would take longer. This transaction occurred in March. Early April, I was offered the position and began packing up my life.

17

In June I received an email requesting I send my transcript. "But I sent it already. Both the company and your university sent me a confirmation," I reminded the department chair. "Yes," he wrote back, "but it needs to be sealed. When I handed it to Mr. Cheong, the seal was broken. I opened it."

Apparently arriving with a seal was not good enough. Like a young boy at Christmas, Mr. Cheong needed to be the one to open the package. Irritated and unable to fathom the logic, I neither wrote back nor ordered another transcript. Eventually, seeing no way around the nonsense, I contacted the transcript company and ordered another copy.

A week or so later, another request, this time for my diploma. Again, I reminded the department chair that I already scanned and emailed it. "Yes," he emails back, "but we need the original and it must contain an apostille from the Korean consulate." An apostille is a raised thick gold seal that proves a document's legitimacy. My diploma measures about 17 x 14, not an easy document to send through the post. Several colleagues with overseas work experience warned me against mailing it; it could easily get lost, and replacing a diploma is difficult. Additionally, I refused to mar my diploma marred with a second stamp. Wasn't the raised one from my college authentication enough?

Apparently not.

More troubles followed. Mr. Cheong consulted the Korean Embassy in Korea who insisted that the Korean Embassy in the States perform the authentication. When I phoned the embassy in Washington, a woman explained that the consulate doesn't authenticate documents. "Not for two years now," she said. I shared this information with the department chair who wrote back insisting that they do. My diploma will not be accepted otherwise.

Several emails later, in pursuit of the cheese, I headed to the Korean Embassy in Washington D.C., a two-hour drive if there's little traffic, as much as four hours if the Beltway clogs. A woman at the embassy repeated the information I received on the phone; they don't authenticate. I handed her my email with the university's request. She glanced at the paper, then gave it back with a slight shrug and no suggestion of help. There is no cheese on the counter, no scent of curd anywhere.

In Kafka's *Castle*, K arrives in town at night weary from a long, cold journey to start a job as a land surveyor. He tries to find a room at an inn, which is fully booked, and is offered a bed of straw. At midnight, a peasant wakens him to explain that the traveler must receive permission from the Castle to reside anywhere in the town. "How do I get permission," asks K.

"From the Castle," the peasant replies, "but it's closed.

"Then how do I get permission," asks K.

The boy then insults K for his impertinence and coarse behavior. "Were you raised by pigs? How dare you!" The Castle's logic and authority, always flawless, should never be questioned. For the rest of the novel, K struggles to reach the Castle and establish his new life, but every step of the way is thwarted, each townsperson leaving the room or crossing the street when the outsider approaches.

It's midnight when I'm awakened by the woman from the Washington embassy. Straw beneath my cheek has left swollen, itchy welts. "But who is in charge?" I say to her, wanting to follow protocol and wishing she had not disturbed my dreams.

"How dare you ask who? Who—or whom—is a question only a Human Resource Director can ask. You have no right. You are vulgar, rude. Did a cow raise you?"

I pursued acquiring an apostille, which I learned can be obtained from a state office in Richmond, four easily traveled miles from my house. There's a catch though. The clerk won't authenticate my documents until my papers are notarized by a bank. The bank clerk explained that since the documents originated in New York, I must go to New York. I leaned over the counter heatedly, my chin jutting out like a blunt weapon. I refused to go to New York. With a few exasperated grumbles, I somehow convinced the state worker to give me the

19

apostille.

There's more. Keimyung asked for a letter from the university where I was last employed. Despite a resume that lists twenty plus years of teaching experience, Keimyung wanted confirmation that I had taught for at least a year. An email or fax won't suffice. It must be sent on letter head stationary with the signature from the department chair and, of course, it must be sealed. The chair wrote me the letter within hours of my request, I placed it an envelope with several other papers, and brought all to the post office. The envelope never reached its destination; I learned much later that it landed on the desk of a Korean professor who reads no English and didn't think to pass it on to someone who does.

I'm asked a third time for my transcript because, yet again, another eager soul has opened the Christmas package.

The letter from my past employer is very much sought after. When I requested a replacement letter, I learned that the chair left on vacation and won't return to the office for days. Her secretary made a copy of the letter and signed it. So much for legitimacy. Her making a copy and signing it gets replayed several more times like rehearsals for a play which may never get staged. For one reason or another, the letter leaves her desk yet gets destroyed while crossing the Pacific by a rogue wave or a giant jellyfish or a pterodactyl swooping out from behind the cloud of extinction. At this point, I considered enlisting a military dolphin or Green Beret to navigate the obstacles and ensure the documents reach their destination. The secretary wisely manufactures a small stack.

Every day, the pickled scent of *kimchi,* not cheese, wafted into the maze. Every day I turned a corner, only to discover my progress to be illusory and my goal unreachable. To leave the country, I needed a visa. To get a visa, I needed a confirmation number from the embassy in Korea. To get a confirmation number, Washington needed to see my contract from Keimyung University. To receive a contract, I needed to have my visa. I'm scrambling with the chicken coming before the egg or the egg coming first or perhaps it's all tofu. Meanwhile, every night, the bed of straw scratched my cheek and a cow and pig sharing the barn with me mooed and snorted in bestial laughter. Each day I wondered if all roads masquerade as detours and who, if anyone, dwells in the Castle.

"Perhaps you can phone the appropriate person," I suggested to a stranger with an official sounding voice who wakens me.

"Phone? You want me to phone?" he said gruffly. "There are no phones."

I pointed to one on the wall.

"That one is for show," he explained. "It accents the brown weave in the carpet and the antique lamp."

"Then a real one," I pushed, "one that works."

He stepped to the wall, lifted the receiver, and dialed. He then spoke in a hushed voice with someone on the other end before hanging up.

"No one is home," he lied. "Everyone is on vacation, but they want you to get permission immediately."

"How?" I implored.

"How dare you ask how! Only detectives and priests and lawyers can ask that question and only they can answer."

I'll spare you further frustrating particulars of numerous emails, letters, and phone calls, none of which yield progress. A week before classes are to begin, I had no visa, no plane ticket, little reassurance, and renters ready to move into my Richmond house. It was looking more and more likely that my new job may fall through and I needed to consider which friend to move in with.

Then, either the result of a seismic jolt or a dish of excessively spiced *kimchi,* my contract and confirmation number mysteriously appeared in my email. I returned to the embassy in Washington and that night purchased a plane ticket.

For my trip to the immigration office tomorrow, I'm hoping to encounter no obstacles, but my hopefulness seems quaint and foolish. I slip a notebook and my stack of official papers into my bag to prepare.

I've yet to figure out how decisions are made in this country.

Something as seemingly simple as securing a room at my university keeps me wandering around the campus amazed.

The department chair has asked me to dance and read my poetry for an upcoming festival at the university. I agree to the reading, but explain that I need to train a partner for dancing and will need a practice room. "It can't have a concrete floor," I explain. The next day, the chair assigns me a room with, guess, wall to wall concrete.

To get an appropriate room with a soft or sprung floor, I'm given names and numbers of people to call and learn after no one returns my calls that Koreans avoid the highly impolite No by not responding. What's wrong with the syllable? The mouth needn't open very wide and doesn't reveal cavities or uneven dental work, if that's the concern? It's easy to pronounce and never produces spittle.

I employ my dutiful assistant Juno to help get me a room in the gym. He's danced on the concrete floor with me once, felt the soreness in his joints, and is motivated to find a suitable replacement. I'm also hoping his request spoken in Korean will yield better results than me.

"They want to know if it's for official use?" he phones from an administrator's office.

"Of course," I reply, then hang up.

He calls back a few minutes later. "They will only say Yes if we have twenty people using the space." Twenty is the magic number to justify using electricity to power the lights.

Yesterday, an American colleague coached me in how to get anything accomplished here. "Lie if you have to or pretend ignorance. Better to say you're sorry after the fact than wait for permission which may never happen."

"Yes," I say confidently, "we have twenty."

If we multiply by three the six people I've been training, then add two, the sum is twenty. It's also the first word in the title of Jules Verne's classic novel, *Twenty Thousand Leagues Under the Sea*. I am an English teacher plummeting the depths of Korean logic for a narwhal. Yep. Makes sense to me. "Twenty it is," I repeat. I offer to sign the form. I can also find a stamp or apostille if needed.

Eventually, I assure myself, I'll get better at leaping over cultural hurdles. I'm less certain about washing clothes.

Blah Blah Blah

Until recently I interacted with the world through written words. The bold or delicate lettering on cereal boxes, newspaper headlines, cooking instructions, airport kiosks all conveyed vital bits of information. Now words are indecipherable doodles, abstract graffiti, irrefutable signs of alien existence. A brain aneurism, stroke, or other incurable neurological ailment cannot be blamed for my newly acquired illiteracy. One word sums it up for me: Korea. Maybe three words: moving to Korea.

You don't realize the repercussions of losing your ability to read until, like luggage, it gets left on the tarmac or stuck on the conveyor belt between countries. Tasks once simple become bewildering, time intensive enigmas. Take, for instance, washing clothes. Yes, that routine task that commonly takes little thought. Not so here.

None of the five machines in the laundry room in my building look like washers from home. Top doors fold open like accordions. Front door ones look like they swing open but mysteriously remain locked. Red, green, and white buttons in Korean *Hangul* characters mark the top and front of each machine, helpful instruction to the person who can read them. I choose a front loader because the buttons are fewer, my chances of success greater. I feed the machine coins, the door pops open, and I toss in my soiled clothes. Then I start pressing buttons like a jazz musician improvising with single notes and combinations until reaching a welcome groove or, in this case, the pour of water. I'm thrilled when the machine drum fills with water. Unfortunately, after an hour, the hoped-for music turns flat and atonal. The view through the window of my front loader shows my clothes floating in dirty, sudsy water, having missed a few necessary cycles. I press a few more buttons and, luck on my side, more familiar sounds. Another thirty minutes pass, the water drains out, and my clothes are ready to dry.

This is where the going should get easy, but doesn't. The door won't open. I apply various strategies: gentle taps, a vigorous jiggle, a yank. Like the caps of childproof medicine bottles, no press or twist or lift leads me successfully to their contents. I press buttons again and again, hoping that the machine's circuitry will intuit my desire or demonstrate compassion for my perseverance. No luck. My clothes remain locked within, no rinse cycle able to wash off my agitation.

Eventually a Russian tenant who has lived in the building a year explains that a coin is needed to open the door. "Like this," he says, obviously forgetting that coins got me this far. He gallantly inserts his money. Still, the door won't budge. Twenty minutes of failed attempts later, I'm ready to smash the door and go sock-less, or worse. A second, then third tenant assists and somehow the door jerks open. Malfunctioning machines and illiteracy make unsuitable partners.

Other tasks unleash less frustration, but no less confusion. Try removing cash from an ATM with all twelve buttons written in the same unreadable code. Try reading a menu, a utility bill, bus schedules, cooking instructions, department memos. Colleagues' text messages, a primary method of communicating here, look the same as the spam that appears daily on my cell phone, every first and last letter in *Hangul*. All gets indiscriminately deleted now that I've learned the location of the delete button. I do so at the risk of ruining my reputation. Colleagues who may have sent messages about a department meeting or a text book likely assume I'm a snobbish American too proud to reply.

Unable to read and with access to only a few spoken phrases, I point a lot, even though pointing here is considered rude. I'm advised to use several fingers or the entire hand and wave or clamp it open and closed. I'm tempted to use my elbow or foot but don't believe that will go over well.

In the States, I'm an avid reader. Every word dispatches a world of pleasure, insights, information. My eyes can't stay away from billboards, t-shirt slogans, bumper stickers. I long for the days when I can read the covers of books and their contents, when I can distinguish a flyer advertising an event worthy of attendance from a flyer best suited for the trash. Once stepping off the plane onto this Asian peninsula, I became a renunciate cloistered from easy communication, words swirling outside my ears, never fully entering or reaching comprehension. More and more ascetic as I abide, then await the retreat of storm surges at my heart, it is my silent voice I increasingly hear. No need to spell. No need to translate. In another few weeks of isolation, perhaps I'll start hearing the voice of the divine, that is, if I can distinguish it from my own mental spam.

My colleagues, many of them linguists, assure me that learning to read is easy. A few hours is all that's needed to learn the alphabet. So far, my Yankee ingenuity is blocked, my usual curiosity incompatible with the new program, Korean language firewalled behind years of reliance on English. When I look at the letters, my mind refuses to register the new shapes, a bug of denial causing them to disappear. My attention turns to the surrounding colors and pictures before all goes blank and I need to reboot.

The collateral damage, so far not fatal, extends to speaking. Take the difficulty in pronouncing names. Although many sounds in Korean can be found in English, many do not. For instance, Keimyung University, the common spelling, is not pronounced as you might suppose; the k sounds more like a g. When I get in the taxi, I ask the driver to take me to *"Gim-yung-dae,"* the last syllable the word for "university." Korean is full of numerous diphthongs, two letters merging into a sound not found in English.

A typical name exchange sounds more like a volley of sounds, the ball continually flying out of bounds.

Said professor and I meet in the hall, bow. My partner serves his name first.

I attempt the receipt: "Kung Yawn Gone," I mistakenly pronounce. He serves again.

My attempt, "Can Gan Yung." Another ball out of bounds.

Another serve.

"Kgang Yen Kgoon, Kang Yeon Gyeong." My attempts continually never make it over the net.

Several awkward smiles later, I bow and accept defeat. When I see him again a few days later, I've forgotten the order of the sounds since Koreans use surnames first, forenames after, politeness and memory lapses stirring into a potent soup of ineptitude. Used to westerner bungling, it's no wonder so many Koreans adopt English nicknames. Few of us ever trip over Judy, Edmond, William, or Sue.

Koreans' ability to speak English surpasses my paltry attempts at Korean, although there are causalities. My identity has shifted, my name a challenge to pronounce. Korean tongues cannot wrap around the sh and ryl sounds of my name. Students go for generic and safe, Professor, which meets the Confucian requirement of addressing an elder by the title of her position. The adventurous have eroded my name into Pal-la, Plan-ta, Che-real, Say-real, Shay-lull, and my favorite, Say-lo. I've also been called Virginia from a colleague who mistook my home state for who I am.

I've asked the grad students in my Current Affairs class to come up with a Korean name for me. Names represent something about your character, so they asked which trait to emphasize; I left the naming up to them, assuring them it would not affect their grade. I am now Soo Ji, the first syllable meaning wise, the second distinguished.

Daily exposure to a new language corrupts not only the original language, but also other files nearby. The other day in the hallway, four westerners approached me and assumed we spoke a common language. By the way they looked at each door, then at a notebook in hand, I could tell they were lost. "*Là où est professeur* Park," one asks. "*Je ne sais pas*," I answer, stunned at the quickness of my French.

That's part of the problem. Weekly, I encounter students and

26

faculty from Russia, China, Japan, Uzbekistan, Spain, Germany, and elsewhere. These languages accent or mangle my Korean attempts. My mouth goes into international spasms, lips, mouth, and tongue twisting every which way in a battle for clarity. What comes out is Korchinaglish or Spuzbekish. It's no wonder I frequently hike the trail behind my apartment. Rocks, trees, and I speak the same language: quiet. There I needn't worry about my name nor my identity. Only activity: walking, climbing, hula-hooping.

Over the weekend, Juno's parents take me hiking and show me the 1998 Olympic Soccer Stadium, an amazing architectural feat of steel, fiber glass, and concrete that looks like billowing waves, then treat me to dinner afterwards. They pick me up from the subway where Juno explains he wouldn't be joining us. "My mother speaks some English," he offers. "My father has good vocabulary, but he can't make sentences." He assures me that his father is not a spy for North Korea. The South is vigilant to weed these persons from their country to stop any leaks, benign or otherwise. "Not as bad as it was when I was in grade school," he adds, explaining whispers among classmates about uncles with inexplicable, suspect behaviors. The closest I can get to understanding spying is cheating on a test, but no student caught ever got jailed and tortured from stealing answers.

I had hoped Juno would join us. He is my translator, someone with whom talking comes easy, my entry into this mysterious country, a customs agent who waves me on despite knowing about the contraband in my luggage. We laugh at each other's jokes, despite humor being a common casualty in crossing the language divide.

They drop him off at their apartment complex, the door between difficult and easy communication closing. His mom turns to me from the front seat and shows me Juno's replacement, a thick, plastic covered Korean-English dictionary.

"I reach, too," says his mom.

"Reach? Reach for what?"

"No, no," she corrects herself as she blushes and covers her mouth.

27

"Teach. I teach."

"Where do you teach?"

"No, I administrator."

"Oh, you have an important job."

"Not important."

I wonder if she's being modest, I've said the wrong word, or she's misheard me. Maybe she thought I said she does "importing" or that I believed she was "impotent."

I drop the topic and move on.

When I speak in Korean, I omit sentences and phrases. Single words only for this kindergartner. "*Bop*," I say while sitting on the floor at the restaurant, proud to have learned the word for rice. "*Muel*," I add, requesting water from the waitress who has shuffled over to our table. And so the afternoon goes, the three of us stumbling with conversation, the translation burden carried primarily by Juno's parents since their vocabulary is more extensive than mine.

An afternoon of communication fumbles wipe me out. Exhaustion comes readily when attempting to scale the Tower of Babel which offers no easy footing.

When I return home from my outing with Juno's parents, I lie down exhausted on my bed. Barely has my brain recharged when my cell phone rings. I stare at it, the screen illuminated. I do not move. It rings again and my staring continues. Rarely am I sure these days what sounds will emerge from my mouth. Such surprises, uncommon turns of phrase or plays with sound, are welcome in my poetry. I lure them onto my tongue and page, experienced enough with English to know what is said, and comfortable, too, with only a twilight of understanding. But in the land of *Hangul*, I have no lingual dexterity and am unclear when my tongue has hit the mark and when it has crossed into impropriety. Answering the phone, clearly communicating with the caller, my fingers fumbling with the keypad, a scroll up, down, or sideways, is a test for which I constantly receive low grades. I extend my hand, results forthcoming, the unknown not a cosmic mystery, but what fits into the palm of my hand.

My ongoing frustrations, however, are about to lessen.

Cooking for Tango

Moony grabs hold of my arm and adopts me as her mother within a half hour of our meeting." Warm heart," she says of me. Her mom died soon after Moony's birth and would be my age if alive. Moony pulls family, friends, and, in my case, a stranger, around her like a shawl. A Richmond friend of mine met her at a gallery in Daegu while exhibiting his paintings as part of a cultural exchange between countries and he gave me her contact information. She refers to him as Uncle, the appropriate name for a younger woman and older man.

We meet in downtown Daegu, a confusion of streets and alleys that require navigational aid; none come with street signs, and shops luring potential customers with neon, tacky plastic scrolls and tinny music blaring through speakers further crowd out sense of direction. We retreat into an upstairs cafe.

"You come to my wedding," she announces after a few sips of coffee, and stretches her fingers and fashionably manicured nails on the table. Everything about her, her hair perfectly clinched by a bow, the rouge a softer shade than her lipstick, and the sheen of her pink dress, are aimed at attracting a mate. Her eyes light up when she talks about her boyfriend who she met ten days ago and intends to marry. As stand-in mother, I warn her about her hasty decision, but she's convinced. "He's from Daegu, my hometown." Common geography, like blood type, determines compatibility. When we meet a few weeks later, she tells me he's proposed. He wants her at his side at all times. Over the next several weeks, she phones me the updates.

A colleague tells me about a boyfriend's proposal. They enjoyed frequent conversation about art and philosophy and traveled to

29

Germany and France together. "He said that once we married, I could do whatever I want—as long as I cook two meals a day." Preparing two Korean meals demands hours of preparation, buying the ingredients from various food stalls, cutting the vegetables and meat, steaming the rice, creating the broth, cleaning up afterwards. Two meals could easily consume the day. She refused.

Moony wants to cook. "I make good *jin* and *kimchi*." At 28, living in Seoul and working at a translation company, she recently accomplished a significant part of her dream, purchasing a Louis Vuitton purse, which she did during a business trip to Paris. She thrusts the treasure in my hand. I look it over as if inspecting a peach for bruises, pop open the clasp, and peer inside. No one has ever described me as Park Avenue or Paris chic. Fashionista police gave up on this parolee a long time ago. "Nice stitches," I say, hoping my comment pleases. I hand back the ripe fruit of her labor.

Satisfied with my response, she switches topics to another part of her dream. "The right man must be kind, smart, handsome, with good job," she explains. Hers, a grad student, features three of the four, the final one of job, she hopes, forthcoming. "He work for good company soon."

I'm happy with my brown backpack and, for dressier occasions, my black mesh bag. Whenever possible, I ditch both for pockets. She accepts that I may not want a Louis Vuitton bag, the price too high, but she cannot accept that my accessories exclude a husband.

"Why no husband," she asks.

I say nothing, the mere mention of a husband enough to rip off the small scab forming at my heart. I twist in my seat and tense my lips, hoping my tear ducts remain closed, and I can avoid a public display of grief.

"I find you husband: kind, handsome, smart, with good job. Do you want Korean man," she asks, as if deciding upon a restaurant or ordering from the menu.

"*Bulgogi* is okay, but not too spicy," I reply.

"Soup, too?"

"Yes, a sense of humor is important."

"How tall? Does height matter?"

"I would love a side of French fries. With skins if possible."

With weddings on her mind, she invites me to her cousin's ceremony an hour's train ride away, in Busan, the second largest city in the country with a population of four million, Seoul with a populace of eleven million. A few days later, we sit side by side passing one rice field after another while she coaches me on a few phrases, niceties perhaps, but I suspect other motives. "Repeat: *Meo ci seo yo.* You are nice and handsome. *Ye peo yo.* You look very pretty. Say it, say it," she nudges with her elbow as she introduces me to a cousin on the stairwell of the wedding hall, a monstrosity of wedding kitsch, a litter of plastic flower arrangements amid Baroque free-standing hard plastic columns, and upstairs, a gallery of photos with the wedding couple in halo, every limb and chin angle angelically positioned.

"Now," she urges when she introduces me to her father in the lobby outside the main room. He speaks no English, and after repeated stumbles on my name, the r and l an impossibility to pronounce, I introduce myself as Soo Ji, the name given me by my grad students. True to or in opposition of its meaning, the distinguished Soo and wise Ji, I withhold telling him he looks pretty or nice or handsome, but bow instead, a gesture that wins me a spot in the family photo. A professor in a marriage photo portends good luck. Best they don't know about my pending divorce, considered bad luck, or my backpack.

Primarily a western style wedding, the bride in a rented white gown walks behind the groom in a black tux, also rented, up to the dais to a recording of "Here Comes the Bride." A friend of the family, an elderly married professor, speaks at length about the value of children, obedience, respect, and marriage. He stands at a pulpit, his hands reaching emphatically toward the lucky couple. When he announces the couple wed, in unison they bow from the waist to their respective in-laws. The groom then demonstrates the sincerity of his devotion by lowering himself to the floor for several push-ups. Between the raised and lowered elevations, he shouts words of love to the ground and to anyone within hearing range. Immediately after, the family departs to the music of Elton John's "Daniel" to begin the Korean segment of the ceremony.

In an adjacent room, the nervous couple have changed clothes for *jeogori*, traditional yellow brocade silk robes with long billowing sleeves. They sit on the floor at a table to partake in formal introductions and receive good wishes for the happy (read: fertile) continuation of the family (read: patriarchy). The bride's family sits on one side, the groom's on the other, all on silk floor cushions. The rest of the wedding guests walk next door for the buffet.

I'm not eager for a husband again. Mine changed his mind about the importance of vows. He came with a house salad, choice of entre, and dessert, and no amount of flossing or hikes up the mountains rids him from between my teeth. I need a good reason to marry—to remarry—something more than fine stitching and pockets.

Korea is still largely a land of tradition. Men want a woman to cook, clean, and tend to children. The woman is expected to carry out his and his parent's wishes to the neglect of her own. A husband and wife focus on family to the exclusion of much else, the very reason several of my students intend to avoid marriage. Shin Ye wants to focus on career, become her own boss. Sang Hwan refuses to give up playing soccer. Women with jobs outside the home, an increase to their workload, are expected to maintain their duties as wife and mother, frequently without the man's assistance. If marrying me, a Korean man would awake from his dream of domestic happiness in a stupefying tangle with the blanket.

"Wife, where is breakfast?"

"In the kitchen."

"Freshly made?"

"In the refrigerator."

"You prepare it?"

"*We* prepare it. After my yoga and meditation."

"We? What this word mean, we?"

If a man says Cook, I say Read. If he says Jump—or Cook or Clean—I say Walk. Walk away. As an American feminist, I believe in equality and choice. I accept no man, or woman for that matter, telling me what to do, particularly if it is based on an antiquated tradition. I can't subscribe to a belief unless I question, understand, and experience it as beneficial, only then integrating it into my life in a personally meaningful way.

Unless there's music, that is, the right music: flute, guitar, cello, bass, piano, and bandoneon—tango music, and its complement, tango dancing.

Lily, her chosen English name to help us westerners avoid bungling her given name, is a forty-something pharmacist who has invited me to a *milonga*, a tango party at a conference center on Palongsa Mountain. Like many of her generation and younger, there's a growing interest in western practices and traditions. She hopes one day to open a wine bar despite wine, a recent arrival, costing three times the price as in the states. For now, she contents herself with tango.

"Tune, tune," instructs my first partner, a banker and singer in the band. I'm new to tango, my dance background restricted to modernist and improvisational forms, not social dances, and he gladly shows me the steps. He clutches my right hand, places my left hand on his upper arm, and wraps his right hand around my back. Synchronizing motion, tuning, he explains, is paramount, like saying hello with the whole body. We rock from side to side tuning to each other's rhythms. "The man is always in control," he says mid-beat. "The man leads, the woman yields. But the man must give her enough room to do her own thing and dance her pleasure."

He steers me around the floor with his left hand. A shift in pressure pushes me to the left or right, backward or forward, all in time to the music. "Back, back, side," he says a few times before I memorize the instruction.

We dance for three songs, a *tanda*, the expected number for each couple before the man escorts his partner back to her seat. This arrangement is part of tango etiquette as is the necessity for the woman to await the man's invitation onto the dance floor. He leads me to a chair, and thanks me for the dance. There I sit. Alone. Unexpectedly I find myself back in high school, wondering if any guy will cross the room in invitation or accept mine onto the dance floor. Because of the coolness factor, high school boys preferred shoving, grabbing, and running with fellow guys on the football field or basketball court, not joining us girls on the dance floor. Fortunately, the men at this gathering prefer the flesh of a woman to a rubber ball and my seat remains vacant the majority of the evening as numerous partners guide me around the floor.

The tango style here is characterized by a close embrace, small steps, and quick, syncopated footwork. If my partner holds his torso firmly yet flexibly, I can maintain my axis and share his easily while sliding or lifting my feet. Couples typically share an open embrace for the first dance and, depending on comfort, the man may pull the woman in closer so that chest or belly or forehead touch for the second and third dances.

The skill and comfort of my partners vary widely I learn, and when men determine the steps, they also determine the missteps. A few partners interpret our close embrace by locking me in an inflexible grid of their motion with little room to breathe, let alone dance my pleasure. They manipulate my hand and back as if I were an electronic gadget shoved across a desk and dropped into a briefcase. Their hold, I hope, speaks more about their ability and less about their psyche. A few step on my toes, our legs collide, and we race across the room out of synch with the music. "I sorry," I hear. "I sorry," I hear again. Sometimes they smile awkwardly. I await an opportunity to do my own thing, in the least, to breathe expansively, but also to pivot, spin, bend, lunge, movements that reflect my dance training and, likely, my American psyche.

Luckily, I am also asked to dance by relaxed partners who provide greater leeway. They insert a foot between mine, stop my motion, cause

34

a change in direction, invite me to hook my leg around theirs or slide it away. With their firm but allowing embrace, my feet move quickly or indulge in a long, slow stretch to the side or back, or trailing up their leg.

My background in improvisational dance leads me to faux tango, movements with the flair and kick of tango but not its precision. I've seen enough tango performances to know the feel and look of the dance, but a lack of lessons lends itself to my making numerous mistakes. My experience, however, with contact improvisation, a partnered improvised dance with weight sharing and close touching, allows me to easily connect with a partner. I fearlessly turn my body toward my partners' and align our energies and the reach of our flesh. I follow their lead, read the signals of their hands and angle of their torso. Somehow my imitation works, and we generate a rhythmic flow and kinetic connection that transports us around the room carried by a graceful Argentine wind. I welcome this overdue respite from my constant tripping on cultural toes, an ongoing strain from fumbling over my foreignness in the classroom and marketplace.

By evening's end, word has spread that there's a modern dancer in the hall with great balance. I am also the foreigner, the only foreigner, the object of numerous circumspect glances, eyes peeking out over the shoulders of nearby couples.

During a rare moment of me sitting in my chair, Lily comes over. Her face is flush either from dancing or drinking the wine available in an adjacent room. She points to several people seated in front of the window. "That one, he's a pharmacist like me. That one is an architect. That one a doctor of Chinese medicine."

"Which one is the doctor," I ask.

"That one. He's also interested in the connection between dance and spirituality."

"Introduce me," I press. My hope during my stay in this country is to write an article about Buddhism, another about shamanism, and a third about Chinese medicine. The doctor not only embodies two of the three—he's also Buddhist—but my interest in dance and spirituality. It's hard to contain my excitement. "Can you introduce me?"

We walk over to him, my body tingling with anticipation, and he quickly follows through on Lily's introduction by asking me to dance. He puts out his hand, I take it, and by the end of our *tanda*, he says his first word. "Again?"

"Yes," I beam.

We dance not only a second, but also a third *tanda*, his signals easy to read, our transport around the floor like two sailboats on calm seas. As he ushers me back to my chair, he says, "You tangotic."

"I would like to talk with you sometime," I say.

He nods in a way that suggests he doesn't understand much English.

"I visit your office?" I say changing my word choice.

He moves his head side to side, as if saying no, then holds up a finger. He pulls out his wallet and hands me his business card. He understood something in the exchange.

Can, a tango teacher I danced with earlier who has eyed me a few times throughout the evening, approaches Lily and me as we head toward the patio and eventually her car. He speaks to her, runs his fingers through his thick black hair, and she turns to me. "He says he wants you to come to his *milonga* in Daegu.

"Tell him yes." I turn to Can. "Yes!"

When Moony texts me the next day to find out about my weekend and update me on her fiancé, I tell her I've met not one, but many.

Spilling Tea, Kissing Pears

Students tucking their cell phones and i-Pods into their book bag or back pocket watch as I step onto the small wood stage with a white board and podium. I scan the attendance sheet which one of my colleagues has graciously translated from *Hongul* into readable romanized names like Park Min-Ho, Kim Jeong-Yi, Choi Hae-Jin. I count the number of students in seats, eleven more than on the list. I'm warned that students will flock to my class, the new teacher, hoping for an easy grader. It's up to me to turn them away if I want. I do. Thirty-four writing students in one class means daily burrowing my head in papers all sixteen weeks of the semester. I've a second comp class and one in conversation, both full, and a graduate class through the Translation Department with eleven students.

"What did you do over break," I ask. No response. "What did you do over the weekend?" Similar response: nothing. No sound emerges from their seated stationary bodies, all with spiked, banged, or free-flowing straight black hair. They wear a familiar college uniform: long jeans or shorts, sloganed t-shirts, sneakers. Most girls don high heels which miraculously they don't topple out from as they walk to class and climb the San Franciscan steep hills of campus.

Most of these students are majoring in English Language and Literature, well aware that in a culture that values knowledge, has few exportable goods, and is jockeying for a prominent position on the world stage, English is highly marketable. Yet students don't want to embarrass themselves by mispronouncing a word or mangling grammar. I tell them I've been in the country several weeks, know only a few words in Korean, and can't read. Rather than describe myself as illiterate, I choose a gentler term. "I'm a kindergartner." I share my admiration for their ability to write in and speak a foreign language. "How is your day going so far?"

Silence. Their eyes focus on me, yet their mouths remain inactive, the rest of their face equally expressionless.

"Will anyone volunteer to answer my question?" More silence. "Do you know the word 'volunteer?'" I continue. Suddenly they come alive. Several pull out electronic dictionaries the size of a cigarette case and punch keys in a race to the last letter. I learn my first Korean word of the day. "Who will *jee won cha*?" I say. Giggles. Likely I've mispronounced the word or used it improperly. Perhaps I've said, "Who will spill tea?" Or

"Who will kiss a pear?"

I've been teaching long enough in the States, Malaysia, and Hong Kong to know what gets students talking. "Whomever volunteers gets extra credit." Four hands dart up. The conversation begins.

Writing essays is not part of the Korean education. Prior to college, Korean students read, listen, memorize, and take innumerable fill-in-the blank and multiple-choice tests. To my surprise, they have never written an essay. They are not unlike American freshmen in my introductory poetry class who stumble over metaphors and figurative thinking and have never read an entire book of poetry.

I assign them to write two paragraphs intended as a diagnostic about what they enjoy doing and what they'd like to do in their future. All plant a piece of paper and eraser on their desks, verbal apparitions appearing and disappearing from the small electronic screens. Some responses, culled from their writing, follow:

I like caramel popcorn payed by my friend.

I enjoy watching the movies but these days I am so busy and I don't have a girlfriend.

I enjoy bed minton with friends, cousins, or family.

I'm interesting in bawling. A month ago I trained that how to play bawling with closed friend.

During my mother and father's summer vacation, we tripped for three days. The first day we go to Kyeung-Ju.

Sometimes I enjoy meeting my girlfriend. Her job is nurse. Although I met my girlfriend once a week, I am happy to meet her. Actually, we met yesterday. We had a good time. We spend much time drinking a cup of

coffee and talking about what did we do when don't meet each other.

Most of all, I really like sitting around alone. Nobody interfere me at least so I could listen to the music or watch movie loudly.

I want to be a English teacher. I like children and children are very cute. I like my teacher six years ago because he is like to me. He is very kind and cool. After I hope I want to be a teacher like him.

All I want is not huge things. I prefer happiness to disaster. I want job that makes me feel satisfied and give high salary than others. My major is English literature, so I will use my major as my strongest weapons.

If I study other languages, I could be a real global person or person by myself.

When I was young, my dream was be a vampire. I knew be a vampire is impossible. Many years have passed since then but I still sometimes yearn be a vampire. Vampire is monster, I know, but charmly, very powerful, and very fast. It can change the body to mist or bat or wolf. It is immortality thing but lonely. Sometimes I think be a vampire ... um ... I'm a strange man, I think.

In conversation class, we've discuss household chores, vacation spots, and how to meet and maintain a friend, a topic that ignites much chatting. I've introduce the term carbon footprint to my Current Affairs students, mostly grade school teachers and businessmen whose ages range from thirty to early fifties. A sacrificial lamb, I invite students to laugh at me when I mispronounce a word, a daily occurrence. I am, after all, a *waegook* (literally, strange person; also stranger; foreigner), specifically a *megook* (American). Already a few students have dropped by my office to chat about movies, a favorite pastime. A student from Uzbekistan whose family runs a restaurant in town handed me his business card and invited me to dinner.

My telling a stranger in the U.S. that I'm a teacher likely gets met with a flat "Oh." There the conversation ends. If I say I teach English, their faces tense in fear of me unsheathing my red pen and slashing their words. People frequently walk away if I mention I write poetry, perhaps hearing "leprosy." Here teachers are revered. Whereas students bow slightly with one another, the head tilting as if both have driven over a speed bump, greeting a teacher requires greater commitment, the entire torso listing forward.

One day I walk to the fitness center with Hyonok, the modern dance professor who studied with many of my same dance teachers in the States. A student greets her on the sidewalk by coming to a complete stop and bending from the waist at a near perfect ninety-degree angle, testament to his flexibility, but more significantly, the depth of his respect.

Teachers are minor deities, real life super heroes. My super powers include constructing complete, error-free sentences with a dash of the pen, banishing wordy adverbial clauses with a single stroke of the delete key. I wield commas, semi-colons, dashes, and ellipses with verve. I fill pages with spells and save others from mishaps of misspelling and other gaffes.

At the hospital where I receive my physical, a precursor to the government issuing me an immigration card, I unknowingly cash in on my deific powers. "Oh, you're a professor," exclaims the nurse who sits up straighter in her chair. "You teach English!" she announces as if receiving news about winning the lottery. "An American!" She squeals in the elevator where I tower above black haired mortals in need of medical care. She escorts me from one floor to the next, holding doors open, asking if I need a glass of water, all done with the pomp of a proud mother. We pass patients shuffling around in their hospital clothes, a nurse rolling a gurney with a woman in fetal position with several drips attached, and a pajama clad man in a wheelchair bending over an ATM machine to withdraw money, his hands bandaged and neck in a beige neck brace.

Before I leave, she asks for my phone number, I assume for the follow up appointment. "You come with my family on vacation. I have two girls. My husband and I take you wherever you want to go."

She hands me a yellow sheet of paper. It may have information about my follow up appointment or her family's recipe for *ttaro gukbap*, a popular Daegu soup of spiced beef and vegetables. Aside from the date at the top, the note is written in *Hongul*. I place it in a safe space in my bag. Batman has his Robin, Captain America his Bucky, and I, capeless and without an indestructible shield, have Juno to help me translate.

Most outings I go on my own without Juno, without, too, calling him to ask what something means, like the plastic containers of toiletries in the trunk of the car of Soyoung, a Presbyterian minister. She, her friend, Kyung Sook, and I finish our scallion and potato pancake, buck wheat noodles with pickled cucumber slices, and sesame noodles with sea weed and peppers. Soyoung attended the same college as me in New York and lived in Queens for almost two decades. Every time we get together, she shows me pictures on her cell phone of her tiny dog, a Shih-Tzu. "So cute," she says with a lovesick gaze. "I'm thinking of buying him a sweater. What do you think?"

Before the meal, Kyung Sook, who owns a piano store, rested her hand on my arm and asked if I minded sitting on the floor Korean style. "She's very flexible," answered Soyoung. With our plates nearly empty of food, her chop sticks resting on her rice bowl, Kyung Sook leans across the table to further test this *megook*'s comfort. "Do you mind nudity?" With my nod of no, we pay our bill, slip on our shoes, and walk the few blocks to a *jimjilbong*, the public baths.

As is the custom, we lock our shoes in a cubby hole on the ground floor, secure our clothes in another on the third floor, and cross the room naked past a snack bar and glass case of underwear, towels, lotions, and hair accessories for sale before entering the main bath hall. The room consists of a few small baths, a central marble one large enough but not deep enough to do laps, a cold bath, a mineral foot bath, and another sizeable bath sided with jets aimed at different parts of the body. Adjacent rooms include a dry sauna stoked with pine, a steam sauna, an *andol* and outdoor spring-fed bath.

Our first stop, the showers, exposes my unfamiliarity with local tradition. Before entering the hot tub at my gym in the States, I squirt a handful of soap from the wall container, rub it all over, and rinse. Here I do the same, minus the soap not supplied. When I meet up with my new friends, they look at me in full lathered surprise. "Go back. Wash," they say in unison, freely sharing with me their not-so-secret knowledge and intent on making me a convert. Soyoung hands me a wet bar of soap.

We reconvene sud-free at the ledge of one of the smaller but hottest baths, about 129 degrees, and dangle our feet over the edge. Eager for heat, I plunge in up to my neck. "So fast," says Kyung Sook whose slender legs have yet to submerge. My arms swish the water, creating small whirlpools. As long as my knees bend, no part of me except my neck and head are exposed to air. For the next hour, we rotate from tub to tub alongside grandmothers, middle-aged women, and girls soaking and conversing. In every room and bath, a large plasma screen TV hovers overhead, all tuned to the same channel. Men in opulent 16th century Choson Dynasty costumes brandish glistening swords, one stern face staring down another while women and children in billowing clothes look on with clenched hands to lips, their honor and lives at stake. Safely below, we women sweat and dip, hands casually resting at the bath's edge or hidden within the water. We wear folds of flesh fearlessly, modesty of no concern, though my flat, muscled belly prompts envious jests from a few women.

I'm relaxed, happy, delighted to finally bathe after weeks of malfunctioning bathroom plumbing in my apartment which, until

43

repaired, sprays no hot water. We go for what I believe is our final dunk, the hot mineral bath in the open air, and I'm pleased that the strangeness of this custom hasn't rattled me. There we sip sweet fermented rice drink, *shikhye*, the rice husks floating at the bottom of the container like small crustaceans. I'm ready to towel off and go home, unaware that the soaking is preparation only for what follows.

My fellow veteran bathers lead me to the lower ledge outside the large, central bath. There Soyoung hands me a small yellow abrasive cloth. She slips hers on, a mitt that goes as far as her fingers. "Scrub hard," she instructs while watching me. I apply my mitt to my left arm and slide it from upper arm to shoulder. "No, scrub harder," she urges. The cloth scratches my skin, pain competing with pleasure.

"Harder," insists Kyung Sook who, disappointed with my skill, demonstrates the correct technique by pressing down hard on my back as if scouring a pot. "Scrub until you turn pink," she coaches, my conversion incomplete without a sacrifice of skin.

However much I failed at scrubbing, I now excel at pleasing Kyung Sook. "Look! Noodles!" she blurts. Noodles are peels of exfoliated dried skin. Mine are healthy, sesame colored noodles, the result of a spent tan and distressingly brief, cold showers.

Her comment grabs the attention of Soyoung. Both set to work immediately, Kyung Sook tackling my arm while Soyoung scrubs my leg. Layer upon layer of rind, days, perhaps years of cutaneous history, grief and disappointments, fading and deeply etched memories, all happily peel away to reveal tender, hopeful flesh. "Splash, splash," they instruct. "Splash!" I dip a plastic bucket into the bath and pour water over myself. Streams of sudsy water carry my noodles to the drain where they join the wash from fellow bathers alone or paired up, all scrubbing toward exfoliant heaven.

When I was a child, my parents frequently took the family to eat at Chinese restaurants. Before the arrival of the fortune cookie, my forehead and the skin around my eyes tingled and swelled. Unaware that an allergic response to MSG was to blame, I believed my frequency in eating wanton soup and chicken chow mein was reshaping my Caucasian shaped eyes into Asian ones. As I towel dry and claim my clothes from the locker, I marvel at my newly softened skin, glowing and a shade lighter, I'm convinced, than during dinner. As we return to the car, Kyung Sook says, "You come again? I take you."

"Yes. Definitely yes," I say without hesitation, assuring this neophyte to pubic bathing if not a reshaped eyelid, then at least a cleaner presence in Korea.

There's yet another test for me, an outing that challenges expectation. It's the weekend of Chuseok, one of the country's most important holidays. Koreans travel from every part of the country clogging highways to join family and celebrate the eighth lunar month, the harvest moon, to eat vast quantities of food and leave fruit, rice crackers, and other offerings at ancestral graves. I join the exodus but for an alternative activity, to hike in Palgong-sa National Provincial Park with Kyung Sook and her friend Won Hee. Soyoung, busy with church obligations, is unable to join us.

"You climb?" asks Kyung Sook.

"Hike," I reply, believing I'm filling in a gap of her spotty English with a more suitable term as two water bottles slosh in my back pack.

"No jacket? You be cold," says Kyung Sook as she eyes my sleeveless shirt and jeans. Both wear color coordinated, long sleeved zippered nylon pullovers, baseball caps, and gloves and insist I'll need warmer clothes at the peak.

It's muggy, about 90 degrees, typical of a sweltering summer day in Virginia. We've walked only ten minutes, but already, likely a result of my new spicy diet, I'm sweating profusely, my shirt as damp as a contestant's in a wet t-shirt contest. The woods resemble the Shenandoah Forest with ferns, pines, spruce trees, and a stream dodging an avalanche of stilled rocks. Unlike the trails in the Blue Ridge Mountains, however, with natural contours forming the path, here thousands of rocks have been dragged into place by industrious workers to help climbers step up the mountain—and, yes, I've switched my word

45

from "hiking" to "climbing." We ascend, rock after rock, one monotonous step after another, like a step machine at a gym without the whir of the rotating shaft nor the heart rate monitor or calorie counter. No gentle switchbacks to ease the ascent either. I trail behind the women, watch their feet lift and lower onto the rocks, this my vista, Gortex and rubber, nothing bucolic. Climbers have two choices: up the steps or down. We've parked the car at about 2000 ft with the goal of reaching Pong Bong peak at 3800 ft. Somewhere exists a formula to calculate the number of steps; my imprecise calculation leads to me conclude that whatever the figure, it's too much.

At 3000 ft, we rest on a boulder near a stream to sip water and eat energy bars. An animated conversation erupts between Kyung Sook and a man seated on a nearby rock. I ask the man through Kyung Sook who translates about his sizeable, well-stuffed backpack. He answers by removing the contents. On the ground, he spreads a bottle of aspirin, gauze, acupuncture needles, and other bottles and sprays I can't identify, a feast of first aide. His impressive collection fits in with plastic signs that hang from trees every hundred yards or so along the trail of a phone number to call in case of emergency. Koreans, I think, are precautious, an assumption that soon proves itself incorrect.

As a foreigner, it's up to me to learn the language and, so far, my schooling consists of several memorized phrases and a few letters of the alphabet. I've gotten used to listening to my Korean acquaintances on outings without knowing a word of what anyone says. As the minority, I don't feel comfortable continually asking for a translation. Like a latchkey child, I amuse myself with my own thoughts and observations, periodically commenting or raising a question. Kyung Sook breaks my lingual isolation and asks, "What your shoe bottom."

I show her my tread. "Why do you want to know?"

She nor anyone else answers. A few minutes later, I hear, "Let's go," and the man leads us away from the steps to a narrow path. Trustfully or foolishly, I follow.

My feet now meet dirt, uneven in places, an exposed root crossing the path here, a divot formed perhaps by a titanium hiking pole there. My knees are grateful for the change. The repetitive motion of the stairs strained my thigh muscles, my knees threatening to swell and ache. The welcome uneven ground happily awakens previously ignored muscles of toes and calves into action, the entirety of my legs pulsing. Gratitude soon turns to concern when the terrain leads to a rock wall—flat, hard, and stubbornly vertical. With the nimbleness of a monkey, our guide grabs hold of a tree jutting out above him and pulls himself up. "We're following," I ask in disbelief, wanting to hear "No."

Won Hee shoots me a look; obviously, no one communicated with her either. I wedge my fingers into a crevice, another, searching for a depth and width that fits my fingers precisely. With hands secured, my feet similarly graze the rock for their own niche. Once my body is clinging firmly, I grab hold of the tree and yank myself up monkey-see-monkey-do. Once complete, I gasp, relieved by the achievement. I'm assuming the difficulty unique and the trail will return to dirt—or steps—but I'm wrong.

Very wrong.

The wall cascades into another wall, this one higher and surrounded by other walls with jagged tops and unforgiving landings should any of us slip and fall. Kyung Sook clutching a rock a few inches away turns to me and offers the first English she's spoken since our rest. "I regret," she says. "I regret. I make mistake!" Won Hee's eyes wider than usual mirrors my own fear. She attempts the ascent first, screaming while she holds the rock tight and as motionless as a lizard. Our guide has already scaled the rock and throws down a purple nylon band which she grabs. He speaks nonstop. His voice is loud, insistent, lyrical, providing instructions for her ascent.

Now, I say instructions, but I could very well be mistaken, given that he's speaking Korean. Overwhelmed by the beauty of the rocks, he could be reciting poetry or talking about his passion for hip-hop music. When my turn comes, no one translates his barrage of words. "Are you boiling water for rice?" I imagine he yells. "Why boil? Use the pressure

47

cooker! The pressure cooker! Slow, yes, but better! Much better! Fluffier. Doesn't stick to the pan. Never sticks. Plug it in! Plug it in! Do it! Do it now!" Half way up, I look over my shoulder, the ground swirling about 75 rice-free feet below.

In my composition class this past week, we discussed structuring an essay and I introduce students to the words "metaphor," *eun yu*, in referring to the "skeleton," *gol gyuk*, of the composition. All eagerly scribble the new words into their notebooks. As I peer below at the ground, I expect to see not the metaphor, but an actual *gol gyuk*, a few bones worth, evidence of previous failed climbs. I'm wishing someone taught me the words for "treacherous", "life-threatening", "foolhardy", "left leg", "right arm", and "help."

I cannot look down. Nor can I look up. Both threaten balance. Both reveal the spin of the earth increasing in speed. My body locks against the rock, one foot finding a vestige of friction, a hand seeking a ridge big enough to wedge my fingers, a knee pressing into a semblance of security. Sight, progress, and safety get measured in inches.

I succeed only to meet the next challenge. Our guide tosses his back pack through a crevice only several inches wide. It lands somewhere silently, invisibly on the other side. Then he squeezes himself into the crevice, a black hole that moments ago absorbed his backpack. This next dimension swallows his entire body. Following, I crawl through the dark opening, a portal about to absorb my fear and possibly my entire existence. Rock scrapes my shoulders, belly, and thighs. On the other side awaits a rope that I grab with both hands to walk at about a 35 degree angle up another rock.

Our climb continues with one intimate embrace of rock after another. No equipment, only our soft flesh against stone reaching for achievement to replace fear.

When we finally arrive at the peak, cameras come out from zippered pockets to snap pictures of the marble marker inscribed with Dong-Bong peak. We adjust the focus to capture the adjacent mountains and Donghwasa, the 1500-year old Buddhist temple nestled

48

in a valley below. A fellow climber offers his paring knife to Won Hee so we can celebrate by feasting on her apple and he recounts a climb from last year that ended tragically. Like us, he and his friend climbed the cliffs without gear. Unlike us, his friend fell and now only his mouth moves, the rest of his body paralyzed. I welcome taking an alternate and more popular route down—yes, steps—smooth wooden steps. With a railing.

Before driving back to Daegu, we stop at a noodle shop near a field and Won Hee pours a white liquid from a white bottle into a plastic bowl. I hear "milk," pronounced as something like "milkuk," a problem of language wherein my hearing grabs for a familiar word, biased, too, by a desire to quench my thirst. One huge gulp later, I learn about *mak gul li*, a potent rice alcohol drink. Dizzy yet again, though with no chance of harm during the ride back to town as I slide from side to side from the slippery vinyl backseat and constant road curves, I'm aware that families have returned from visiting their ancestors' graves and are sitting around the table for their traditional Chesouk meal.

No offerings need be left for me that night.

In the Ache of the Beholder

Eating soup with dried fish, rice, or *kimchi* for breakfast has not, does not, and likely will never satisfy me in the same way as a bowl of Grapenuts soaked in milk with a cup of dark roasted coffee prepared in a French press. Though elastic by nature, this saclike organ in the center of my torso refuses to abandon its early morning habit of secreting the appropriate digestive juices to break down anything other than Grapenuts and coffee. As much as I want to believe otherwise, my open-mindedness imposes limits when it comes to my stomach, particularly first thing in the morning. In preparation for my move, I packed a few boxes of cereal and bags of coffee to last me several weeks. Dedicated parents and loving friends agreed to send replenishments when my supply dwindled and, thanks to them, my stomach digests with American enzymatic glee.

For the rest of the day's alimentary activity, mind and belly shift standards, open to local culinary offerings. Okay, not entirely open. Out of necessity, the mind employs a few tricks that the belly is slow to catch. One ploy involves not asking about ingredients.

Mind: "Just lift the metal chopsticks. Prod the food until it balances between the two sticks and transport all across the table toward the lips. Drop the food in your mouth, not on the table."

Belly: "I'm hungry."

Fellow diners point to the *yubu guksu*, noodles and fish cakes in a broth: "Do you like it?"

Mind translates the question: "Do you like our country? If you don't, why sit at our table?"

Belly: "I'm hungry. Can I start now?"

The youngest person pours beverages for those older. It's rude to pour a drink for yourself or to take a mouthful before an elder. Additionally, when toasting, the younger person must be sure to keep the elder's glass above his own.

Mind: "Try it. It's good. Very tasty."

Fellow diner, referring to the *sujung jeongul*, a seafood stew: "Is too spicy?"

Belly: "Woah! Quick! Where's the water?"

Mind: "Not at all. It's fine."

Eyes, feet, liver, genitals, intestines, brains, and other body parts make regular chewy appearances in soups, stews, and noodle dishes. Fellow diners pluck such treasures expertly with their chopsticks, allowing a drip over the rice bowl before unloading the morsel into their mouths.

Belly: "What!"

Mind: "Nothing."

Belly: "No, I heard something. Did you say eyes, feet, liver... " At this point, gut instincts alerted, Belly announces its presence by making churning sounds and demanding attention from fellow diners. They look up while chewing and politely refrain from commenting.

Mind: "Just eat. Have the rice. Or lettuce. How about some lettuce?"

Belly: "What's that gob floating in the soup? What is this soup anyway? Is that an eyeball?"

Mind: "It's... a.... pea."

Belly: "You're lying. I've seen no peas like that in the market!"

Mind: "Did I say pea? I meant pepper corn."

Mind wants to excuse itself from the table and lead Belly to the parking lot for a private talk. Mind won't reveal the gob as coagulated cow blood. Last week, Belly ended up visiting the toilet where it stayed for the duration of the meal.

Korean style eating involves shared dishes, several large and small bowls crowding the table. It's ill-mannered to ask others to pass a dish. Instead, everyone reaches across the table, the very motion that prompted slaps and scolds from mothers and fathers across America. With many an eager eater simultaneously plucking food, I'm amazed by the absence of midair collisions, especially from the beer tipsy. Perhaps Korean air traffic controllers not only land planes, but also direct arms crossing the center grill, chopsticks touching down on radishes or noodles, data transmitting through cellphones and other personal electronics.

Some of the more exotic foods I've braved so far are *bondaegi*, boiled silk worm larvae soaked in a light sauce (avoid), lotus stems and flowers (welcome), garlic soaked cuttle fish with beak (try it), a sweet, green pine tree juice (easily likeable), and ginseng alcohol (spirited and healthy). I've eaten much of the local food; however, if unpronounceable or not identified prior to eating, the names of these dishes digest memory into a readily forgotten mash.

My intention is to avoid eating live baby octopus. The thought of tentacles catching onto my teeth or lodging on the sides of my throat as it resists its fate leaves me squeamish. Octopus fascinate me. Master

51

shape shifters, their boneless bodies squeeze into tight openings in coral and rocks. I prefer to view them from a distance and not have them slime their way across my shoe as one did in escape from its pink plastic bin at a fish market. That said, I've already eaten a small coral reef's worth of adult cephalopods, given that they appear in numerous dishes.

It seems that the difference between one restaurant and the next is not what's on the menu but whether the server cuts the meat with the scissors at the table for you or you to do it yourself. Spicy red pepper sauce slathers many foods, making it near impossible to find a pepper sauce free zone. I like the freshness of foods like seaweed, sweet potatoes, lotus, mackerel, however, too much of anything is, well, too much, and Korean food suffers from homogeneity.

I crave variety.

I crave familiar foods.

I crave food from home.

I roam outdoor markets, squeezing between stalls in futile quest for an avocado. I traipse around Emart up an entire isle devoted to seaweed hoping for feta, olives, basil, whole wheat bread, smooth dark chocolate. During lunch, I fantasize about mixed salads, pizza, lasagna, falafel, lentil soup, to fork, finger and spoon their way to my tongue. When I find 100 millimeters of nirvana at a convenience mart at a nearby hospital, shelves of small containers of Hagen Daz in flavors of green tea and Belgium chocolate awaiting my grin, my grab, my gulp, I willingly pay triple the price as home, mouthfuls of cold creaminess sliding down my throat.

I suffer from dairy deprivation, cheese deficiency, lactose longing. I dine with Daria, a grad student from St. Petersburg, Russia whom I met when Juno escorted us both downtown to co-sign for acquiring a cell phone. We dine at restaurants and prepare meals together regularly, and she, too, suffers from the same malady, her eyes darting around food stalls desperate for a taste of home. When we spot an Indian restaurant upon leaving a concert, we sprint across the street, ignoring the light and cross walk. Once seated inside the restaurant, we pass over the curries and biryanis to glory in bowls of thick ambrosial white yoghurt.

52

Food cravings I expected. What I didn't expect was to hunger for beauty. Visual beauty.

Downtown Daegu and Ganchang, the area immediately surrounding campus is—I hesitate to use the word, but in this case, my usual tact must bow to a recognition of reality—Daegu architecture is, well, ugly. One apartment building after another rises unremarkably upward, all white, all rectangular. Nothing to inspire awe. Nothing to ignite marvel. Nothing to lure me inside. Instead I look away; I would cross the street or walk another route if it promised better scenery. Convenience stores, hair salons, restaurants, florists, and other shops, typically three stories high, absent of color and design, squeeze streets with bland nonchalance. They bore the eye. My retina and cornea hunger for activity, enticement, any sort of stimulation. My eyes want pattern, dazzle, hard lines juxtaposed by soft, curves elongated in steel or marble or wood. My eyes want surfaces that offer intensity or simplicity, depth of thought, anything other than dull.

Bland exteriors as well as interior spaces share one feature: utility. Buildings shelter. Rooms accommodate. Plastic pots hold plants. Open spaces store parked cars, discarded boxes, trash bins and their overflow. Visual composition is simplistic, much like my student's writing—to the point and without flourish. Plumbing and electricity may be hooked up, but there's no conduit for aesthetics, no place where design, texture, shape, and color delight the eye.

In the late 60s, President Park Chung Hee intended to raise the citizenry out of poverty. During previous decades, Koreans suffered from staggering poverty, the result of several decades of gruesomely brutal Japanese occupation, military rule, and then the division of the country into two separate countries. Much of the peninsula reached such incredible levels of hunger that people resorted to eating bark, a substance that scrapes its way through the intestinal tract. That someone is so poor, their ass bleeds, is a commonly used saying that refers to this period.

President Park wanted to transform the country, to abandon its agricultural roots for industry. People flocked to the cities for newly created jobs in electronics, steel, iron, cars, textiles, furniture, footwear and other goods intended for export. The president assured everyone a home by razing small, single family traditional dwellings to maximize land use. With an approving nod from the government and blessings from citizens, developers bulldozed small, contoured gardens and meandering stone walls, and tile roofed houses. Stomachs and bank accounts filled while history and beauty got discarded as debris.

I hold Korea's rise from poverty in mind as I walk to the bakery or head to the subway. Nothing in my experience compares to the deprivation of these people. My hunger, at worst, lasts a few hours, likely the result of negligent shopping habits that keep my refrigerator full of condiments but nothing to put them on. Always I have a choice of when, where, and what to eat. Always a well-stocked supermarket or restaurant nearby quells the temporary grumble in my belly.

Despite decades of hardship, Koreans have not invaded their neighbors nor have they sulked off into victimization. Their cities look like many in the U.S. with efficient, multi-lane highways, multiplexes showing first run American movies, well-lit gas stations, fast food chains, ATMs, dry cleaners, and nail salons, a range of services most Americans take for granted. Signs of past hardship are not apparent. The last few decades have created a comfortable life for most, some people outrightly wealthy. Korea's recent story is success. With this in mind, I rise from my chair in applause.

But then I sit down. Walks through town drain me. My feet drag along the pavement, my spirit slouching a few feet behind as if carrying a bag of potatoes. This is not marital grief. This is something else. My eyes seek to alight on form and a richness of color that goes beyond simple repetitive squares of white concrete, to mingle with shape and design. This part of culture shock I didn't expect.

I arrange to meet Daria on campus in the International Lounge. She is more mature than her years and I welcome her company. In the cushioned chairs, faculty watch a large flat screen TV showing CNN. At nearby tables, foreign students sit with Koreans and practice speaking English. We position ourselves near a shelf of travel books and I tell Daria about my longing for beauty.

She stares into my eyes with the intensity of an optometrist. I expect her to say she's located a bend in my cones and rods, but my yoghurt consuming cohort reveals something else. "Me, too," she admits. "St. Petersburg has some of the most beautiful buildings in the world. Every day I used to walk past wonderful buildings and marvel. I was having these thoughts today. I thought I was crazy. Now I don't think so." She pushes her strawberry blond hair behind her ears.

"I'm finding out how important beauty is to me," I say. Not as essential as food and water, beauty sets into motion soulful satisfaction. Beauty is the spark in darkness, the strum of a guitar string, a warm hand in winter, the leaf sailing to the ground, the *mot juste* of the writer that delivers readers home to imagination. Beauty knows the difference between soup simmering on the stove, carrots, celery, onions, and spices carefully blending, from water poured into a Styrofoam cup of ambiguously flavored, industrialized instant noodles heated in the microwave. "It feels like I'm drying up."

Try talking to a Korean about the absence of visual beauty and they look at you as if you're speaking a foreign language. Ask them about beauty in general and they'll lead you to a favorite hangout, the *noribang*.

A *noribang* is a small room for singing, a private *karaoke* lounge. Koreans love to sing and welcome any occasion to do so, in private lounges, in the classroom, on the street. If happy, sing. If sad, sing. If worried about the stock market, sing. If the room next to yours at a conference breaks out into song and interferes with your ability to hear a colleague deliver a paper on Jane Austin and Christianity, no one requests the singing stop.

"Why no sing?" many of my students ask in the hall on my way to the campus coffee shop, their face dimming when I explain memorizing no lyrics.

If it weren't for subway riders' preoccupation with text messaging, gazing endlessly at themselves in hand mirrors, and abiding by the rule to speak quietly, I'm convinced many would break out into song. Korea, the Musical. Subway Riding, the Musical, *Kimchi* Eating, the Musical. Refuse an invitation to a *noribang* or request to belt out a tune on the spot and expect conversation to halt abruptly, your rudeness burned forever in their memory.

After a poetry reading in Seoul, the soon, but not soon enough to be married Moony and her friend insist I go with them to one of their favorite song sanctuaries. We pay our room fee, get drinks, and sit at a small table to thumb through the thick song book. Moony punches in the song numbers for "Killing Me Softly With His Song," grabs the mic, and turns to the four monitors. Duplicate scenes of daisy fields and scrolling lyrics appear on each screen.

Her friend grabs the second mic for a duet. Both assume diva position, heads facing an imagined adoring audience, left arms lifted like a flag waving overhead. Without a need to read the words, they pipe the song, hips in swing. A spare synthetic melody and beat accompanies their voices, sharp, strident sounds that drown them out. Subsequent ones similarly leave much to be desired. Adding to the poor sound, the cheap microphones degrade their voices into mediocrity. Yet none of this spoils Moony or her friend's fun. When Moony selects the next song, she phones her fiancé and serenades him, and he stays on the line until the end, remaining for a second song, her smile constant.

Then the inevitable moment arrives: my turn. I thumb through the odd collection of English artists: Paul Anka, Pink Floyd, Maria Carey, Metallica. I flip pages forward, back, then repeat the process. I finally settle on the Beatles' "Obladi Oblada." I grab the mic and position myself before the monitors. Penguins waddle across a frozen terrain on the monitors, the lyrics popping up soon after. Moony presses a button which turns on a mood-enhancing, multicolored disco ball which floods the room in a swirl of light. I'm smiling. Sorta.

As a teenager in the back seat of my mom's car, I learned how to manipulate her to turn the radio from her abominable Easy Listening station to my teenage-cool Rock and Roll station. Sing in the worst way possible. Stretch a note to sound like a suffering donkey. Twist melody to the point that ears shut. My braying worked. Within seconds, her hand reaches for the dial and I look out the window with adolescent contentment.

In the *noribang*, I work the angle of the mic to amplify my voice. Most of the mic head picks up no sound. After Molly does "her pretty face," I figure out the right angle. I stand for "life goes on" to better use the bellows of my lungs. I sing to the best of my ability. Friends, family, Mom, recent acquaintances, be thankful that exorbitant international cell phone rates prevented me from calling and subjecting you to this donkey's punishing last brays, mediocrity plummeted to an insufferable low.

Moony and her friend do not pull the plug on me. Instead they swoon in delight, clapping and striking the table while urging me to pick another song. I pass over David Bowie, Elton John, REM, Bjork and choose Suzanne Vega's hip-hop version of "Tom's Diner." They sing with me after the man has "poured the coffee" and dance to the repetitive doo-do-doo's.

We leave the *noribang* arm in bacchanal arm, singing our way to the subway, the ninety minutes spent cajoling the mic without injury to my voice or the ears of listeners falling short of appeasing my hunger for beauty. I am, however, temporarily satisfied attending a Puccini opera at the newly opened theater on campus a week later, those voices well worth sharing via cell phone. The clarity and timbre of their vocal range vibrate every part of me. The rapture and boldly resonant melodies during selections from "Madame Butterfly," "La Boheme," and "Tosca" land upon the torn tissue of my heart like hands of a skilled masseuse. For the first time in too long, my heart swells in welcome of the influx of sound and quivers of emotion.

Yet the ache persists. A type of loneliness. It longs for home, to rest in familiarity. Perhaps a single brush stroke of paint will do. Or these words. Or maybe something not quite of this world.

Healers, Shamans, and a Sandwich

I don't count the innumerable people I've met over the years who say they recognize me from a former life. I make no attempt to explain the phenomenon. The doctor of Chinese medicine who I met at the tango party at Palongsa Mountain is the latest. "My soul knows yours," he says.

Dancing with him was easy. Our initial "tuning" which established a nonverbal communication took seconds. We needed only one dance to glide around the floor as if we'd partnered for years. His signals are clear; a light but firm press of his hand or angle of chest cues me to turn one direction or the other. When he tries new moves, extending a leg or arm or introducing a twist, his focus permits me to venture into untried material easily. But there's something else at work here, a strength and fluidity to his subtle energy, his *ki*, the Korean word for *chi* (Chinese), or *prana* (Hindu). He's devoted years to meditation, tai chi, and other body practices. On this level, too, what I call sympathetic resonance, we meet, my years of meditation, yoga, and other somatic practices coming into play.

In the weeks since Lily introduced us, my Korean language skills have improved little. One morning she phones to say, "The doctor invited you to his clinic." As Lily's elder, she refers to him by his position in the same way that my students call me Professor. She rather than he calls because his English skills, he believes, are insufficient for setting up a meeting.

After a twenty-five minute subway ride from campus, I climb the stairs to his clinic and take a seat in the waiting room. Acupuncture clinics are as common here as corner convenience stores in the U.S. In the half block walk from the subway exit to the clinic, I pass two. The waiting room reeks of ginseng, a pungent, unfamiliar earthy smell that causes my nose to twitch. A room of his clinic is devoted to chopping, sifting, boiling, and extracting healing properties from this root and from a cornucopia of barks, leaves, roots, and powders, all stored in jars

58

on two walls-worth of shelves. A major ingredient in many a medicinal cocktail, Korean ginseng is known for its potency in treating ailments like high blood pressure, allergies, diabetes, sexual dysfunction, and fatigue. The root is made into tea, liquor, added to soup, and eaten straight, raw consumption not advisable without medical supervision.

His nurse motions for me to follow her. She takes me to a room with a raised *andol*. After I wait on the floor a few minutes, the doctor comes in and positions himself across from me, crossing his slender legs. He wears a peach mandarin style waist length coat with macrame clasps. He glances at my face but says nothing. Between us, like a still life painting, is a bamboo tray with a small ceramic kettle and two cups. He brings the painting to life by flooding the tray with boiling water from an electric water heater. With great ceremony, he moistens the tea leaves, discards the water, pours more water, soaking the leaves and letting them settle. "Tea thirty years old," he says, his first words as he fills my cup. I sip the few ounces before he refills my emptied cup.

After the fourth refill, I motion that no more is needed. He then invites me into his main office where I take a chair beside a two-foot high plastic spine. He treats patients with a blend of acupuncture and chiropractics, the ancient techniques of eastern medicine incorporating western ones. Like the rest of his clinic, scrolls with Chinese calligraphy cover walls alongside framed images of vertebrae and human bodies mapped for acupuncture points. He takes my hand and presses two fingers to my wrist. "Oh, broken heart. Very deep," he says reading my pulse, not once looking up while he grabs my other hand to confirm the weakness of my lung meridian.

"I treat you. Come," he says as I follow him into the treatment room, a row of several heated beds separated by curtains. The nurse instructs me to replace my shirt and bra with an opened back gown. Once covering me, I lie face down, hear him chant softly, then feel hands palpating my back as if smoothing dough on a baking sheet. "Very curve," the doctor says, discovering my scoliosis.

There are a few soft clangs before I feel slight pinches as needle after needle is inserted along my back and neck, a hot pad placed on my lumbar soon after. Immediately, energy begins to migrate up and down the *ida* and *pingali*, the central channels of *ki*, a relocation of tingles and stirring in my arms, hands, neck, everywhere, my body and psyche in deep rinse. I fall asleep, wake up, fall asleep, and wake up again, the light of consciousness flickering on and off.

When I get off the table twenty or so minutes later, I'm lightheaded, my feet unsteady, unsure of the floor. He takes my pulses again in his office. "Broken heart very deep," he repeats. "I repair." He looks directly into my eyes, a penetrating look that moves beyond superficiality. He knows nothing about my history, the reason for my coming to Korea, and I'm unwilling to share details and risk crying. Besides, I came to him to learn about his medical practice, not for him to learn about me. Then he stuns me by adding, "Curve spine I straighten."

"Straighten! It's possible?" No western doctor ever offered me a chance of removing the curve, only preventing it from getting worse. Is this the eastward pull I felt from the States, my body somehow clued that the idiopathic conditions contributing to my curvature might be alleviated? The pronouncement alone perks my spine, the muscles holding each crooked vertebra in place seemingly relieved at the prospect of the gift of bilateral support.

And so begins regular visits to his clinic for a healing cocktail of neck cracks, needles, and a mouthpiece. The latter is based on Fascia Cranial Structure Technique, a procedure he developed with a colleague that is based on the role of balancing the jaw in order to send unimpeded signals to the hypothalamus. This part of the brain regulates the pituitary and pineal glands which globally impacts the body, improving its overall functionality. Years ago, in treating his son, he discovered the connection between braces, pulled teeth, and a curved spine, all part of my history, too. During treatments over the weeks, we talk—with the assistance of what's become our best friend, Google Translation—about acupuncture, herbs, Zen, dance, creativity, and *ki*. If no other patients await treatment, we chant and meditate together.

I traveled to this peninsula to earn money to assume the loan on my house in the States. Friends urged me to reconsider my decision when the Castle seemed intent on blocking every move with bureaucratic boulders, the university and embassies on both sides of the Pacific uncooperative. Yet I prevailed. At the time, I wasn't sure if stubborn determination or something else behind the scenes pulled me here, something vague, unnameable, insistent. One afternoon, the doctor describes my soul as Korean. "My destiny to return home," he says matter of factly. The home he refers to is not the U.S., but Korea. Me Korean? I glare at him in disbelief. I'm as foreign here as a vegetarian at a pig roast. Could it be residual effects of my consuming MSG as a child?

"You Korea," he says. "We connect. Spirit connect. Connection deep." I look at him stunned as his nurse hands him a note.

But he's not the only person that's said that to me. Comments from encounters with monks, shamans, and madmen, not the usual Walmart shoppers, have contributed to not a string of coincidences, but a rope's worth. Hemp or flax, I don't know, but I'm paying attention. Intuition, usually a whisper, lately is speaking in a loud voice, increasingly with a Korean accent. The more I peer into this society, my own cultural blind spots reveal themselves.

Hyonok, dance professor and colleague from the university, agreed to go with me to Kanghwado Island, about thirty miles northwest of Seoul and a few miles from the DMZ, the demilitarized zone, an area 2.5 miles wide and 151 miles long that separates north from south. No people are allowed entry into this heavily guarded area, the reason why wildlife, including rare plants and animals, flourish. Here, as close as she can get to her birthplace in the North, lives Kim Keum Hwa, the country's most powerful shaman. Hyonok agreed to introduce us, but at the last minute, is requested to attend a meeting on campus, so alone I ride the subway downtown to the hi-speed KTX train to Seoul where I take a taxi, express bus, then another taxi. Seven hours after I've left my apartment, my taxi turns up the steep mountain driveway of Ms. Kim's retreat center, a neo-traditional, two story building constructed of wood, mud, sliding doors, and heated floors. I step out of the vehicle to the sight of a dead pig in an aluminum pot, the sound of drumming, and uncertainty about which wood door to enter.

As my stay in this country lengthens, I've gotten accustomed to strangeness and risk. I enter cars and trains with recent acquaintances to sightsee or attend an event in an unfamiliar city, not sure about what I may find or how to return to my apartment. So far no one has held a knife to my throat or dumped me in a ditch. Violence here is limited to suicide and traffic fatalities, Korea receiving the unwelcome honor of ranking at the top in each of these categories worldwide. Fearfulness and a closed heart are more common in Americans, not these people who readily greet you with an affectionate smile and insist upon sharing a meal and a song. With this in mind, I remove my shoes and add them to the lineup on the steps. A hand opens the door to welcome me in.

Inside is a large hall with more than a dozen people standing in deeply hued silk *hanboks*, traditional dress. Mandarin oranges, apples, bananas, kiwis, and colored rice cakes crowd a counter the length of the room, the wall above covered in water colored renderings of animal guides and *bodhisattvas*, enlightened persons who have postponed their arrival in nirvana to help those still struggling with existence. Small tables contain brass ornaments, bottles of *soju*, a popular distilled rice drink, and other food offerings intended for the spirits summoned for the occasion. A woman escorts me to a side room. She slides open the rice paper paneled door and there in front of a vanity sits Ms. Kim, a slender, robust seventy-nine year old, hair pulled back into a bun, her face etched with a history of a divided country, communications with spirits, and stories that challenge many a western imagination. "*An yang haseyo*,"—hello—I say, then hand her a note from Hyonok that contains my introduction and reason for my visit. She reads the note, looks me over, and invites me to sit with her for lunch.

I follow her back to the hall, now lined with meal tables. She motions for me to sit beside her, across from a smiling elderly man who I learn is her ex-husband from forty years ago.

Ms. Kim is one of about 300,000 *mudangs*, shamans, a third of which live in Seoul. About 90% of *mudangs* are women, male *mudangs* primarily living south on Cheju Island. That the profession is primarily women is no coincidence. The first documented *mudang* dates back to 19 BC when the king of Koguryo, a region that eventually became Korea, requested a healing. Buddhism arrived about 400 years later, then Taoism in the 7th century, both traditions influencing shamanic practitioners. All changed, however, with the arrival of Confucianism in the Yi Dynasty, the Choson Period, in the 13th century, its successors remaining in power for 500 years.

I don't know who is older, Ms. Kim or her ex-husband. As the youngest at the table, I wait for one of them to begin eating. Not only does the eldest take the first mouthful, but that person also sits slightly higher than others at the table. Their head height appears about even and I'm unsure if I should slump to appear shorter.

Confucianism is patrilineal and patrilocal. Not only did men hold government jobs and other positions of authority, but all ritual centered on them. Women were subordinated to serving the needs of the husband, raising the family, and preparing and cleaning up meals. Strict guidelines, many of which still hold today, determined status and behavior based on age, gender, and profession. Shamanism, concerned with nature, less important than culture and ideas, the domain of men, was pushed from the public sphere. Women welcomed the practice with its focus on rituals for restoring the health of family and members in the community as a source of power and expansion of their domestic duties. This role continues to this day, *mudangs* also sought as beneficent presences at ground breakings for new homes and businesses.

Ms. Kim goes first, grabbing a few unroasted nuts prepared in a sauce. My taste buds never developed a liking for them nor have my chopsticks ever managed to capture their slickness. Another woman arrives at our table, bows, then kneels to give us each a cup of water. Before returning to the kitchen, she bows at our table again.

Ms. Kim had no intention of becoming a *mudang*, but destiny had another idea in mind. To escape the fate as a comfort woman to the Japanese who occupied the country, her mother quickly married her at age fourteen to a boy a few years older from a nearby village. She went to live with his family who treated her as a servant, the mother-in-law often beating her as punishment for faulty knitting and cooking skills. After several months, fearing for her life, she ran away back to her family. At the time, her village was plagued by typhoid which she contracted. Highly contagious, she never returned to her in-law's home.

More and more frequently, she exhibited signs of *sinbyong*, the illness associated with the call to a *mudang's* life. She suffered from headaches, uncontrollable screaming bouts, tinnitus, frightening premonitions, and disconcerting visions, like people riding tigers, which she couldn't discern as real or not. Her grandmother, a *mudang* herself, recognized that the gods had chosen her granddaughter to be a *mudang*. She escorted her to *Jung Waltaepo*, an important ceremony marking the first lunar moon of the year. For the first time in years, Ms. Kim's debilitating symptoms disappeared.

The three of us eat in quiet. She grabs chunks of fleshy mackerel, *kimchi*, and strings of dried fish with her chopsticks and pushes her bowl of rice toward Mr. Kim for him to finish.

When her grandmother's health weakened, Ms. Kim apprenticed herself to another *mudang* for the next eight years. It was then, she met her neighbor, a man whose wife of six months suddenly died. The two eventually married and moved south to Incheon when the war broke out. She has been unable to visit her home in the North ever since.

By the 60s, S. Korea was westernizing. The military government prohibited the ancient practice and burned whatever shrines and ritual items they found. Arriving Christian missionaries and Jehovah Witnesses vilified *mudangs* regarded as witches and consorts of the devil.

Ms. Kim was adamant about continuing the practice while her husband, unable to cope with public scorn, pled with her to give up the profession. She refused, which put tremendous pressure on their relationship, and eventually he had an affair which brought about the

64

demise of their marriage. He married this woman but she died after several years. Then his business failed and his children estranged themselves from him. He blames his bad luck on abandoning Ms. Kim and has since returned to receive her forgiveness. I watch him as he lowers his eyes to hers, a surrender of his will to hers.

Cho, a film maker and main drummer for this *kut*, ceremony, squats beside me and invites me upstairs. "I try to be with her as much as possible," says Cho who considers Ms. Kim his spiritual teacher. We come to a sizeable hall with a huge bay window overlooking the surrounding mountains. At the far end of the room is Ms. Kim's private altar with her personal pantheon of helpful spirits, paintings of tigers, rabbits, Buddha, Confucius, Zeus, General MacArthur (here because he helped during the war), and others. Bells, knives, and other ritual trinkets rest on a shelf near three fur coats hanging on the wall.

"Ms. Kim is very powerful," explains Cho. "From an early age, she could balance barefoot and dance on knife blades. Not every *mudang* can do this." He has witnessed her do this many times without losing a drop of blood.

"Oh," I say, as if the feat is relatively normal, an extreme sport like bungee jumping.

"Why do this," I ask, recalling drips of my precious fluid while completing a much easier challenge, cutting cucumbers for a salad.

"Proves her strength to the spirits," he answers. Apparently, vengeful spirits are intimidated by a *mudang* who can enter a trance deep enough to reach benign spirits who spare her from slicing the skin of her feet. Always good to have friends, I think.

We return downstairs, the hall once again turned into a space for ritual. I lean against a wall and watch as woman after woman, all disciples of Ms. Kim, take turns standing and dancing before Cho and four other musicians. The women cry out freely, sometimes mumbling, and turn to the woman sitting quietly beside me. A *mudang* herself, she lost her life purpose on moving to Japan with her husband and requested this *kut*. Ms. Kim tosses a knife to a doorway, the blade's direction determining the day's luck. I can't see if it points to the door or kitchen, but the lack of alarm in the room portends promise. She then cuts the air with a sword, followed by the waving of flags. The eldest woman, perhaps ninety, joins Ms. Kim to spin, then grabs a pitch fork. An explosion of sound, shrill horns, clanging cymbals, and an insistent drum beat accompany their moves and shoves my usual calm outside the hall. My ears, seemingly confused by the clamor, shut out the noise, let it in, shut it out, let it in, dizzying my thoughts and increasing my heart beat.

Throughout the ceremony, various people pass through the hall as if what's taking place is nothing more than folding laundry. At one point, the flutist takes a break to thumb through a store catalog. A woman in the corner files her nails. Ancient and modern Korea collide with exquisite invisible circuitry when a friend from Daegu texts me: "What are you doing?" I don't hesitate to type: "Watching a shaman stab a pig," then hit Send.

After the initial stab, the elder *mudang* stands the pitch fork on end. Fellow *mudangs* skewer hind quarters, forelegs, chest and other parts of the pig's carcass on the teeth of the fork, the head mounted last, the snout open and stuffed with 10,000 *won* bills.

There are a few breaks during this several-hour ceremony. As I drink green tea during one, an elder shaman approaches me. "America?" she asks. I nod. "You very sensitive. Have shaman energy," she says with a grin before walking away. During another break, I step outside to feel the blaze of sun on my skin and breathe air that is free of exhaust fumes so common in Daegu. I walk down the driveway past an amphitheater for outdoor ceremonies to two *janseung*, twelve-foot high carved wooden totem poles who guard the property from demons. Cho joins me.

"The ceremony bores you," he asks. He witnessed me earlier go from sitting upright to sprawling on the floor. Traditional Korean homes and retreat centers have no chairs or couches, and hours of floor sitting pain my back. "Not boring at all. My back started hurting."

"Your back?" he repeats.

"Yes."

"You are resisting the spirits. Many shaman feel it right here." He points to a spot on his back, the very place of my pain. A week earlier, the doctor identified the spot as *yung dae*, the place where my spine is most curved, also the acupuncture point that, if energy is blocked, produces asthma and a lack of spiritual faith, both, yes, part of my history.

There is when the twine on the string of coincidences thickens into a rope, when my western inclination toward skepticism frays. One can easily step over, even ignore a string, but the thickness of a rope requires effort and a large step. Lately I'm lifting my leg higher and higher.

About a year earlier, while visiting my brother in California, I took a day trip to Pacific Beach in San Diego. As I strolled along the boardwalk, a man in his mid-eighties bicycled over to me. "I'm so happy to finally see you," he began, his eyes tearing. "I've been waiting more than half my life for you. I could see your glow from over there." He points to a burger stand on the boardwalk several hundred feet away. "I would hug you, but then I wouldn't let you go."

I thank him for his kind words, and we talk briefly before I continue my stroll along the boardwalk. California, I reason, is full of such people. Perhaps he says this to every woman walking alone. As if hearing my thoughts, a woman approaches and asks what we discussed. "He's friendly," she confirms. "He's been looking for a special one since he left New York. He talks about this every time we meet, but he's never met her. He was a bank vice president, you know."

A few weeks after my encounter, I'm walking on the sidewalk in Richmond with milk, apples, and a few other essentials from the grocery store when a Baptist preacher stops me. "Excuse me for being so forward," he begins, "but I had to comment on your glow." Coincidence that he used the same word? Over the next several weeks, strangers at bookstores, cafes, and on the street say the same thing: I'm glowing. One woman hands me her bible and explains that Jesus is coming into my life. The book is dog-eared, yellowed; I thank her before handing it back.

When you live in a city with dogs as pets, it's common that neighbors ignore the pooper scoop law. My nose or slight slip alerts me to the stinking smear on the sole of my shoe. If you step on a pile of uranium, does this scentless element leave behind a radioactive signature, a glow? Can I explain my luminescence by this? Or is this the *yung dae*, the spot on my back softening, opening, and radiating heavenly energy?

"What would I need to do to become a shaman," I ask Cho with a nonchalance more typical of a query about getting a job as a gas station attendant.

"Get customers." I'm unsure how serious he is.

Ms. Kim invites me to stay the night. I go for a short walk along the road with Hyonok who arrived late in the afternoon. I see stars for the first time in months. We walk past barbed wire fences and military outposts. Frigid air turns my exhales into vapor. I make rings with my breath and wonder about the number of N. Koreans trapped along the DMZ by the barb wire, shot as they tried to escape south. How many drowned in the nearby Bukhan River, hoping to ride its current to freedom, given it runs into the Han River flowing through Seoul? This waterway which holds the allure of escape for northerners is also the cause of nervousness for the South, the North having threatened to dam the water upstream to flood Seoul or cut off the water entirely. Ms. Kim arrived before the fence posts, before the water wars, but what anguish did she suffer as she risked her life for freedom? How often do her neighbors, eating the bounty of food on their tables, cry for their estranged family who, in order to appease their hunger, grow a personal garden hidden from the government, its discovery leading to the capture and torture of the entire family? The silence of the night, punctuated by a single dog barking, shares no details.

When we return to the retreat center, Cho leads me to the upstairs hall where everyone has spread out their bed rolls for the night. I unroll mine, slip inside, and await sleep. It's possible that tiger spirit or Buddha roamed the hall that evening, but if they did, the ceaseless snores of *mudangs* blanketed any audible evidence.

By midday, I'm riding the subway into Seoul, the first leg of my trek back to Daegu. I meet a seventy-five year old man, a retired dean of public administration from Yonsei University. He tells me about his experience as a soldier in the Korean War and thanks me, as a representative of the U.S., for our help. Suddenly a man across from us bolts up from his seat and lets out a cry that gets everyone on the train looking. He dances drunkenly, like a boat pitching side to side from rough waters, the same way some patients amble through the halls at a psychiatric clinic where I've worked. He gazes at something far away, a place beyond the train, its sway causing him to wobble further. He falls, then quickly gets up, only to pull my acquaintance from his seat to join him in dancing. Arms held high, they whirl a few times before I, too, am grabbed for a threesome. As abruptly as he began our dance, he now ends it, but still holding my arm tightly, he says, "She make Korea happy. She have light!"

My acquaintance takes advantage of the pause in the commotion to lead me to another subway train. "I apologize," he says again and again. "Life is not always easy. Maybe he lost his wife. He needs medication."

I get off the next stop, Itaewon, hoping to buy souvenirs before taking the KTX, the hi-speed train, back to Daegu. I emerge from the underground to a bustling city street, glad to spot the American food chain, Subway. I want to order a piece of home, familiar and comforting, something that does not adrenalize me. Usually I order a six-inch veggie, but a glance through the glass case at the browning lettuce and ultra thin tomato slices turns my attention to the teriyaki chicken which I order instead. I carry my sandwich to a table, unwrap the paper, and bite in. To the unhappiness of my tongue, I discover mayonnaise, thick, sweet, and very un-teriyaki. Too late do I recall that Koreans believe adding mayonnaise Americanizes food—any food. As the teriyaki mixes with the creamy dressing in my mouth, the familiar mixes with the strange. It's gotten harder to know these days which is which.

Some Kind of Vegetable

Minji's brother lends her his GPS for our trip to Namsan Mt., a few miles from historic Gyeong-Ju, the Confucian center of the country. Hwan Yoon, my student of English and dance, suggested our contact improvisation dance class celebrate school Korean style with an overnight outing with ample food, beer, and *soju,* the popular rice alcohol.

When the committee chair for Fall Festival, an event showcasing the talents of faculty and students from the Department of English and Language Arts, learned I dance, she requested that I perform. "It's not a solo dance," I say, preferring as agreed a few weeks earlier, to read my poetry only. "I need a partner."

By partner, I mean one with skill, not a mere few hours of training. It takes time and effort to stretch and strengthen an untrained body, to get it cooperating with the mind. This partner must learn to be receptive enough to handle impromptu lifts, rolls, and falls with grace and no injury. It takes time and effort to know when to hold, when to let go, which activity is going with the flow and which stems it. I want to demonstrate balance in poetry, how I partner rhythm and syntax, sound and meaning. I'm curious to speak in a room where I assume few listeners will understand me. I expect my American words to be a voice in the woods, an unfamiliar spirit like an unidentified insect concealed by foliage, the full impact of my voice clipped by the language divide. I'm prepared for this, but not the awkwardness and physical risk that comes with dancing with an inexperienced partner.

"So who will join me," I ask during one of our sessions, the date rapidly approaching. No one offers. All laughter and banter comes to a sudden stop. "Hwan Yoon?" He smiles. "Seonghee?" She shakes her head vigorously. "Juno? Anyone?"

With no takers, I close the door to the studio and drag my feet up the stairs. A student comes to my side, softly voicing yet another lesson in Korean etiquette and a privilege that come with status. "Juno will do it."

"He said no. You heard him."

"He's your assistant. What you ask of him he must do."

"Not possible to touch you," he warns me, trying to remove the contact from the improvisation.

"You can," I say, giving him permission to transgress the cultural norm that says a male should not touch his elder, especially a woman. I roll my back against his, lean my arm into his, feel his body tighten in fear and unfamiliarity.

On the night of the performance, numerous students and faculty already seated, Juno pulls me aside in the back of the theater. "I have an idea," he says with a nervous chuckle. "You tell me when to lift you, when to spin. Just whisper. I'll listen." His voice trembles. Beads of sweat have formed on his forehead and we haven't even stepped onto the stage. He's never stood before an audience, let alone danced in public.

I agree to his plan.

We situate ourselves on the stage, I lean sideways into him and feel his body stiffen, blocking all routes to improvisation. "Roll," I whisper. "Bend your knees," I say.

"Lift now," he asks. No, but he's already grabbed hold and if I resist the strength of his clutch, I do so at my own peril, his full weight bearing down upon me.

"Okay," I whisper as I yield to his momentum and seek to support myself on the flesh of his shoulders and neck before gliding back down to the floor. Not a sound from the audience.

"We done?" he whispers.

"Yes," I say, hearing him exhale deeply and forcing a smile as we bow to the clapping audience. So much for the joy and magic of spontaneously arising movement.

Fourteen of twenty-two students agree to attend our overnight celebration, but by the morning of the outing, the number dwindles to five. Yena's parents won't let her stay overnight if boys are present. Eun

Young's parents tell her she must start looking for a job, Hye Jin got sick, Daria is working, and the students from Germany, the Czech Republic and Brazil already boarded planes for home.

Juno, Hwan Yoon, my Chinese colleague Mona, and I squeeze into Minji's tiny car. Despite an electronic map and two calls to the *hagwan*, the traditional hotel where we'll be staying, our hour and a half trip stretches into three. Every raised narrow lane over rice fields and twisting mountain roads, none with road signs, dumps us further lost into the countryside. Juno suggests we return home, but the rest of us refuse. We've prepaid for an overnight of relaxing, dancing, and eating. I grab the container of caramel popcorn from the back window and peel open its top. "Lunch?" I offer. Hungry hands spill a few kernels onto the floor.

When Hwan Yoon returns to the car after asking yet another stranger for directions, he announces beside me in the back seat. "We're on a journey."

There are two ways to define journey. One is a simple trek, like driving to a grocery store which may, depending on the driver and companions, be easy enough to accomplish. Get in the vehicle and go. Sit back and watch the scenery. Steer the car and avoid a collision with nearby motorists. Extend the idea of journey and, whether going to the gas station or crossing the country, each encounter carries an awaiting insight formed by a collision of perspectives, of cultural, historical and personal markers. Every parking spot, missed turn, or run-in with a stranger broadcasts a hint signaling a message, a whisper of wisdom, or a shout. This class—no, all my classes at Keimyung University—in fact, my entire slippery life demonstrates the changeability of everything. Nothing sticks, or not for long. To hope for a specific outcome or grasp after anything as stable leads to trouble, stress, an argument with and, perhaps, outright denial of reality. Impossible to root in one hemisphere only, one state, emotion, or geography.

A few weeks into the semester, after innumerable phone calls, Juno helped me reserve the dance room for our contact improvisation group.

72

Mistakenly I believed the room issue solved, yet without fail, every evening before class, the guard wraps his hand around the keys and refuses to unlock the door. He acts as if he's never seen me before. Every facial muscle tenses as he yells at me while crossing his hands at the wrist in the shape of an X, a familiar Korean gesture, a sign that bars me from entering. Maybe he dreamed about me stealing the ballet barre and believes I've returned for the mirror. Or he sees me fouling his beloved culture with a revolting form of western dance that throws the neatly ordered Confucian gender divide into hormonal disarray. Each time, I explain that I've filled out the required paper work to reserve the room.

"It's me. Remember? Professor Pallant. I'm authorized to use the room." I'm speaking in English, of course, none of which he understands. We go through the same ritual each week. He rants to demonstrate his power and I say my piece, some nights with less patience than others. Then Juno or another student speaks to him in Korean and phones someone from the administrative office who then speaks to the guard. A minute later, the guard smiles generously like a family member glad to see me and, keys jangling happily, he leads the troupe of us down the hall and steps to the studio door.

"Lean into your partner. Relax. Use as little effort as possible," I urge my students whose flush faces reveal strain. "Follow your breath. What arises each moment, your awkwardness, your ease, a slip toward the floor, your hesitation—all of it is your material. Use it. Feel only this moment. Attend to the place on your body where it meets your partner. What is taking place there? Heat? Pressure? No leader. No follower. One movement spills into the next like a drop of water meeting a stream." I watch students lose and regain balance, their shirts untucking from their pants, an arm sliding past a knee, quiet erupting into giggles.

I teach them how to focus on bodily sensation, to step away from the trap of thought and a judgmental mind. Notice what is happening with the muscles in your back, your neck, your leg. I could easily be teaching a class in Buddhism: Follow emptiness, the rise and fall of breath, the sun greeting the moon, one thought dissolving into the next. Let all preconceptions fall away. Let the purity of each moment rise up. Your own mind is unsubstantial like the sky.

The focus on sensation, so pivotal to the dance, to locating your partner as he or she presses or tugs at your body, which elicits a response in kind, helps generate a solid connection and flow within oneself and with another. This very practice is akin to the Buddhist idea of *vedana*, which refers to focusing on sensation as a means toward enlightenment and the end of suffering. The intent of contact improvisation is more humble, practical, and immediate. Create art. Let your body partner with another. Pay attention to prevent anyone from bonking their head. And yet, there's an unintended consequence; the movement of body lightens the mind.

Ideals fall short of their intention sometimes. Focus narrows significantly when you're lost, hungry, and tired, and you punch the GPS keys harder than you might otherwise, your mind fixed on a specific outcome, in this case, a hotel room and a meal. Minji requests Juno press the keys more delicately.

We drive past mine quarries, soy bean fields, Confucian academies, Presbyterian churches, a dog tethered to a pole. Our car is a cruising *noribang* as we sing to pop music from the stereo.

In the week leading up to our outing, in fact, my entire life of late, I've let go of expectations. Easy to be reminded about improvisation, impermanence, and emptiness when attendees dwindle from fourteen to five, when food meant to be bought before packing ourselves into the car awaits our purchase at the store, when the map Hwan Yoon printed at home omits a few key directions. We'd arrive when we arrive, well fed or not, likely tired, and maybe, just maybe, we'd return to Daegu.

By the miracle of persistence, we find the hotel perched behind a grove of pine trees halfway up a mountain. The guys unload the vehicle and carry our backpacks and bags of food to our room with a marble *andol* and a large window facing a stream. As the *ahjima*, the elder woman, my role is to do nothing but be served. "Maybe Korea know something

74

good," says Mona, also benefitting from her age. According to Korean etiquette, Minji, the youngest woman, cooks. The guys prepare the room, then go outside to cut wood for our outdoor grill.

As dusk arrives, I announce, "I'm going outside for a walk. All of you, please relax." Before I close the door after me, I see Juno turn on the TV.

"I go with you," says Hwan Yoon.

"I don't need an escort, but if you're offering company, then okay."

He grabs a flashlight.

Two rows, about thirty, brown clay *kimchi* pots, the vessels that for several days or months ferment the cabbage into a dietary mainstay, form a wall between us and the stream. We find a dirt path that leads down to the water and hop rocks, careful not to fall in. Pine trees surround us, a common sight once you leave the city. Several years earlier, the government sanctioned widespread replanting; during the period of starvation and poverty, nearly every tree was felled for firewood. During the Japanese occupation, men regularly cut and shipped trees across the East Sea to their country. I've seen few trees older than twenty years and those more than a few decades are honored with a fence and a plaque stating their age. Learning about the barbarity of the Japanese, I've questioned maintaining my devotion to Zen, given that my practice follows a Japanese lineage. How can I agree to a practice from a country that forced every Korean to destroy their identity and take a Japanese name, who institutionalized raping its women, who beat and treated the men like rugs, who transported every resource they could find, tea, water, trees, silk to their own land? Is it fair of me to judge an ancient tradition by the relatively recent policies of a government? Or blame monks for policies for which they likely held no sway?

Like my meditation rock up the path behind my apartment, the mountain permeates calm. The trickle of water washes away my parade of thoughts: the tyranny of territorial conflicts, the misdirections of the car ride, the constant pressure to prepare for class, my struggle to understand and be understood by Koreans, embassy woes, the rawness of my heart from marital strife. Each thought winds its way around the rocks like sediment or a leaf spiraling in an eddy, eventually carried downstream. Vitamin N, (n for nature), as essential as other vitamins and minerals, evident in the natural rhythms of water and wind, reinforces a similar flow in my body. My attention returns and settles into the present moment.

From somewhere in the heart of the mountain a bell rings. Its low clear resonance like a breath, long, deep, and overdue, cascades against, then inside me, vibrating the cavity of my torso. Each wave of sound falls silent before another resonant peal begins. I lose count after four. The purity of its vibration seizes Hwan Yoon and me. We look at each other, pilgrims summoned to walk upstream.

Up a ledge of the stream sits a Buddhist temple where we discover a pavilion with a six-foot high bell, its mallet still, suspended by a hook in the shape of a dragon. We follow a rhythmic knocking emanating from inside the main temple. We remove our shoes and enter. The peace of the space is palpable, soft and warming like a scarf. Beneath an elaborately painted turquoise, red, white, green, and blue ceiling, a monk is hitting a rounded piece of wood while two others bow repeatedly. One gets us cushions, and after several rounds of chants, the two exit. Hwan Yoon motions that he, too, is leaving. I stay, welcoming the site of hundreds of tiny Buddhas surrounding three large gilded ones on the center alter. The remaining monk turns to me. "You stay? Thirty minutes bow and chant?"

"Yes," I reply, hungry for calm, something deep within me sighing.

We bow together.

Typically, bending down, forehead greeting the floor, is no problem. Never has flexibility or shortness of breath been problematic. But now, with each bow, something pierces, like hundreds of stinging bees angry that I've disrupted their hive. I try to ignore the discomfort, explain it as an allergic reaction, an irritant that will soon subside—the path of peace is frequently laden with obstacles. When it persists and I finally look down, I find my pants covered from ankle to thigh in prickers. I'm tempted to brush them off right there, but reconsider. The scatter of my discomfort would eventually become the discomfort of another. I could go outside but the dark would prevent me from locating the prickers. I opt to stay. With each bow, I remove them one by one and place them in a small pile beside my cushion to later cast outside.

The remaining monk, Zhong-ho Lee, used to be a computer specialist until embracing Buddhism full-time fifteen years ago. He finds great comfort in the practice, yet is sad that fewer and fewer Koreans seek it out. "Busy with capitalism. Buy, buy, buy," he says. Kumchasa Temple, a satellite temple to the main one in Busan, used to oversee dozens of temple stays, retreats for practitioners, each year. With attendance down and only a short Sunday service, monks are the primary users of Kumchasa.

In that cold temple surrounded by trees and protected by mountains, there's a charge to the moment. Perhaps it's being only two people in a spacious temple over 1400 years old and knowing that numerous others before us have participated in this sacred practice of stillness. Or it's his penetrating gaze and brown knitted hat that covers his shaved head and accents his cheeks. My awareness shifts to my breath, to his, and that a few-minute walk away, my students are firing up the grill and twisting off the caps of beer and *soju*.

"Where do you live?" I say. He looks at me perplexed, so I use different words, a language problem perhaps. "Your home?"

"Nowhere. This temple, that temple, Buddha."

How many times in my Richmond Zen group did I chant the Three Refuges: refuge in Buddha; *dharma* (teaching); and *sangha* (community)? How often do I tell my dance students that home is the body? My privations of late, my lack of dairy, breakfast cereal, visual delights, the familiarities of life in the U.S., buying a house from half a world away, separation from loved ones, the grief of losing my husband, and a pending divorce have contributed to a big fat sense of homelessness. I've become a global vagabond, an itinerant English teacher selling verbs, commas, and other grammatical properties on available street corners despite essential possessions like changes of clothing, a handful of books, a bed, sink, and toilet measuring several grades above a beggar. If it weren't for my lifeline back to the States, Skype, the last moorings would have unfastened a while ago, and I'd be an empty soda bottle adrift on the East Sea somewhere between here and Japan.

Like the temple bell, Zhong-ho's comments resonate deep within me, a stirring, every layer of my body echoing his words. Home is breath. Home is *ki*. Home is flow. Breathe deeply enough and find family, friends, cheese, Grapenuts.

I return the next morning to meditate and again after dancing and packing the car, this time with the students. "Just ten minutes," I tell them. I had not, at this point, learned his name and considered featuring him in an article. Ten minutes extends into tea, cookies, and a lengthy talk in Korean, all of us crammed around a low table in a small room away from the cold wind. Juno translates, that is, he tries. Zhong-ho speaks rapidly, at length, and without pause. I watch his lips, his eyebrows, and study the collar of his shirt. If it weren't for my periodic interruptions, "What's he saying?" I'd have heard no English the entire time. Fifteen minutes of Zhong-ho's words leads Juno to say, "Something like the mind has layers, an onion or some kind of vegetable."

"That's it? That's all he said?"

"No," he laughs, as if caught cheating. "It's difficult to explain. I don't know the words in Korean or English."

The talk continues for two hours. Two hours of Buddhist stories and wisdom that my ear hears as waves of sound, a low yet comforting modulation, a voice that concentrates chaos into an order with its own irresistible nonsense. When we finally get up to leave, Zhong-ho turns to me and says, "You come back. Your practice deep." Interesting that he understands the poetry of my silence and senses my meditation which began years ago, when I was sixteen.

It's me who starts a conversation in the car. "What are you guys thinking?"

Juno speaks first. "He really makes me think. I never question my thought before. Not to this degree."

Then Minji: "I think to use the practice he talked about. If have a question, sit with it, meditate. After ten minutes, write first thing that come to mind."

"I'm hungry," announces Mona.

At the bottom of the mountain, we stop for dinner. When we leave the restaurant destined for Daegu, we don't get lost. I'd like to say the same about relationships.

Stumbling on the Curriculum

Every Sunday afternoon at his web design office, I meet Can, who's become my tango teacher since meeting him at my first *milonga* on Palongsa Mountain. When I arrive, I run my fingers through the thick fur of his dog Chicho, an Alaskan Malamute, chained outside, and push open the glass door. Can gets up from his computer to brew coffee. Not quite brew. First, he plugs in a portable burner to roast fresh beans. Then he crushes them with a hand cranked grinder. Next, he presses the grounds through a manual espresso maker, a sleek but somewhat medieval stainless steel contraption that involves lots of pouring, rinsing, and pressing. There's more to the processes, but by now my attention has turned to surfing the internet and viewing his tango videos. Forty-five minutes later, he pours us cups of espresso and we talk.

Can and I are making "pottery" (wink, wink). We're engaging illegally in English lessons. Or perhaps not quite so illegal. We exchange no money, therefore, there's no taxable income to report; we barter in tango lessons. By far, the best *tanguero* in town, on the floor he dances with a grace most people are lucky to have while walking. He performs *ganchos* (leg hooks), *boleos* (swinging kicks), *sacadas* (foot displacements) and other tango moves with fluid force and ease. He struts across the

79

floor in simmering connection with each partner, their legs continually braiding and unbraiding. I'm told his lessons are expensive and he rarely teaches, so I'm honored to be taken in as his student. The coffee is good, too.

Tango lessons take place at Salsita, a tango club downtown, accessible via a narrow alley crowded by a tailor, small tucked-away restaurants and shops selling shoes, children's clothes, and housewares. Salsita is a windowless room with mirrors, a bar with too little heat, few places to sit, and, like so many public places, a co-ed squat toilet.

Instructions begin with finger tips pressed against the mirror for *ocho* practice, the woman's main step, her feet making a figure eight. Always the torso faces forward, hips twisting after, legs following. Can's instructions are precise. Continually he corrects the placement of my hand, the angle of my back, how we breathe together, the direction of my chest, and which muscles gets used in which order. When he introduces a new move, I watch with the attentiveness of an interning surgeon. Yet despite my best efforts, my cuts regularly miss the intended fold of skin. "Again," I request, needing to see how far one leg slides away from the other. "Again," I request, having missed how the toes point.

Though my mistakes spill no blood, continually he stops me and says, "Your case." He then demonstrates how my kicks are too low on his leg or I'm using my thigh, not my calf. "Too strong," he says. Then to compare, he says, "My case." He shows the correct move, the swing of my leg aimed higher on his thigh, nearer his groin, gravity not muscle returning my foot to the floor.

From years of dance training, I'm well aware of the gap between the image we have of ourselves, the movement we picture ourselves doing, and what the body manifests. Patiently he tries to get me to narrow the gap and erase it entirely. He taps my foot with his, yanks it into position his hand. He pushes my hips away from him or pulls me in close, then closer.

I'm learning tango, but there's another subject I've unknowingly signed up for, and it's hard to distinguish one from the other. "Wait for man. Always wait. Give him complete attention," says Can. His chest faces mine, his wavy black hair falling into his eyes. We're to dance like magnets drawn to each other.

"You need not wait for the man," says Sung Ho who lived two years in Georgia and Virginia. "*Tangueras* in Korea abide by too many rules, don't know how to feel free," he continues.

Another partner: "It's your role to make man feel good about himself. He feel good, then dance well. Then woman dance well."

Am I learning tango, male-female dynamics, or Korean culture? I suspect D, all of the above.

Take Hauk, for instance. After watching me dance with Sung Ho, he escorts me to the side of the room for instruction. "You not follow well," he says unsmiling, as if my failings will bring about the ruin of the entire club. He provides verbal instruction, then guides me around the floor. Mostly we walk with breath rhythmically synched—nothing complicated, something I've a good handle on. He gives me meager opportunities for *ochos* which I gladly take. "Oh. You learn quickly. Very good." I don't explain that Sung Ho encouraged my bold moves and invited the spins, hip perches, and lunges. I also don't say that Hauk's signals conflict; one moment his hand presses me left, but before my foot has lifted off the floor, he signals me to go right or straight, the equivalent of driving with the left blinker on, but turning right at the corner. He remains oblivious to my balance and the moves of my feet.

What prompted the spontaneous lesson? Was it genuine concern for my learning? Did the improvised moves disrupt his definition of tango? Did my seeming to break rules challenge the Korean proclivity for obeying authority? Or was he jealous that I danced two tandas in a row with another man and he wanted to not only partner with me, but possess me, a behavior I've witnessed in many men and women off the dance floor?

Tango is, after all, a dance of romance and passion. Where else do you hold a stranger in intimate embrace, feet sliding enticingly along a shin, legs twined, partners united in breath in time with music? For the duration of the music, every dance reveals a short-lived affair, a courtship, a glimpse of a life lived in union. A sweaty hand meets a warm hand, a forehead tucks against a neck, hips graze, feet commingle. Hope and attraction mix with fear and flaws, the execution of each move hinting toward a relationship off the floor.

Partner 1: Our legs twine before he aligns his foot with mine, pushing it away from my center, extending my stretch... We're seated in first class on an airplane headed for Maui. We leave our hotel bed only to watch the sun set or rise or to call room service to order champagne, oysters, steak tartar. Three months later, we meet in Nice France and sip wine on a patio while a violinist serenades us before we climb down the stone steps to the beach.

Partner 2: We clutch hands and glide around the room, our torsos relaxed, our feet syncopated to the music... We've parked our car, a married couple, and search the aisles at Target for the advertised sale on patio furniture. "It's this way," he says, motioning past the toy section. "Let's go to linens first and get the pillow," I urge. He eyes the camera section yet gladly follows me.

Partner 3: Without tuning first, he pulls me in tight against his chest and steps on my shoe... We've gotten an apartment together. He spills his morning coffee. In the afternoon he's fired from his job. It's all my fault. Why didn't I pick up his shirts from the cleaners? Why did I arrive so late at the restaurant? What's wrong with me? Doors slam. Plates rattle in the cabinets.

As they dance around the floor, partners date, marry, purchase cars, a house, dentures. Yin meets yang. Strength meets surrender. Leader balances with follower. Tuning encourages a blending of male and female energies. Yet it's a dance, only a dance, muscles in musical simpatico. Compatibility on the dance floor, however elegant and pliant—or full of fumbles—likely does not mirror a similar relationship once the tango shoes come off. After the third dance, the man escorts the woman back to a seat, a six or seven-minute affair terminated. Upon her chair, she crosses her legs, eyes potential suitors, and awaits the next invitation onto the floor.

Yet there's much to be learned about relationships on the floor beyond the timing of muscles, and it has everything to do with your axis. Axis, your central support, the spine both stem and root, pliant yet firm, works with gravity. Knowing your axis helps position you in balance. Maintaining center, back straight, elongating from the crown of the head to the tail bone, prevents toppling over. It keeps you squarely in yourself, not dependent on your partner. Lean into him, but not too much; he leans into you, but not too much. Feet slide, lift, and hook. Partners balance alone but also joined. In connection, partners respond to the subtle changes of motion and energy in the other. Both bear the responsibility of bringing home the bacon, I mean, the dance.

It may sound like I know what's going on. Not fully. One evening Song Ho pulls me in tightly for the close embrace and I follow reluctantly. His grip is firm, too firm, my ribs pressed in rigid discomfort against his torso. "Lean, lean," he urges.

"More?"

"Yes."

I lean.

"More," he urges again.

"More?"

He nods. I lean further.

"More," he repeats.

My body, slim by American standards, is not as lithe as the rest of the women at the club. Two of their legs could fit into one pant leg of mine. My belt could round their waists twice. I don't feel him rooted in his center, but with his insistence that I lean further, I comply. Sure enough, with my shoulders wedged into his chest, the thrust of my weight upon him, his arms and back begin to shake as he struggles to steady himself and keep me on my feet. Like a drunkard who's imbibed one drink too many, I begin a slow, uncontrolled descent to the floor, he grabbing hold of my arms ever so ungracefully to yank me back up.

Can is my sounding board. As we sip espresso in red and yellow ceramic cups and Chicho squeezes as best he can beneath my chair and rests his head on my foot, I share my questions: How do you do the close embrace? When is it okay to improvise? Is there ever a time when the woman can take the lead? Koreans, I tell him flatly, confuse me. What do you think about Americans anyway?

I know I've leapt from talking about dance to discussing my difficulties in adapting to his culture, but periodically my frustration needs voicing. In and out of the classroom, on and off the dance floor, like a monkey learning through observation, I politely follow the lead of my native hosts. If they slurp their noodles, I slurp. If they excuse themselves to blow their nose in the bathroom, I similarly sniffle in private. (I refuse, however, to cover my mouth when speaking and lower my gaze, a gesture of femininity, one that, in all honesty, rubs my American female sensibility raw.) But when my hosts offer mixed signals or too many examples simultaneously, this monkey doesn't know when to eat the banana and when to swing from the branch.

How do you explain Da-Ook, a professional photographer, who I met at the tango club? He speaks no English and phones Lily, the tango dancing pharmacist, to ask that she call me about getting my picture taken on campus. It's through him, not a campus memo, that I learn about school-wide faculty photos. I show up in the designated photography room in the Life Sciences Building, sign my name on a sheet of paper, and watch one professor after another, all dressed in funereal black suits, stare at the camera. In my dark green corduroys and purple turtle neck, I wait my turn. Once he snaps my picture, I thank him, he smiles, and we wave goodbye to each other.

A few hours later, Lily phones again. Will I go back at the end of the day? He didn't finish photographing me. What kind of pictures? She doesn't know. I ask that she phone him again, but her followup call provides no additional answers. I return to a cue of the black robed and watch the line shrink. When the last professor leaves, he motions for me to follow him. He grabs his camera and a lens big enough to view a night sky and we go to the *honhak-chon*, a collection of traditional wood buildings, a brief walk away. He sets up the camera on a tripod, then steps away to cross his arms, slightly separate his legs, and angle his chin toward the sun. Good simian that I am, I ape his position and he hides himself behind the lens. He assumes more positions which I imitate and he clicks away. A few weeks later, the bartender at the tango club hands me a disk with the shots. I ask Da-Ook with the translation help of Juno to join me for coffee, but my invitation is declined.

How do you explain the dean from the college who introduced himself immediately upon spotting me in the photography room? No other colleagues, male or female, have gone out of their way to cross the room or knock on my door to say hello. He phones a few weeks after our greeting to invite me to lunch. I accept, assuming we'll meet in the faculty lunch room, though aside from foreigners, rarely do men and women sit together. He drives us to an expensive restaurant with a private room, ceramic vases boasting their craftsmanship in illuminated cabinets. He offers to order me a glass of wine which I decline.

"How do you like Korean food," he asks, as is the customary initial question.

"I like it," I reply, which is mostly true. Once you venture away from campus, the culinary offerings are more varied. From here, we talk about the Puccini opera we both attended, work by Van Gogh, a favorite artist by many Koreans. We're laughing, he's telling stories about his children, and I ask him questions about his book on Christianity and economics, a topic that for whatever reason, he refuses to discuss. As our meeting continues, the aim of our lunch remains unclear. Do I exhibit American directness and ask?

When the tea arrives, I believe I may have found the answer, at least a part. "The president of the university asked me to find out what keeps our foreign faculty happy? Do you have complaints? What difficulties do you have? How's the salary?"

My list is long. "A booklet provided upon arrival at campus with information about class policies, housing, shopping, hospitals, immigration procedures would be very helpful," I begin. "Access to a computer printer, a calendar in English about events on campus, an unlocked classroom, a heater in my office, the scarcity of female faculty..." I stop after about the eighth item, unsure if lengthy grievances will lead to a termination of my contract, not improvements of conditions.

It's when he asks me about my blood type that I suspect a motive beyond the president's request. His query is not about donating blood since blood banks refuse donations by foreigners. Koreans ask about blood the way Americans ask about astrological sign, to determine compatibility. I avoid answering. He also wants to know if all American women are like those depicted in "Sex and the City." "I watch only because my wife likes it," he says in likely cover of the truth, an admission like men who admit to enjoying *Playboy* primarily for its articles. He notes my similarities to the character Cary Bradshaw: writer, born New Yorker, curly-haired. When the plum juice dessert arrives, he asks about getting together again.

"I would enjoy that." Then for emphasis, in case he has other ideas in mind, I add, "to talk." We drive back to campus. I've not heard from him again.

Poema, the western nickname chosen because it's also the name of his favorite tango song, escorts me back to my seat. "May I sit down next to you," he asks shyly. For the next thirty minutes, he shares heartfelt stories about being an exchange student in New Hampshire, worries about the economy, his desire to buy a car. I don't know if he's interested in talking to me out of foreigner curiosity or wants a friend or a date. Many Koreans, men and women both, quickly open to me with tales of sorrow and joy, then invite me to share a meal. We punch the other's number into our cell phone. Such an exchange in the U.S. plants a seed of friendship, a followup meeting, yet few ever call, unless in need of English lessons, the germination of friendship a rarity.

One of my colleagues lived here for seven years. "I have yet to make a Korean friend, "he admits with disappointment. Every foreigner I speak with says the same thing. We're treated with civility in the classroom, office, or during mandatory after work drinking parties, but sincere lasting friendship is rare. Koreans welcome us foreigners, but only to a point. The university's mission is to hire forty foreign faculty by the year's end, but when the administration fails to include us in events and doesn't address our gripes, we leave the school and the country. I hear a similar story from exchange students.

All Koreans know their place socially. Not only do they stay in touch with college buddies, but they also stay in touch with classmates from grade school; and if for whatever reasons you miss the yearly gathering, one of your teachers may call the following year to insist you show. You honor not only your parents and grandparents but ancestors from hundreds, even thousands of years back, your patrilineage well documented, making the dinner table at holidays very crowded. Only in the last several decades has the border of this country opened to outsiders. But there's a huge gap between waving you in at the immigration counter with a passport stamp and welcoming you through the front door of their home.

There's much that's confusing. Open displays of affection between romantic partners is frowned upon—unless you're a college student in your twenties walking around campus snubbing your nose at several hundred years of Confucian tradition. Limited displays of affection is permissible between friends of the same sex. Young persons who follow tradition won't say the name of someone who's older, even by a few years, nor call them a friend, a moniker applied only to people of the same age. Were Poema, who is younger than me, to maintain formality, he would call me Elder Sister. As the elder, I, however, get to call him Poema. So if someone shows interest, do I assume we're friends and only friends? If someone ignores me, is that a sign of romantic interest? It's like I'm back in fourth grade with Bruce pulling my pig tails and sticking a living mouse in my desk not because he hates me but because he wants to hold my hand on the playground.

One night at Salsita as I await to be asked onto the floor, Can comes over with a plate of *mondoo*, dumplings. He plucks one with his chopsticks and places it carefully in my mouth. He does the same with a strawberry, except without the chopstick. I accept his offerings. I don't try to interpret the meaning of his actions.

Chicho rubs his head repeatedly against my leg and whimpers when I walk away. When I throw a rock in the street, he runs to retrieve it and returns with a lick to my hand. We have, if not an understanding, at least a familiar routine.

Can agrees to answer my question about Koreans and Americans after smoking a cigarette which he does outside on the sidewalk. When he returns, I repeat my question, "So what do you think of Americans." I've put him on the spot, but as teachers, continually we challenge each other. He encourages me to kick my leg higher up his thigh than is comfortable and I get him to correct a bungled pronunciation of an English word.

When he returns, Can sits down before replying, "You white."

"And?" I say, not quite understanding the color reference.

"Koreans," he starts, then turns to the computer to find the English words, "look up to whites."

"What!" I say, astonished by the admission of racism and my own ignorance.

"I afraid to talk with you."

His fear is loaded. It was Americans who aided Koreans in fighting the communist invaders from China and the North. It was America's model of democracy and progress they tried to imitate to lift them out of poverty when the Japanese occupation ended. Depending on the generation of the person you talk with, either we're revered or resented. The attitude becomes even more potent when you add educational pressures to the blend, that Koreans spend ten or more years of school learning English. Year after year, classes are devoted to learning grammar and vocabulary from worksheets and textbooks, all followed by national tests. Rarely do students speak with native speakers unless parents save enough money to send their child overseas, a financial burden many parents accept. Low grades and failing is met with punishment by teachers and parents, and shamed students often resort to killing themselves by throwing themselves off the balcony of their high-rise apartment.

"Do you think I care if you mispronounce a word or mess up on grammar? I just want us communicating—somehow." Then I add, "I'm sorry I don't speak Korean."

"Korea," he responds, "difficult." Because of varying levels of formality and formality dependent on age, status, and familiarity, a challenge even for native speakers, foreigners rarely figure out the proper noun and verb form to use with whom.

A week later at a tango party in Daejon, a city two hours away by car from Daegu, Can asks me to dance. I'm tired from the ride squeezed between fellow *tangueros* in the backseat, and as is often the case, his superior skill unnerves me. "Test," he says jokingly. I drape my hand in his, direct my torso toward him, and lift my right foot in readiness. That's about all I do well for our tanda. I falter with each beat. When he sticks his foot against mine for the *sacada*, I hop over it—mistake. I lean my torso back, also a mistake. My body is as stiff as a locked doorknob. Every one of his lessons slipped out the car window somewhere along the highway. We don't dance again that night.

After dropping off fellow passengers in downtown Daegu, he drives me to my apartment. I'm assuming our lessons the following day will be canceled; it's already 4am and he can blame tiredness rather than disgust in my lackluster dance for us not getting together.

"Lessons tomorrow?" he says.

"Really? After my pitiful dancing?"

"Only two month you tango. Two years, no one dance with me. I terrible."

"You want to continue?" I say.

We arrive at the guard house near my apartment building and he gets out of the car to light up a cigarette.

"Yes," he says without hesitation.

The guard doesn't exit the building to ask for I.D.s. A spotlight illuminates our faces. Like Chico running after a tossed rock, Can and I have a familiar routine. And some understanding.

My relief is short-lived, complicated by gender and class, generation and degeneration.

Lady's Night

"Your turn. You decide."

"What do you mean?" I ask.

"Us guys decided to do whatever you want," says my Irish colleague Dave as he lights another cigarette and blows the smoke away from the table. He, among the quartet of men—Dean from Kentucky, Daniel from Arizona and Stevie from Scotland—help me with questions and difficulties concerning students, the department, the culture, anything from explaining the lack of heat in our offices to translating a grade sheet, even escorting me to my apartment from a questionable part of town. They look after me like concerned brothers, which is why on this night, as with others, it's difficult to turn their invitation down.

The expectation for Fridays is that colleagues socialize together after work. On several occasions, I have dined with the entire department, usually to mark an event like a professor retiring. The Koreans in our department mostly go out with fellow Koreans and expats go out with fellow expats. There's a reason why I often decline my colleague's invites: they drink. They don't just drink; they consume. Liter after liter, they guzzle enough malt liquid to irrigate a rice field. The merriment ends only when the can slips from their fingers, the head falls on the table, or their Korean wife or girlfriend summons them home.

One time, Stevie showed up for our weekly department meeting with a bandage below his eye, the tape not fully covering the reddened skin beneath. "What happened," I asked, pushing my notebook aside and leaning across the table.

"I'm told I fell off the curb." He blushes but only slightly. Apparently, in an inebriated haze, he got up from his chair at one of the sidewalk cafes where expats gather, pushed a few patrons out of his way, then walked to the side of the road and tipped over like a top on its last spin. He landed face first in the street.

I have witnessed many Koreans in a drunken slump on a stairwell or in someone's helpful arms being carried to a car or bed and eventual sobriety. Drunkenness is tolerable, even expected, a chance to remove the Confucian mask that demands "saving face," all behaving respectfully in accordance to social hierarchy and top down management. Imbibe a few drinks and show one's true face, be it a sneer, swing of the fist, smile, or whatever genuine emotion remains otherwise concealed by the rosy facade. Many business persons won't agree to a deal before completing this rite of passage. I'm not sure how my colleagues profit from their boozing because I usually depart before their masks are fully removed.

We finish dinner, a platter of assorted sausages and *pajeon*, my green onion pancake favorite. My colleagues have each consumed four or five beers, I only one, and we've crumpled our toilet tissue onto our plastic dishes, many restaurants relying on a roll of toilet paper for use as a napkin. "How about bowling," I offer. The sport holds little appeal, but I'm hoping the knocking down of pins pushes aside the lure of the can.

We pile into two taxis and exit a half block from the bowling hall. "Pit stop!" announces Stevie as he points to a corner mart where all queue up at the register to purchase six-packs or several sizeable cans of beer. I wait in the taxi in silent, unheeded protest.

At the bowling alley, we exchange our footwear for bowling shoes, secure an open alley, stow beer beneath our seats, and choose from among the various blue, purple, or blue weighted balls. A cascade of pops, cans opening, serves as prelude to the start of the game. One by one, we position ourselves several inches away from the foul line to throw our first ball, movie talk filling the time we await between turns.

"Did you see *The Host* playing at the Plex? Not as good as *Dragon Wars*," says Dean.

"Are you kidding? The monster was even more ridiculous," replies Dave.

"More?" says Dean, preferring movies from any country other than Korea. "What do you mean more? Taller maybe, and eating more people, but not believable at all."

"Like it matters if it's believable?" Dave rolls his eyes. "I go for the laughs. Hey, it's your turn, dickhead!" Dean lifts the ball from the rack and with knees flexed and elbows loose, sends the ball rolling down the alley.

After several turns during which they debate the merits of various actors, plot lines, acting ability, and realism of certain scenes, the topic shifts to work. By now, several empty cans idle on the table and floor.

"I'm having difficulty with Chinhwa," snickers Dave. The student handed in no homework all semester and believes himself exempt because his mandatory military duty, an obligation few men welcome, begins next month. My guess is he's more anxious about his future than uninterested in school. He doesn't share the incentive as do recruits in the North with their guarantee of regular meals, civilians otherwise scrounging for whatever food they can find. The South mandates that all able bodied Korean men in their twenties serve two years, recognizing the need to prepare as best as possible against the most militarized country in the world, the fourth largest army, and a massive chemical and nuclear arsenal. Even a recent admission by a N. Korean official at a political gathering in Beijing who inadvertently spilled the truth that, contrary to the official story, his country did blow up the S. Korean jet liner in 1987 which killed all onboard, is not enough to motivate young men to serve.

"He hasn't turned in a blasted assignment for me either," says Dean.

"That bastard! I'd like to throw his sorry ass where it belongs," says Dave.

"Your turn," I remind Dean.

He sets down his beer on the ball rack, tosses his ball, and knocks down four pins. Hoping for a strike, he claims the ball for his second run, meanwhile knocking his can to the floor, no one but me noticing the small approaching stream.

"His brain is as useful as a turd," says Dave.

"A bastard for sure. Shite!" exclaims Stevie, whose frequent use of British slang suggests that, despite being a Shakespeare scholar, when it comes to "casting the lustful eye of an old fop at the fairest of them all," he prefereth the slang, not the poetry from the isle of his homeland.

"F—ing A!"

"What a dick!"

"Good try," I say in response to Dave's gutter ball, trying to steer the banter from completely going there as well.

Although I'm not the target of their assault, my ears close themselves to their verbal venting, their negativity fouling sound and, it seems, the air around me. I look around at the fluorescent lights, counting how many bulbs illuminate the room. I study the shape of the numbers on our score board to learn if the 6's and 9's are as round or clearly marked as the other numbers nearby. I watch the clerk at the counter adjust his hair and glasses as a small squad of girls approach. My eyes dart around the space, my attention seeking a shelf, a shoe, a wall, any alternative but the ongoing swigging and bluster of my colleagues.

Daniel, the one colleague I willingly seek out for coffee from time to time, takes the seat next to me after wiping up the beer on the floor. "I apologize for these guys. They mean no harm."

"I know," I say, the muscles of my jaw tensing. Already my exit strategy, not improving my game, is uppermost on mind. He knows that before the slurs and slaps and who knows what else, I usually excuse myself from the night's festivities.

"Another round," exclaims Dave. "My treat." He's referring to the game, but Stevie uses it as a prompt to purchase more beer. "Same brand, guys, or you want something new?"

I stay for a second game. Daniel instructs me in using the twist of my wrist to better control the ball. He places his hand on mine and torques my wrist gently before pointing to the arrows on the lane. "Aim for the arrow, but aim a bit to the right to compensate."

By my third turn, the frequency and volume of maledictions have increased. Were this an American television show, the number of beeps replacing the cusses would surpass the dialog and sound like the monotone of a heart monitor machine alerting staff to the stopped pulse of a patient. Between turns, I shrink further and further into the plastic chair. "Guys," I start, intending to tone down their banter, unwilling for us, me, to be seen as emissaries of the west. "Guys," I repeat, trying to steer the exchange to a topic of substance, to at least get their attention.

Dean takes a seat near me, but rather than turn towards me, he pulls out another beer from his bag.

Daniel polices Stevie. "Hey man, you're cursing pretty loud."

"Shite," he yells back as he attempts to position himself at the lane. "What do I care what anyone thinks! Don't bust my balls. F—k!"

This is where the bad turns worse. Like his last turn, Stevie tosses his ball straight into the gutter. "What's wrong with this ball," he yells. "A piece of f-k--g crap!" When he takes his second roll, the ball misses the gutter entirely. Instead he with ball attached at the hand are thrust into the neighboring lane. He careens to the side like the Tower of Pisa, one leg wobbling, the other leg buckling in turn, gravity asserting swift victory as he topples down to the glossed floor. The ball thuds beside him, not once loosed from his hold. He scrambles to his feet, the round appendage still attached, only to have him slip again like a balance-challenged novice at an ice rink, his skates sliding away from under him. A pair of Korean players using the lane containing the sprawl of Stevie wait patiently for it to clear. I imagine Stevie rolling down the alley cussing, one arm reaching outward in search of his can, the pin setter stilling his body before sweeping him away.

"Stay, please stay!" pleads Stevie, wiping spittle from his chin, as he totters toward me. I'm untying my laces, deciding whether to walk home or take a taxi to the lonely oasis of my apartment preferred to this comedy of errors that fails to entertain and promises no happy ending.

Several nights later I receive another invitation, this one from the doctor. On the first Friday of each month, he gets together with several of his friends, only men, wives not welcome. "How is it that I can join you?"

"I ask. Say you write article about me, maybe them. They agree."

The doctor picks me up from a subway entrance since no line takes me to the part of town where his friends gather. We drive past Lexus, BMW, and Mercedes dealerships, a concert hall, furniture galleries, and a host of buildings with twinkling colored lights before reaching a Japanese restaurant. A *maître d* in a blue silk dress and high heels leads us upstairs. She pulls back a transparent brown curtain where awaits his friends, all in suits, white shirts, and ties. Once she steps away, she pulls the brown edges closed. The men stand and offer their hands. I shake their hands but also bow before I'm directed to a seat in the middle of the table, a small chandelier lighting the empty plates and glasses, bonsai plants situated in each corner of the room.

"What would you like to drink," asks the chemistry professor. "Beer? *Soju?*"

I glance at the drink menu on the table. "Wine. Anything red."

"Great," announces the lawyer sitting diagonally across from me stroking his tie, glad for the opportunity to order a bottle.

"Wine much better than beer," confirms the owner of a gym and health spa.

"Yes," I confirm, "I welcome the antioxidants, but I've never enjoyed beer." In recent years, I mostly avoid wine, having developed an allergy either to the sulfites or something else, my bronchioles typically closing after a few sips, my breathing compromised. Hard alcohol sits with me no better.

"You know about antioxidants," asks the plastic surgeon.

"I know what foods are healthy and which to avoid. I know not to drink milk from China."

"You know about that?" says the surgeon, his and the other's ease with English impressive. The Chinese have been exporting milk tainted with melamine. The chemical increases the volume of milk, but as a hardener typically used in plastics, it tends to clog the kidney. Several infants have died, yet the Chinese so far refuse to accept responsibility, profit trumping health.

As *udon*, noodle and fish soup, shrimp tempura, sesame seaweed, and a host of unfamiliar yet tasty dishes arrive, it is they who ask most of the questions, not me.

"She write poetry," offers the doctor who asks them to translate the conversation for him to understand.

"What do you write about?" asks the surgeon. Topics of poetry by Korean women are restricted to nature, heftier topics like social issues or politics the domain of men. There are few bold women like Yi Yonju who broke ground by writing about pollution, poverty, and prostitution. "I would guess your words," he continues in a charming tone, "are as graceful as you." He lifts the wine bottle to refill my glass, then puts it back down when he sees that it is nearly full.

"Dance, too. Tango and contact improvisation," adds the doctor, as if providing them a better glimpse of my resume.

Each man takes turns interviewing me, an eyebrow rising now and then as if surprised that I can speak with more than an um or oh about each topic. We talk about how the administration at my university treats me, how Korea's legal system, originally feudal, only changed in recent decades, modeled, in part, after the American system. We debate about the merits of western medicine versus Korean medicine which is largely subsidized by the government. They have difficulty understanding how in a country as wealthy as the U.S., so few people can afford health care, the cost for these men low, their country a medical destination for many Americans, especially for plastic surgery.

All have traveled to the U.S. for school or business and they proclaim their favorite sites.

"The Grand Canyon," says the gym owner, "nothing is more

amazing than that. Korea has mountains but nothing cavernous."

"The Statue of Liberty," says the professor, as if in competition.

"My daughter has lived in New York since college. She likes the city very much," says the lawyer.

When one of the men's phone rings, he glances at the number appearing on the screen, rises from his chair to stand on the far side of the curtain. He talks briefly, curtly, as if annoyed, then moves further away from our gathering to where his voice can't be heard.

"My wife," he apologizes as he takes his seat at the table soon after.

"How about dessert," asks the lawyer. "I bet you'd like dessert."

"That's okay with me."

The waitress brings a plate with sweet rice cakes and ginger tea.

When it's time to leave, the men speak in a hush with each other in Korean, making it impossible for me to know what they're talking about. When one poses a question to the doctor, he says, "No, no," then waves his hand.

One by one, they say their farewells, shaking my hand American style.

"Most entertaining," says the gym owner.

Before I exit the door, the professor pulls me aside. His face, jovial before, now pales as he tells me he is recently widowed.

"I'm sorry," I say.

"Perhaps you can find me a nice Korean woman," he says.

"Okay. Sure..." I stumble, flattered and offended in the same mouthful.

"I take you to subway," the doctor says as we cross the parking lot to his car. "They go to *noribang*."

"Don't you want to sing with them," I ask.

"Not tonight."

Something tells me their *noribang* is unlike the one Moony and I visited in Seoul. Ours included a waitress that delivered drinks and fish chips, but the wait staff at other *noribangs*, I'm told, provide additional, exclusive "adult" services in private rooms behind closed doors. I'm curious to know where they're headed but don't ask.

The surgeon follows us to the car and stands jingling the keys in hand. "The men and I agree. We like you to join us next month."

I don't know what to say. How is my presence welcome at their private meeting, but not their wives? I doubt any of the men will share tales about meeting me with them.

As we drive several blocks, my American identity loosens then slips, lifted off like a transparent curtain. In its place steps a modern *gisaeng*, Korea's equivalent of a *geisha*. We share many of the same credentials: schooled in dance, poetry, and the arts; able to talk on a wide range of topics; considerate (although far from polished) of local etiquette. For hundreds of years, Korean kings considered *gisaeng*s integral to their court. These women were prized for their intellect and aesthetic sensitivity and given food, housing, and fine silk dresses, a slave arrangement that disappeared at the start of the twentieth century. As Koreans retrieve their cultural heritage damaged by Japanese occupation and American influences, the position, minus the ownership, is experiencing a small revival.

I welcome their invitation, don't quite know what to make of it. I'm glad to not have to lift any of them off the floor. I'm glad to not be asked for any backroom services. A poor fit among my western colleagues and a novelty to the doctor's friends, I don't know where I belong nor what, given the choice, I want. Identities that once held sway in Richmond don't carry the same traction here. Here I exist in the margins, a foreigner in a culture that prizes homogeneity and ancestral purity. For a woman to survive, she is encouraged to follow the dictates of men. Where do I belong? What am I supposed to be doing in a land that doesn't recognize or accept who I've been and how my life has unraveled?

Regularly my raw heart swells, every encounter tugging at and tearing the tender flesh. Most nights and weekends, I grade papers and prepare for the next day's classes while tucked away in the burrow of my apartment. Often, I climb the trail up the mountain that overlooks

98

Daegu to meditate and be among trees. Regularly I retreat into the safety of solitude which builds the strength to ride the waves of emotion with its surges of sensation, the pulls of dark and release of light. The body has its needs, its innate flow; to that I surrender.

What Endures

Deon has agreed to be my husband. I haven't mentioned him before, but there's good reason. Last night was only our first outing together, dinner. Mostly, we bump into each other in the hallway of the apartment building or on the sidewalk while walking the hill to class.

We went downtown to the Holy Grail, a restaurant so named because its primary clientele are westerners who wrap happy fingers around forks and knives, watch a plasma screen TV showing Cirque du Soleil, and, most importantly, eat dishes like quesadillas and Greek salads. Cheddar and feta exist in Daegu because the owner, a Canadian, responded to the call of the dairy deprived. The space is a haven for Americans and other native English speakers who occupy every table and seat at the bar. Some of the wait staff and a few customers are Korean but all gather here for the same reason, to escape the constraints of the country.

Deon, a Canadian teacher in the education department, and I are sharing gripes. As head of a program that teaches Korean high school teachers English, he's fed up with his students' lack of follow-through and inability to reflect. "Do you know how hard it is to get a decent conversation going?" He leans his arms on the table, his chest leaning toward me for emphasis. "These are adults. Adults! Can you believe it? Not a bone of reflection in them."

I've heard similar complaints from other western colleagues. Korean education's emphasis on memorization omits analysis, synthesis, and reflection. "They're taught to repeat, not come up with something new," I tell him between sips of water.

"They've got to get over it. They have to break out," he says with a clenched hand that raises above the table but never strikes it.

"You can't just issue a command like that." Now it's me leaning toward him, my hands however, relaxed in my lap. "They probably don't know how. Besides, you may be a professor, but really, you have little status here. Why would they listen to you? You've been hired to teach English, not critical thinking."

Deon spent four years living in Japan, another country dominated by hierarchies and obedience to rules. His intolerance of Koreans surprises me, but only to a degree. For foreigners, every moment is rife with difficulty, whether it's something mundane like washing clothes or more complex like directing a program. We adapt the best we can. We lower our standards or toss them out altogether. For instance, the faculty living in International House have learned to climb over the fence at the guard house. As long as I'm not wearing a dress and pantyhose, it's easy enough to hoist myself over the metal barricade that gets pulled across the street each night. Both hands grab the rounded metal, and like an gymnast on parallel bars, I hoist my legs up and swing them over onto the other side, my dismount, although not Olympic grade, improving each time. The gate locks because the university imposes an eleven o'clock curfew for students. The faculty building is located at the end of the road next to student housing, several feet of pavement linking student curfew to faculty inconvenience. If we return home after 11, carrying bags or preferring to be dropped off at the front door, the gate will not open. Faculty with cars, when lucky, can get out of their cars and hoist the gate open, closing it after them, but only if the guard has not locked it. No amount of complaints have altered the policy. As stipulated in his instruction manual, the guard closes the gate at the appointed hour, and nightly, if not preoccupied with watching TV, he views the video monitor as faculty and students hop over the gate, instruction for reinforcement of the rule apparently omitted.

Every now and then, we foreigners reach our limit. We break. We refuse. We rip the plug from our new but malfunctioning heater from the wall. We shove the stranger who knocks into us in the subway station, something Deon did twice on our way to the restaurant. We gripe. We pack up our suitcase and leave, as did the colleague in my department who I replaced in August. I reached my limit earlier in the week. The event in isolation isn't the culprit, but the accumulation of daily and weekly affronts. Mine took place at the bank when a transaction that should have been simple stretched into five exasperating days.

I sit at the edge of my seat at a bank cubicle. A clerk explains that the money I transferred via the ATM a few days earlier had gone to the wrong person, even though I punched in all the right numbers. The bank couldn't retrieve the money without a lengthy investigation which they were unwilling to do. "Very sorry," says the clerk.

"I think I misunderstood you," I say tapping my pen and clinging to rapidly eroding politeness, the muscles of my mouth tightening. "Did you say the bank can or can't?"

He repeats what sounds like a blend of both words, his accent blurring the distinction.

"Can or can NOT?" I say again, my teeth clenching, the volume of my voice increasing. If I make a stink about the situation, flail my arms, yell, throw a chair, give in to chaos, behavior I've witnessed in Koreans, my chance of getting the situation favorably resolved increases. This is my moment, the breaking point. I'm ready to toss my bank book on the desk, a useless piece of paper, march past the guard without bowing, and purchase a ticket for the next plane back to the States. My pride and a firm belief in civility struggles with the rise of an outright tantrum. Right, it seems, at the tipping point, a call comes in from one of my expat colleagues inviting me for coffee. The invite douses my fire, although not until she hears an earful of invectives from me.

"We all reach that point," she sympathizes as we sip cappuccino and I agree to go furniture shopping for her new off-campus apartment on the twentieth floor with an amazing view of cliffs jutting the

Nakdong River.

"Do you know that the chair of my department asked me not to date any of the faculty?" I say to Deon. We place our orders and he asks what's on tap. The waitress, a Korean, doesn't understand what "on tap" means.

"She told me she's looking out for my best interests. Best to not be seen with any men on campus and start rumors." Faculty in the university are about 80% men. Other than the chair who recently replaced the one who hired me, I am one of two women in my department, she a tenured Korean professor who has shown no interest in getting to know me. That leaves no one, other than accommodating foreigners, with whom to sit in the lunch room.

When I first arrived, I was advised not to stick out or cause trouble. Koreans value collective unity over individualism. Standing out, a demonstration of individuality, is viewed negatively, synonymous with being selfish. Most residents of this city wear black or navy. Students tell me it's slimming, and they don't want color to attract attention to themselves. To stand out is unacceptable. At all times, blend in. Well, for me, that's impossible. To begin with, my hair is blonde.

Yes, blonde. Most westerners would describe my hair as brown or brunette, but any hair color other than black is called blonde. My hair is curly, naturally curly, something no hairdresser in town knows how to cut. My students continually ask about the product I use to make it that way. My eyes are brown and hazel and double-lidded—without the help of surgery. I wear cheerful colors like green, purple, and orange and slip my feet into flat or low heeled shoes, not high heels. My ears are not wired daylong to a cell phone or iPod. I do not whisper when I speak, will say yes if I mean yes and no if I mean no. I show emotion with those younger and older than me without resorting first to drinking, and more and more often, I hug friends and students. Though I don't smoke cigarettes, I would not hide my habit in a bathroom stall as women smokers do to avoid being spit upon by a morally superior elder. Being unmarried is suspicious, divorced even worse, so on that front, I avoid details.

The incident in the bank, the final straw, led me to being unashamedly, unabashedly myself. Deon knows what happened with the doctor, a period when I behaved circumspectly, believing I was respecting customs.

"It's okay that we talk," I ask the doctor after the nurse removes the acupuncture needles and I return to the chair beside his desk. "Okay, yes," he reassures. I ask questions. Lots of them. He graduated at the top of his class from med school. I want to learn details about the chiropractic technique he developed and learn about five-elements Chinese medicine. I want to get to know the body's meridians, how energies run through the body, and understand the thoroughfare that my deep grief has slowed almost to a halt, the channel of *ki* that the doctor says is broken. I want to better understand the many seemingly numinous experiences of mine over the years that have left me puzzled. In the process, I learn much about him.

During the communist invasion, his father was captured and placed in a stockade. Many captors indulged in torturing prisoners, each week slicing off an ear, finger, breast, whatever body part struck the fancy of the moment. Metal bars bound his father's legs. For months, his body was ravaged by cold, then hunger, then heat, mosquitoes, fever, and increasing weakness. No standing, no walking, no washing. It was an American soldier who finally released him and placed his feet back on the ground, although by then infection rampaged his body. With slim chances of survival, he prepared to join the spirits of his ancestors. Yet the soldier delivered him to an American doctor who placed him on his treatment table and injected him with a hefty dose of penicillin, a previously unknown and unavailable drug. The doctor saved his life.

"America save my country, my father, let him marry my mother, birth me. I thank America. I thank you."

It's hard to accept thanks for an event for which I played no role. I tell him about my Richmond neighbor Vern, a veteran of the Korean War. Vern and I often chatted while we sat on our front porches or when we'd run into each on the street while walking to the grocery store. About two years before my leaving for Korea, he agreed to heart surgery to treat a wound from the war. According to his surgeon, all went well, yet Vern suffered serious side effects. Within months of his release from the hospital, he lost forty pounds, couldn't stomach food, and would walk bent over only as far as the corner before needing to turn around out of breath. Almost daily, he suffered panic attacks. He lived with an elderly, infirm sister who was unable to care for him, so it was me who sat with him on the rusty chair on his porch to calm him and slow his racing heart and increase the depth of his breath. And it was me who biked up the street to the pharmacy and grocers, sometimes as often as twice a day.

"You angel," says the doctor, what Vern, later placed in a residential facility, also calls me.

"Your energy pure," the doctor says to me one night at Salsita as he escorts me back to my seat where my bottle of orange juice on the bar awaits. "Your energy special. Very rare." Then, as he's done before, he asks if we can dance a second tanda.

The tango club is not the best place for conversation. The setting at his clinic is better, but the language barrier continually tests our patience, and many threads of conversation are left to dangle. If normal talk speed is 60 mph, we rarely go faster than 10. Either I'm thumbing through his English-Korean dictionary or he's punching in letters on his keyboard.

He types Korean with one finger into Google. An English word appears as if by magic on the screen. Imperfectly he pronounces "hypophysis," a word I don't know.

"Look this word up," I request, "P—i..."

"B?"

"No, p. Like pig."

"A—b..."

"No, l—m—n—o—p."

The conversation crawls along. Sure enough, "hypophysis" is a synonym for "pituitary."

104

Once, talk disappeared for an altogether different reason. I know that needles stir the body and I've been grieving the loss of my marriage for over a year, but I wasn't prepared for needles prompting a tsunami of tears. As I sat beside the model spine in his office, every dike and canal carefully constructed to hold back emotion crumbled, rebar, concrete, and rock reinforcements carried off by the force of the wave. I hold my forehead with one hand, half covering my eyes, the deluge wrecking all attempt at speaking, every noun, verb, and adjective, every syllable swept away. He grabs a tissue from his box, rolls his chair closer to me, and dabs one cheek, then the other.

"I apologize," I say finally, tilting my face in his direction, trying for composure.

"No apology. Must cry. Let go despair."

I have no choice. My body and its need to release emotion take over.

The cries are, at least, within the range of a normal response to loss. Yet whatever words he may use to describe my energy, the meridians, or the impact of balancing my jaw and straightening my spine, there is something more going on, something inexplicable about our relationship, each visit and exchange providing mounting evidence.

According to him, Korea is yang, America yin. We helped restore Korea's yang, but America's yin is still broken, our spirituality not receptive but divisive, one religious sect out to dominate another, one's ego so fragile that it, too, needs to conquer another. Additionally, an over reliance on reason has pushed away any trust in an inward, subjective experience of intuition, self and body which bares the interconnectedness of all life.

For him, healing me has personal and national consequences, and he pursues my treatment with great devotion. I go to the clinic about once a week, although the severity of my curved spine requires greater frequency. He suggests I come more often, but it's hard to do with a full teaching load and hour and a half round-trip travel time. He starts sending me text messages to check on the quality of my energy: "Today

105

bright? Today tired? You dream? What you eat?" He explains how a dreamless sleep is deeper and more beneficial physiologically. Based on my body type—we're all dominated by metal, wood, water, fire, or earth—he suggests I eat lotus roots (easy), beef (double the price as the U.S. but doable on occasion), tangle weed (don't know what it is), apples (welcome); I'm to avoid mackerel (difficult), alcohol (easy), ice cream (impossible). Some days I need ginseng to fortify my strength, other days the stimulant would be too potent. He calls himself my Energy Upgrade Man.

Each week, he fits me with a new mouthpiece. He places strips of silver between my teeth, gets me to close my jaw, and lines up my teeth. With one hand cupping the outside of my jaw, I make a loop with my thumb and forefinger on the other hand. He pries my fingers apart, the degree of my strength determining how many strips to add or remove before he presses and folds dental putty fitted to my bottom teeth that will eventually go into my mouth at bedtime.

Each week, my head rests in his hands and I try to relax before he jerks it to the right and left for deep cracks. Each week, he creates traction on my spine by pulling my head and elongating my neck. Each week, like fence posts tilting from wind, needles line my spine and form a half circle at my neck. Each week, the nurse places a heat lamp angled at my neck and a hot pad on my back to intensify the effect of the needles and returns to remove them when the timer goes off. Every night, I sleep a little longer, a little deeper, the bags below my eyes growing lighter, my overall energy increasing, the pain at my heart softening.

Not since the family doctor would push aside hair that had fallen into my juvenile eyes or phone my mom to ask about my wheezing have I had this level of medical attentiveness. This, I imagine, is what American doctors might do if they didn't fear malpractice suits or strangling rules by an insurance oligarchy. They would display what attracted them to the profession in the first place, helping and serving the interests of patients, not profit margins.

The doctor receives immense satisfaction from being "helpable," one of his Konglish, Korean + English, words that as a patient, not his English teacher, I refuse to correct.

One afternoon while getting up from the chair to leave the clinic, placing my notebook in my handbag and grabbing my coat, I thank him for his services. I bow, shake his hand, give him a quick hug. "You are most kind and... helpful." I'm tempted to say his word, but don't.

"You are helpable for me."

This I don't understand. Other than help pay for the run of his office, how does a patient help a doctor? I remove my coat.

He finishes writing notes on my chart and closes the folder. He presses the speaker button on his phone and asks his nurse to bring us grape juice. "The purity of your energy upgrade mine. I better doctor because of you. My hands stronger. I no tire. I feel bright. Much I can do. Last year, the year before, low energy. Now I feel, Wow, can do."

"But what have I done?"

"Your existence. Your being." The nurse brings in a tray with two cups of juice which she places between us on his desk. The thick purple juice captures the light streaming in through the window. He hands me my cup before taking his. As the liquid slides down my throat, I wonder how this elixir will affect my chemistry, or his, why he asked for this, not the ginseng drink or herb tea which he's asked for previously.

"You remind me about my dream." His dream, not the type of sleep, is to own, not rent a clinic, and to assist more patients. "You help me. My energy up because of you. I know now this dream come true."

"How?" I'm stumped on the mechanics. Is he meeting an accountant? Realtors? How do you go from renting to owning a space in a place like Korea where property is so expensive?

"You make me believe."

"*Samadhi*," he texts me when I asked a few days earlier what he wants from life. *Samadhi* is a type of awareness where the gulf between people along with usual perceptions of time and space collapse. There is no desire, no wanting. Each moment is perfect exactly as it is. Yesterday and a week from now is as nearby as this moment. I've had this experience, or something like it, usually after hours of dancing, muscles flush with exertion, but sometimes, it occurs with no known cause. Once it took place as I viewed unfinished paintings in an artist's studio. I was able to view the completed paintings even though the canvas contained only a few brush strokes. I also knew details of his life before he shared any with me. Then, as with subsequent instances, my awareness is like that of an eagle in flight, keenly focused on every curve, color, and movement on the land, able to see distant ridges and rivers as if they were immediately below my talons. Linear time coalesces into a concentric point of continuous nows. I seem to float from conversation to a walk in a field to driving to sitting at my cubicle at work to eating and sleeping with utter satisfaction and a depth of knowing that to this day I find impossible to accurately describe. Trying to explain it is like telling a joke that no one gets, adding the caveat, "I guess you had to be there," except there is no joke, only my own riddle and questions.

A few days after my last visit to his clinic, there's a noticeable shift in our relationship. I had left my cold office an hour earlier because shivering got in the way of concentrating on reading student papers. Back in my apartment, I'm reading one sent via email and suddenly tire. I lay down on my bed. Normal enough. I consider getting under the blanket for a midday nap, but become aware that there's a presence in my room, the heat of a body that is not mine. I close my eyes and flash on the doctor. It's his body that I feel, his body that I hear in the quiet of my apartment. Isn't imagination great, I think, yielding to what seems like a movie of my mind as he walks around the room and sits beside me on the bed. We exchange no words but I feel his usual calm. Eventually his image and my thoughts grow fuzzy. Soon after, without having napped, my tiredness disappears and I return to reading my students' paper.

Days later, I mention the incident to the doctor. "I know," he says. "I sent you my energy. Felt you tired. Wanted to raise your energy. I needed your help with patient. Big man. Thick body. Your energy strengthen mine." He admits this as if our energy exchange was as common as sending email.

We previously discussed non-duality, how thinking isolates us and walls ourselves off from another, caging our mind and limiting awareness. Westerners, in particular, are conditioned away from believing in non-physical connections. We're taught that matter, mind, and spirit are each separate and we often value one while neglecting or disparaging another. On the level of spirit and energy, he explains, we're all connected, but so busy thinking and trapped in a snare of logic, we rupture our *ki*. We not only disconnect from our own body, but other bodies as well. "Follow body. Follow energy. We not alone. You and I spirit together."

He discusses his visit to my apartment as if an ordinary house call with stethoscopes and pill vials. The incident gets me questioning my own dismissal of non-ordinary phenomena, the one in the artist's studio and others like it. Why do I so readily discount such experiences?

Of the more mundane, I frequently know who's phoning me before I pick up the receiver. In an age of caller ID, I don't pay much attention to this ability. But I've had many more events, some dramatic. Once a friend and I were reading poetry while basking on the rocks in the middle of the James River in Richmond. The river rushed around us, blocking out the sound of cars and trucks on the nearby bridge, and muffling the rumble of a passing train. A woman sat on a nearby rock engrossed in a book. My friend and I read a poem aloud, discussed the language, the images, and then turned the page to another poem. Suddenly, the noise of the river disappeared. All sound vanished but one, a cry of help. I immediately saw in my mind and knew that the woman, now gone from her rock, was being attacked in the woods. I stood and insisted my friend follow. Sure enough, we found her kneeling below trees, a man raping her and later, I learned, promising to slash her neck. My friend and I chased the perpetrator away and we drove her to the hospital.

I was grateful that we intervened, glad that I heard her call and responded. But I can't explain how I heard her voice or how, in the weeks following the house call from the doctor, I hear him speak or feel him beside me while I'm jotting down notes for class at a café or walking home from class. "We all connected," explains the doctor. I've since listed in a notebook the times I've experienced voices, visions, and premonitions, surprised to fill up both sides of two pages, quitting only because my wrist ached. What do I do with such abilities? I don't even know what word to use. Guidance? Paranormal? Primordial awareness?

One day, he asks that I come to the clinic early. He wants to take me to lunch. He drives us to a restaurant at the top of a hill in a residential neighborhood. The exterior is landscaped with carefully placed stones and pruned bushes. Inside is an active fireplace, the only one I've ever seen in Daegu. A waitress seat us near a large window overlooking the city. I won't call it beautiful, but it's the nicest restaurant I've been in so far, with, perhaps, the exception of the Japanese restaurant, this one with table cloths and brass napkin rings. The menu lists various cuts of steak, each description of its preparation and side dishes in elegantly scripted English. He insists I ignore the cost and makes sure I know there's ice cream for dessert.

Without our good friend Google at the table, conversation is spare.

"Is delicious?" he asks as I cut into my medium rare steak ornamented by roasted asparagus.

"Yes."

"Important you eat meat every week. Your body need mu-chee." (tr: much). Red meat apparently works well with my body type. He lifts his knife, his fingers finding the appropriate way to wrap themselves around this foreign utensil.

He tells me something else. He tells me something I already suspect, that he loves me. "What I do? I on-yee (tr: only) want you happy. You happy, my happy." He sits upright, the suppleness of his slender body ready to receive whatever response I may supply.

I do not return an admission of love. My grief and his unavailability push aside acknowledging the full extent of my affection for him.

Several of my students have expressed their love for me. They give me handmade cards with simply drawn images of hearts and flowers, the type one might get from a nine-year old, not a college man or woman. I wasn't sure how to respond to the first card from a twenty-six year old guy, but my worry dissipated upon receiving several more from gals and guys, casual affection and respect, not romance their supposed intended purpose.

The doctor, however, is the type of man I would consider dating: older than my students, gentle, quiet, intelligent, considerate, embodied, a reader, dancer, and meditator. But there's a bit of problem, a huge problem: he's married. Welcome to my soap opera. In this episode, neo-traditional Korean man meets post-modern, neo-feminist American woman.

In one of my conversation classes, my students ask that we talk about choosing a marriage partner. They discuss the topic in small groups, each student instructed to come up with the three most important qualities. One by one, I write their answers on the board, items already listed receiving a check. After all twenty-four students report, eight of them guys, I tally the check marks. In number one position, the partner must make a good living. Number two, family. Number three, friendly and personable. I'm surprised that love doesn't appear until fifth place.

This generation is past by only a few decades the custom of arranged marriages. Now it's students, not their parents, who choose potential partners, although parents still hold considerable sway. Although women have entered the workforce, if they want assurance of economic comfort, they marry a man with a secure job. Getting along with family is important because you marry not just your partner but the entire family, for women, the in-laws having as much or more influence as your spouse. All behave dutifully, obeying elders according to Confucian guidelines, great power going to men and in-laws. But where does love fit?

I don't know the circumstances that led to his marriage, but I do

111

learn that eight years ago she left him for a man with whom she secretly shared an apartment. Clandestine relations are commonplace. Better to save a marriage, or maintain its pretense, than to divorce. To divorce goes against family and country. Extramarital relations maintain social stability and salvage a marriage and are, therefore, tolerated, a reason why Love Hotels can be found in many neighborhoods throughout the city. Officially it's men who stray from the relationship, women apparently having no sexual desire. This myth is likely generated by the same people who claim that Korea has few cases of HIV and AIDS (because the population eats so much *kimchi*); that spouse abuse and abortion don't exist (both are common but unreported); and that homosexuality is rare (because so few don't *choose* the western lifestyle).

Many unhappy couples, especially in conservative Daegu, choose to "endure," a word I hear frequently, especially from those forty and older. They fear the wrath of their ancestors and the scorn of the community. Couples stay together for the sake of their children since divorced parents are a harbinger of bad luck and can ruin a child's marriage prospects. Despite the stigma, divorce rates have skyrocketed in the last fifteen years, especially in a more progressive city like Seoul where women are getting well-paying jobs and have less need for a man's income. Those who stay unhappily married attend holiday gatherings and other public events together, wearing a mask of matrimonial harmony while behind the scenes, behind the public face, they lead separate lives, perhaps owning a second home, sometimes in another country.

The doctor's daughter, a teenager at the time of the split, and his mother, requested the separated couple get back together. After a year apart, he and his wife reunited and attempted to mend the relationship with new shared activities like taking tango classes. He discovered great joy in the dance and she found tedium. Tango became yet another wedge in their relationship, she insisting he quit, he refusing, the gap enlarging with subsequent attempts at shared activities that neither found mutually satisfying.

112

"Would you consider leaving your wife," I ask one day. No, he say,s because his daughter and son, though in their late 20s, have yet to marry. I'm not interested in a secret relationship, I tell him, if that's what he's proposing. He's not, he replies. Our connection, he explains, is spiritual. "We deeply alike. Deeply connect. I with you when you go back to U.S. I with you always. In spirit." His words both reassure and disappoint me. Having already been on the receiving end of betrayal, I was not about to assume the role of betrayer, despite my loneliness.

Here's where the drama of the soap opera heats up. His wife finds messages on his cell phone about his inquiries into my health and screams that he can text no woman. She takes his cell phone and hides it, something she's done many times before. She opens files on his computer and presses Delete. She tells him she will poison herself. She phones the chair of my department and threatens to post stories about me on the university website and get me fired.

Drama like this I do not want.

The chair phones me. "His wife is crazy. She made little sense on the phone," she says. "It sounds like she knows she has no marriage. She's very unhappy." But here's the clincher. "In our culture, regardless of the facts, a woman such as yourself is guilty. You're a foreigner. Rumors and scandals cannot be tolerated at our school. If you don't stop visiting his clinic, we may have to let you go."

Guilty, without trial, by reason of gender and nationality. Every good deed has its punishment.

The doctor stopped dancing at Salsita. I stopped going to the clinic. We stopped texting. To ensure some treatment continues, he sent me a box of apples, thirty-five pounds worth, each one the size of a grapefruit. In an apartment that is three *pyong* large with a small refrigerator, no counter space, few cabinets, and an *andol* that would slowly cook my medicine into apple sauce, I've knocked on my neighbors' doors and leave them each a handful.

We've talked on the phone. He tells me about a chance meeting with a real estate tycoon who offered him the hottest property in town.

The new location will assure him of future prosperity and the healing of many patients. He thanks me for the windfall in helping him secure the deal and realizing his dream. He hopes we work together in the future by traveling the world healing people, me sharing my dance, he applying needles. "You shaman," he says, not the first time I've heard this. "My family all monks and healers. You and me, we work together. Maybe we together in previous life."

"How did I help?" I want to understand what I've done or how, should I want to replicate it in the future. I don't even bring up so unwieldy a topic as our shared future—or shared past—the hemispheres of my brain colliding.

"When meet the owner," he explains, "I connect to your energy. Your energy strong."

I want to celebrate his success, have tea or a glass of wine. But because I periodically tremble when an unfamiliar middle-aged Korean woman appears at the front door of my apartment building and I imagine her hiding a poison soaked dagger, I withhold the suggestion. Rash behavior and a strained marriage do not bode well for sharing herbal or fermented spirits, no matter how innocent.

He offers an alternative, a fully Korean alternative. "We sing," he suggests, *noribang*—by phone.

Given my guilt regardless of my actions, I agree to dinner with Deon (male faculty, therefore, off limits). Let the rumors fly! Let untold stories get told! When caught between cultures, a reluctant, curly-haired heroine grabs the *kimchi* pot with both hands and lifts it overhead.

We have a pleasant enough meal. He cuts into his burrito with his knife; I use a fork on my quesadilla. "That's the thing about Americans," he says. "They cut with their forks. What do you have against knives?"

By the time he wipes up the last of his sour cream, Cirque du Soleil gymnasts flying through hoops and landing with perfect balance on a mat, I learn that his apartment, like mine, suffers from short spells of hot water, yet he receives cell phone coverage anywhere in his place whereas I must go out onto my porch or into the hall. "Hard to have a Korean woman as a friend," he says before we agree to leave.

"Or a Korean man."

We get up to pay the bill and our waitress, a twenty-something Korean woman, meets us at the register. "How long you been married," she asks. "You happy together. Communicate so well."

I grab Deon's arm. "Not yet," I say playfully, "but soon."

He smiles before adding, "Can't wait, Dear."

Then I realize how important it is that she knows we're friends, only friends, that we work together, and this only our first time together. Such relationships, I want her to know, are possible. "Do you have any men friends," I ask.

"None. But I want to be like you. Like America. Free."

I pull out bills from my wallet and place them in her hand. She opens the register, places the bills in their slots, and hands me coins. Though I don't recall filling out the application, more and more I'm finding myself an ambassador of change.

Limitations and Freedom

My student Minji, who has taken me a few times to the grocery store since our maiden voyage to Emart, should be returning from taking several weeks of English classes in the Phillippines any day now. I'm waiting to find out the results of the homework assignment I gave her the day before her departure while we ate *juk*, porridge. I urged her to write letters to herself daily, expressing how she appreciates something about her legs, her hair, her humor, anything really, and to note the areas where she's critical. The critical parts need extra care. As we scoop portions from the large bowls into individual smaller ones, my *juk*, pureed sweet potato, hers rice with strips of beef and sesame seed, she surprises me with yet another admission.

Minji sat in the fourth row in my conversation class. Whereas most girls huddle together, taking advantage of the paired seats to lean into each other when called on, she was among the few who sat upright and eagerly contributed to the day's topic. She spoke loud enough for all to hear, a rarity for girls who I constantly plea with to move their hands away from their mouth and speak up—infuriating Korean feminine behavior! When Minji talked, she often turned to address the entire class, her eyes sparkling. Woo-yul, who sat in the corner of the room and worried me when he talked about suicide—his last girlfriend left him heartbroken and a friend of his in similar circumstances threw himself off the balcony of his apartment building—spoke loud enough for her to hear that he admired her pep. He was not alone in his admiration which is why her class presentation surprised so many of us.

Often, I put aside my agenda to take advantage of students' energy, their interests, and the direction of the class. The day we discussed jobs, one student mentioned the importance of having a life philosophy, a vision. Most students stress the size of their paycheck, yet here was a student realizing that happiness was more important than material gain; attitude also mattered. I seized the moment and assigned a presentation for the following class: imagine they had died and a friend or family member was memorializing them at their funeral. What would this person say? What accomplishments get mentioned? What was most valued?

The next day, one by one, students stood at the podium with a memorized talk or a folded piece of paper for reading. Most women shared common accomplishments like being a good mother and devoted wife, and among the men, a vaguely stated work achievement. A few talked about donating money to the poor. Minji typically cheers on whoever is talking by asking a follow-up question or lifting the cover of her electronic dictionary to help a student fumbling over a word, but this day, she was unusually quiet. When every student but she had taken a turn, she reluctantly walked to the front of the room, her feet dragging as if to announce a fatal prognosis.

Everyone watched as she positioned herself at the podium. She removed a piece of paper from her pocket and slowly unfolded it as if to maintain the crease. Then she turned the paper around to show the class. It was blank, not a mark anywhere. She explained that this was the hardest assignment ever given, that she phoned a friend the night before for help. "What make me special," she asked. "What my strengths? What is memorable about me?" She tilted her head downward, hair falling across her face, and began to sob. "I don't know," she said over and over again. "I don't know meaning of my life."

No one moved or made a sound.

"You can sit down if you want," I told her after a few rounds of tears, but she stayed put, holding firmly to the edge of the podium, letting all witness her crying. After a pregnant pause that could just as easily have led to a labored birth as a miscarriage, a student called out, "We love you." "It'll be okay," said another." "You're great," said a third. The outpour of comments continued for a few minutes, coinciding with tears trickling down her damp face.

She didn't speak. Nor did she move.

Eventually she folded her paper and returned to her seat. The classmate beside her gave her a hug. I offered to take her to lunch.

We had spoken in my office before. Then, she wanted to share a secret with me; that she's thirty-two, ashamed of her age, ashamed, too, that she's as yet unmarried, without a boyfriend, and without direction. Two years previously, she transferred from another university where she studied law. Her father ended her studies because he wanted her close by, not an hour and a half away. Keimyung was closer to the family home but farther from her interests, and she has since struggled to find a satisfying course of study.

"I want to travel, but my father not like it. He say no." Her father shoots down many of her ideas. A dutiful daughter, as are most, if not all Korean girls, she is eager to please her parents.

"What I do, Professor?" she says, a question I hear from more and more students who crave my freedoms. The answers I may give an American student—find a job, travel, move into your own apartment, be more independent—hold little weight here. Family approval matters greatly. One is discouraged from pursuing selfish dreams. Veto dreams like schooling or opening a business if it benefits only yourself. Repeatedly I find myself not knowing what to suggest.

"Have courage," I say during a stroll across campus. "Are you strong enough to deal with losing your father's approval?"

She joined my contact improvisation group several weeks earlier. She, like the other students, cross the threshold of shyness into a newfound warmth and play of fellow bodies sharing weight and balance, laughter and connection. For the few hours in the studio, my dance students step out of Korean and Confucian restrictions to roll on the floor or on a partner's back without concern for gender, age, and status. In the process, students question, then relax cultural norms and form strong bonds.

When my student Hwan-yoon suggested we go away for the contact improvisation retreat in the mountains, it was Minji who immediately offered to drive. It's this same retreat where she surprises us all. As we sipped beer and *soju* in the warmth of our room, Hwan-yoon asks my assistant Juno, my Chinese colleague Mona, Minji and me to share something about ourselves that no one likely knows. When Minji's turn came, she slowly admits, "Tuesday, I get plastic surgery on my eyes."

Juno breaks the silence. "Why?"

"So I be pretty."

"You pretty now," say Hwan-yoon, Mona and I nodding vigorously in agreement.

"I'm not. Eyes too small." She points to them and pouts. As in the U.S., plastic surgery is a lucrative industry, image experts continually conditioning us into believing that happiness increases with the slicing and dicing of our skin. The most popular type of surgery here, costing about a thousand dollars, is to add a lid, widening the eye to appear more western, an expected procedure for models. Caucasian eyes equal wealth and happiness. A few hour procedure minimizing a signature Asian

118

feature improves the quality of your life. As many as 40% of Korean women have bought into the idea and opted for the surgery, convinced it increases job and boyfriend prospects. Beauty propagandist can claim victory.

All of us sit up now, no longer sprawled on the floor with a relaxed grip on our drinks. We try to discourage her from following through on the procedure and convince her of her natural beauty. She refuses to entertain our perspective. "I think about this for years. I decide and save money," she says resolutely.

There's no changing her mind. On Tuesday, her eyes will open to greater glory. A new fold of skin will unfold her long awaited happiness. Despite the consumption of alcohol, there's a solemness to the rest of the evening. No one brings up the topic again.

I text her a few days after the procedure to check on her condition. "Swollen and red," she replies.

A week later we get together for *juk*. I study her face, her skin, as always, without blemish. At first, I can't detect a difference. When she removes her glasses, I think I see something, more like a bump, not a smooth continuous crease. I don't mention my liking her pre-surgery eyes; it is she who admits disappointment.

"I can't see improvement," she states. "I feel no different," she says. "Still not happy." The surgical knife failed to remove the fat of her unhappiness. She hovers on the verge of tears, her porridge thickening around the motionless spoon.

Pala, the wife of Can, my tango teacher, is more defiant that Minji. Pala, whose eyes are already wide, naturally or surgically I haven't asked, retired from a short career as news anchor and wants to pursue a Ph.D in French. The problem: the school is located in Seoul. Can refuses to move his web design business, having spent too long building up clients in Daegu. Although not happy about her desire which burdens them financially, he agrees to her commuting or finding an apartment there if necessary. It's his father deterring her plans.

The father phones to ask her to visit him. She sits beside him on the floor and he shows her his blood pressure monitor. He wraps, then squeezes the sleeve around his arm, and presses a button. Higher than healthy numbers appear on a small screen. He explains that the numbers will get higher, his health to worsen, if she leaves for Seoul.

A woman's place is next to her husband, he states. An obvious fact. If she goes, his blood pressure will increase to the point of critical. Unfair that she thinks only of herself and compromise his health.

"What does Can say to that?" I ask Pala who is recounting the story to me in the stairwell at Salsita's. It's chilly, Can has dropped his cigarette butt into a paper cup on the window sill, and they're on their way down. Because she speaks English well and Can doesn't, we talk about him while he looks on contentedly, oblivious to the topic. The reversal, me cutting someone out of a conversation, is a welcome change from me being the one looking on in smiling ignorance.

"He told me I have to work it out myself with his father."

I'm disappointed by his lack of support.

Then she adds, "What do you think I should do?"

"It's important that you do what you want," I say, pressing the American perspective of individualism and self-development. "Find a way."

When she and I talk a few weeks later, she tells me that she might pursue her degree in secret. "I come home on weekends. Maybe in a year, I tell Can's father." Clandestine activities extend to studies, not only love affairs.

Juno does not keep secret from his parents that he's dating Daria, the graduate student from Russia. They meet regularly between classes, lunch together at the cafeteria or off campus, and go to the movies. When Juno rides the subway home one night to share his happiness with his parents, his father insists upon a stop to the relationship. There's one simple reason: she's not Korean. I don't ask Juno if his father worries about maintaining a pure blood line, as is the case with many who after thousands of years of Korean DNA, do not want to contaminate the genes. Many Korean girls date, even marry western men, but it rarely works the other way around. My guess about this inequity is that girls are expendable, but boys, always the preferred child, perform the valuable role of continuing the family name.

Daria and I sit on the grass beneath a tree, her eyes full of tears. "They never even met me. How can they judge me before finding out who I am?"

"Is Juno going to resist his father's request," I ask.

"No. No," she says, as if repetition leads to a sort of understanding which she hasn't yet reached. "Just like that, he broke up with me. His father won't allow us to date. You're an adult, I said to him. Why do you agree so readily?"

"He's my father," replied Juno, as if that one word should explain so much about how the world, the Korean world, that is, works.

"Why can't he be free to make up his own mind," Daria asks me as she retrieves a twig from between blades of grass and breaks it in two. In St. Petersburg, she lived in an apartment for four years with a boyfriend, an impermissible arrangement in Korea, even in the more progressive Seoul. Again, I find myself unable to say anything to support a more welcome outcome.

When the second semester began and I met my conversation students for our initial meeting, I set the rules immediately to encourage them to talk. Their usual excuse for sealing their silence is shyness. They also don't want to outshine others and set themselves as different from their classmates. On the board, I write the word "shy" and put a circle around it. As I've seen on so many signs around the city to curb behavior, I slash the circle with a diagonal mark. "This classroom is a no shy zone," I announce. They enrolled in the class to learn to speak English, and it's my job to get them to utter these strange English phonemes and string them together for the purpose of communication. Their hope is to speak English well enough so that the skill stands them apart from other job applicants. "Challenge yourself to talk." Then I write the word "mistakes" on the board and put a circle around it without the diagonal slash. "Make mistakes in pronunciation. Use the

121

wrong word. Confuse your grammar. If you don't try, you won't learn. Practice, practice, practice!" I don't use the word free, but it's resting on my tongue like a dog who will sprint out a door with a whistle call.

To emphasize my point further, I get them to stand, raising their hands. "Right hand up, left hand up, right hand. Up! All the way up! This is how you ask questions," I say, "and show me you're interested." They grin in welcome of physical exercise.

The assumption from many of my students is that I'm free. I am, after all, from the land where dreams come true, where the poor can become wealthy, the jobless find jobs, where immigrants rent, then buy their own homes, where slaves revolt and become nurses or CEO's. Dreams rise up from the dirt of hope and hard work. The national anthem says I'm free, but am I?

S. Koreans have been competing with their family to the North whose tyrannical government watches its citizens' every move. The North believes the South under constant manipulation from the imperialist U.S. For years, the two Koreas vied for international recognition to legitimize their existence. The South claimed victory with the 1988 Olympics, although the North doesn't accept the claim. Both keep a wary eye on the other and send spies across the border, the South dropping propaganda leaflets by air. Guns are cocked and missiles are readied for detonation. Labor camps that work the unfortunate to starvation and death are plentiful in the North, dank prisons in the South. With a dramatically oppressive regime so nearby in the North and surrounded by Confucian restrictions here in the South, I live with constant reminders of freedom, yet I can't help but wonder how free I or anyone is. I may take a subway anytime I want, at least until 11:30 when the last train runs, and I can speak openly on any topic to students and faculty.

When the former abbot of the Sangwon Temple in Mt. Odae plunged a knife into his belly and wrote a blood-stained note to Korean President Lee Myung-bak, a born again Christian, to plead for an end to the latest manifestation of discrimination, omitting Buddhist temples from official electronic maps, was this devoted Buddhist leader demonstrating freedom? When his followers and fellow monks from 10,000 temples gathered in protest, striking bells, bowing, and praying over the administration's favoritism of Christianity, were they showing freedom? A similar display in the North would never occur. The North allows no dissent because the party line states that all are already happy. Voice a complaint and find not only yourself but your entire family tossed in a labor camp.

Are we responsible for our own mental captivity or freedom? Thinking, explains the doctor, is what keeps me apart from others and from myself. If my mind emptied of all thought, what remains? My question is like the Zen koan, "What was your original face before you were born?"

S. Koreans, for the most part, boast happiness. Officials would have you believe that no one suffers from depression or any sort of displeasure. How do you explain, then, the fact that every subway station installs partitions separating the track from the waiting area, sliding open only when the train arrives? Most know, though may be reluctant to admit, that the partitions, like the many safety guards strolling the platforms and waving their batons, are meant to deter desperate individuals from throwing themselves into the path of an oncoming train. Were those who ended their lives not feeling free? Or am I confusing freedom with happiness? To what propaganda have I succumbed?

We westerners are preoccupied with getting all we want, be it a new car, spouse, or peace of mind. We're set on ensuring that rights provided upon an individual at birth get exercised: to drive a car, smoke a cigarette, carry a gun, burn a flag, choose a marriage partner, determine where and how to live. In S. Korea, no one wants guns (many believe all Americans own at least one because our country is so violent), but they do want their own cell phone and home, among other familiar comforts. The U.S. is a country of I's and me's. You and I are individuals whose separate needs continually bump into the needs of everyone else, family, neighbors, drivers on the road, customers at the bank. Here there are families, classrooms, and companies: we's. The we's progress together toward profit, travel, studies, and harmony. The growing population of Christians put fellow wants on equal footing as oneself; make money, but give it away charitably. Buddhists urge letting go of attachment to desire. One day you have a job and the next week you're looking for one. One day you accept your omission from the city map and the next day you object to the missing information. Freedom comes with welcoming all the winds of change.

More and more I find myself caught between. Between chopsticks and forks and knives. Between hearing Korean and understanding little. Between a welcome fascination for this foreign culture and a wish for the familiarity of home. Last night, craving heat and a solitary dip, I wanted to take a bath without trekking across campus to the noise of the public baths, so I turned on the *andol* and sprawled on the floor, my muscles and bones welcoming the penetrating increase in temperature. Not quite the splash of water, but it worked its own dry magic.

Daria phones and joins me to soak up the warmth of the floor. She was restless, needing to complain about the university's slack academic standards and her Korean friends too fearful to try anything new. As we heat ourselves, lying on one side, then our back, two slabs of meat cooking on a rotisserie, Daria's eyes widen with a suggestion of stirring up a bit of benign trouble. "Let's go downtown and challenge the Koreans."

Ever since I introduced her to the Free Hug movement, she's wanted to create the requisite placards in simple lettering to announce our desire to give away a bit of western affection through the double-armed embrace. No fathers or spouses or generals or police or any other authority to get in our way. Just two cultural crusaders making available to passersby something they are free to take advantage of.

Or not.

124

A Sense of Wings

After my first visit to Ms. Kim's retreat center, I emailed an editor of a magazine devoted to shamanism to see if he was interested in an article about her. Twenty-four hours later, I received a positive response, then contacted the lead musician and spiritual disciple Cho about a good time to return. This time, Yena, one of my contact improvisation students, agrees to go with me. I need a reliable translator. She is nervous about the trip, unsure if contacting the spirit world will upset her Christian views. "The shamans are all kind women, mothers, aunts, and grandmothers," I assure her. "They want to help those who suffer." She knows little about the practice, an oddity given that the tradition in her country is thousands of years old. Years ago, her mother arranged a shaman ceremony, a *kut,* for her own mother who was approaching death, but Yena, twelve at the time, was kept out of the room and not permitted to participate.

Cho called me at my office a day before my scheduled departure to insist upon my coming sooner than planned, in time for the opening in the morning. "Can you come now," he asks. In two hours, the train departs. Both Yena and I alter our plans.

In my apartment, I methodically pack clothes, notebook, camera, and batteries, making sure necessities go with me and don't remain forgotten in a drawer. Finished with time to spare, I plop myself on the bed, once again reviewing my packed items. I begin to shake, a kind of nervous trembling as if something big is about to take place. The reaction surprises me. It's not like I'm the client paying the hefty fee to learn what the spirits and ancestors have to say about my life. My role as observer is much more passive. My shaking suggests another sort of trip, an event charged with meaning, a pilgrimage of sorts, though its significance is unclear. Whatever its meaning, my senses are more alert.

Sure enough, this notion is reinforced within an hour of leaving my apartment. As Yena and I head up the escalator away from the subway, a man who sat across from us talks with her. "He fortune teller," says Yena midway between floors. "He want to share a vision about you."

125

I nod, not knowing what I'm getting myself into. They talk all the way to the top of the escalator. She turns to me to translate, initially confused by pronouns. "He say me—no, sorry—I mean *you* are powerful woman. Recent struggles have passed. Good fortune coming."

I thank him, bow, and ask Yena about the encounter once he continues on his way. "Do fortune tellers just come up to anyone to spontaneously give a prophecy?"

"It happened to me a few times, but they usually warn me about something bad. You lucky. He say only good things." I wonder what compelled him.

We meet Cho in Seoul, eat grilled marinated beef, *bulgogi*, together at a restaurant, and arrive at the center in time for bed. Yena and I are given a private room where we lay out our bed rolls. One of the *mudangs* rearranges our bed to face our heads north in the direction of the kitchen in accordance with *feng shui* principles. Most buildings and landscapes in Korea are designed in accordance with *feng shui* and geomancy principles, both helping to harmonize oneself with the *ki* of the surroundings. Though I prefer my head away from the doorway in case someone enters in the dark and mistakes my head for the floor, I follow through on her suggestion of balancing heavenly and earthly energies. That night I dream about attending a retreat, eating dried fruits with friends, and dropping stones from my pocket into a stream. The stones don't fall to the bottom of the water as expected but float on the surface and are carried off in the current.

Before sunrise, Yena and I join Ms. Kim and her ex-husband on their morning two-mile walk. The ground is covered with frost, and we avoid slipping on patches of icy pavement by stepping on the grass that crunches beneath the weight of our steps. They discuss the client and plans for the ceremony. The client has great fears about the future for herself and her ten-year old son. Her husband's business is failing and he's got a mistress. They fall silent when we reach an area with oddly shaped metal bars, like someone's failed attempt at equipment for a fitness trail. Ms. Kim stands against a vertical bar, rubs her back, and then gently bangs into it with her whole body.

126

As we head back to the center, I offer to help with the ceremony, something simple, perhaps dancing in an ensemble like I witnessed during the last *kut, mudangs* and disciples all shaking shoulders and heads in a group dance—easy enough for me to do. When we return to the center, I'm shown how to cut up white paper and twist them around sticks to make flowers, a single paper bloom stuck into its own bowl of rice. To each door, Mr. Kim adheres slips of paper which say, "Open the door, be delighted and present, fly. Luck is coming."

Everyone meets outside briefly for music and the ringing of handheld bells to mark the beginning of the ceremony. Once back inside the hall, Ms. Kim, wearing a red and white traditional dress, a *hanbok*, red a symbol of luck, white for purity, sings a song that involves greeting the main entry to the hall. She tosses the divining knife toward the door, and like last time, no one displays alarm at its fall. Ms. Kim then summons her coterie of animal, mountain, star, general, and child spirits for blessings. She hops on one foot, spins, and raises her arms. She rings bells, waves a multi-colored flag, then a fan painted with the image of three *bodhisattvas*, enlightened beings. After several bows, she twirls counterclockwise repeatedly, afterward addressing the client sitting quietly on a cushion to tell her there's no need to worry. Then all *mudangs* join her in a group song.

Although some *kuts* last a few days, this one continues for the next nine hours. There are twenty-four sections, written on a piece of paper and taped to one of the drums. Because of her age, Ms. Kim tires easily and relies on the help of others, although it's rare that a shaman works alone. It's also her way of passing on the tradition. She worries, however, that the comforts of modern Korea prevent her disciples from making the necessary sacrifices that open them to spirit energy. She fears her knowledge and experience will die with her.

The *mudang* who dances after Ms. Kim wears a *hanbok* similar to hers, with a high hat and bright multi-colored robe. After a brief dance, she changes clothes and assumes the behavior of a Confucian dignitary. She stomps around the room, and in a voice low enough to sound like a man, she tells the client not to worry, that the downturn in his business is a result of the poor economy. Her husband's infidelity, she explains, is common male behavior; he won't abandon her or their son.

When she completes this section and a disciple helps her to remove her hat, the ceremony takes an unforeseen turn. The music stops. Cho turns to me and says, "Will you dance now?"

"Me?"

I walk to the center of the room expecting others to join in. No one does. All eyes, including the video lens of a woman, a documentary film maker working for a Dutch company, focus on me. A *mudang* approaches holding a white robe and pointed hat. She guides my arms into sleeves which extend several inches beyond my hands, and ties the hat in place. I wave the lengthy sleeves back and forth a few times feeling like a child in adult clothing, except these garments carry a weighty cultural significance beyond its fabric.

"Do you know *gutkari*," asks Cho.

"What?" I say, not understanding the word, a contestant at a spelling bee unable to pronounce let alone come up with the proper letters. My single syllable answer somehow satisfies him and the musicians begin to play.

Years ago, I had a series of dreams about being in middle school, unable to remember the location of my books, locker, or classroom, a classic anxiety dream that resembles my apprehension now. I am exquisitely unprepared, my body cold and sluggish from hours of sitting. There's no opportunity to politely sit back down. There's no opportunity to stretch or envision empowering images to shift my attention from the mundane to the sublime. Unschooled in Korean shamanic dance, I don't know if a spirit pursues me or I solicit one. What moves do I make? How do I start? As instructed, I bow three times to the altar.

With my experience of contact improvisation, sacred dance, and other improvisational forms, I'm accustomed to dancing without a plan, the environment influencing my moves. My inclination is to view the body as sacred, movement a way to open energetic channels in commune with the divine. Change the body's oxygen content and heart

128

beat, and the sympathetic nervous system switches over to dominance by the parasympathetic system. Brain patterns shift and new experiences and awareness become possible. With this in mind, I turn to the four cardinal points, then look around the room at paintings of Buddha, a trio of *Bodhisattvas*, a tiger, Zeus, welcoming the influence of each stroke of paint and color. I am not analyzing the images, only letting them stir me.

The music pierces my ears and wraps around me like a responsive partner who both guides and follows my movement. I alternate between light and heavy steps. I fill my sleeves with air, extend my arms, and take flight, spinning counterclockwise to agitate the unconscious, then reverse the direction for increased awareness. I step near the musicians, then away, step near the client, then away. Heat and energy permeate my body, every tissue of my being tingling as the bellowing of my breath leads to one motion after another. I repeat patterns with my feet and undulate my spine, abandon the pattern and close my eyes. Deeply embodied, taking advantage of the axis of my spine, I'm in familiar territory, comfortable in reaching my arms to the side, overhead, poised in the rawness of the moment, its burn and blows, rises and falls, its ineffable stillness. But the territory is also unfamiliar; a complete surrender to the moment opens me to commonplace impulses but also unpredictable ones.

Eventually, I slow down, halt, believing I've danced long enough, but the musicians continue. Following their cue, I rev up again, energy moving into the sinews of muscle, prompts coming from somewhere deep in my body, the room a blurring reality.

When I finally sit back down, energy continues racing through my body. The dance leaves me brimming with deep breaths, sweat, and heat, a conquest of inertia. The full extent of changes taking place beneath my skin I don't know.

Lunch follows. A few people thank me for my inspiring dance. Before I can process what has taken place, I'm told that Ms. Kim is ready for the interview I've requested for the article. She talks not only about her upbringing but also how she performs ceremonies at the barbed wire fence at the 38th Parallel; she hopes to help reunify N. Korea, her birthplace, with her current home in S. Korea, and heal the rift between the countries. But then she turns the table on me. Like the man on the escalator at the subway, she wants to share a vision. It hadn't occurred to me that *mudangs* are also fortune tellers. She points to me, while addressing Yena for translation assistance. I look to Yena for help. "She say you will travel world helping people. It one of your gifts." My plan is to ask follow up questions. I want particulars. Where will I travel? What specifically will I do? How? But we're called back downstairs before I can say anything to Yena, the ceremony already resuming.

We descend the stairs through the door to the first-floor hall. There on a table near the main altar is the entire cut, dead body of a cow, tail, head, hind quarters, organs all visible, each part laid out like a deck of cards. The site of the pig last time surprised me, but the sheer size of the cow's skinned body, its flesh faint pink and yellow, stops me in my tracks. A few men carry slabs of meat on their bent back from a refrigerator truck outside.

Animal sacrifice is intended to appease angry spirits. Pigs are commonly used, but Ms. Kim chose a cow to prove the earnestness and generosity in rebuilding the husband's business. Ms. Kim's niece and successor paces the room frenetically. An assistant hands her a bowl of the liver cut up into small cubes. She grabs a handful and stuffs them in her mouth, swallowing some, spitting out others. She walks to the table and thrusts her face into a huge slab of meat and bites with the ferocity of a jackal, her face covered in blood. Assistants scurry around her to wipe her face and red droplets on the floor. Then she grabs two legs, ties them with a rope, and hauls them across the floor as if dragging firewood. She abandons the legs, which the assistants take away, and with help, places the cow's head atop her own and prances around the room. When she returns it to the table, she bites the cow's testicles. Meanwhile the client and Ms. Kim are offered bowls of cut up organs. It's hard to tell which makes my heart beat faster, the cow or the raucous music accompaniment.

Another *mudang* pulls out a trident and all work together to place each part of the cow on the blades. The head goes on last, its mouth stuffed with 10,000 *won* bills. All place their hands on the cow and close their eyes in prayer. The trident stands on its own briefly before the cow is lifted off piece by piece and placed back on the table, then hauled away, large parts cut into manageable sizes for cooking.

There's a short break before we're invited outside for the niece to walk on the edge of knife blades. As shaky as the scene of the cow left me, it's harder to watch her slide a blade across her bare thigh, then down her tongue, my imagination hemorrhaging in anticipation of a gush of blood. Unharmed, she then climbs up a plastic chair to the cover of an aluminum drum where she stands atop two blades, balancing herself between two bamboo poles, where she speaks to spirits invisible to me. When she finally steps down unbloodied to the relief of everyone, the musicians close the ceremony.

The client drives Cho, Yena, and me to Seoul. What do you say after such a ceremony? What is appropriate? "Banana anyone," I ask from the back seat, wanting to share the bunch given me upon walking out the door of the retreat center, part of the food bounty from the altar.

The client explains her experience as cathartic and requests one almost yearly as part of her religion. She warns us she won't be saying goodbye, as instructed by Ms. Kim, because it could reverse the promise of good luck generated by the ceremony. When she stops at a gas station in the city, our drop off point, sure enough, her car pulls away without her saying farewell.

One of my tango partners from Daegu who moved to Seoul for a job training meets us at the gas station. The three of us walk to a tea room where we each order a cup, mine pine tree tea. He invites us to stay at his apartment, a brief walk away. His offer is an attractive option. Hotels are expensive and I'm accustomed to staying at homes of friends when I travel. Yena suggests we stay at a *jimjilbang*, a public bath, the common Korean choice. Typically, there's a heated floor where men and women can sprawl, sometimes sleeping side by side. My vote is for an individual bed.

"He's single?" whispers Yena, never having slept at a man's home before.

"He has two roommates. He's a gentleman. Nothing to worry about." The weekend signals two unnerving firsts for Yena: attending the *kut* and now this, an overnight stay at a single man's place.

She agrees to the apartment. He lets us use his bedroom, offering to sleep in a common room. When she puts on her sleep wear, sweat pants and sweat shirt, she races back and forth between the bedroom and bathroom like a mouse determined not to get caught.

On the return to Daegu, I reflect on what it takes to be a Korean shaman and my unexpected initiation into the practice. N. Korean shamans are chosen to the vocation through *sibyong*, the shaman sickness characterized by voices, visions, premonitions and debilitating symptoms, whereas their southern counterparts are chosen through lineage, usually through the mother's kin. Southerners stick with given forms whereas northerners welcome improvisation and the whims of visiting spirits. *Mudangs'* place in society is increasingly tenuous as younger generations distance themselves from ancient traditions in favor of all things modern. They prefer electronic connections over spiritual ones, the former better preparing them for competition in the world market.

Despite my pre-departure hunch about some significance to my trip, its relevance remains unknown. Yes, I've been hoping to make sense of my numinous experiences for which all words fall short, but a hasty conclusion can be misleading and unhelpful. I crave certainty, but doesn't that force a frame around the experience? For what purpose? Comfort? I admit to not fully trusting what tomorrow holds. I may be able to find balance in a dance but still need practice with not knowing, in watching and participating in the slipperiness of life with its constant changes. Otherwise I may grab an answer the way an addict snatches her drug for immediate satisfaction. Like *mudangs* who live with one foot in the common world and the other in a realm beyond, my guess is that the truth dwells on a 38th Parallel, neither north nor south, nor east or west, but in a wild territory beyond the constructs of thought and easy understanding.

English Refrains

It's winter break and I've been asked to teach in one of the many English camps that takes place throughout the year. Camp is partly a misnomer. There are no tents or sleeping bags, no swimming holes or hikes through the woods. Camp, in this case, refers to a doctrine, a common interest, the obsession that Koreans have with learning English. At this camp organized by the Engineering Department, students volunteer six weeks of their time between semesters to taking a class in speaking and writing English. I agree to teach two of the weeks, about eighteen hours total, choosing weeks that focus on small talk, discussion, argument, and interviews.

The Engineering School is a twenty-five minute walk from my apartment. To avoid the main road through campus, I walk up the steep, car-free hill to the open-aired amphitheater with a view of the city below, past the traditional buildings, the *hanhak-chon* with its frozen waterfall and pond, the carp as inactive as the stiff lotus and lily pads. This is my preferred cross campus route, one enveloped by pine, gingko, and chestnut trees leading to the ancient, tile roofed buildings that complement the land and provide a glimpse of a remnant way of life increasingly overrun by the frenzy of industrialization. Though professors complain about the hour that class begins, 9am, I easily show up on time, even on mornings when a blanket of snow makes the stone steps and dirt walkways slick.

First day: small talk, but with foreigners. It so happens there's one in the room: me. I walk to the desk of one student wearing a baseball cap. "How are you this morning?"

"Good," he says as he eagerly scoots his chair closer to the desk and adjusts his cap.

"What did you do this weekend," I ask. He tells me about a Japanese anime he watched at a downtown cinema. I chat with a few more students.

One asks as his first question, "How old are you." A few students know better than to ask this squirm.

"Let me explain the difference between Americans and Koreans.

133

Your question, perfectly okay and expected in your country, is considered rude in mine." It's imperative that a Korean ask this question to establish rank and determine which grammatical form to use, but for Americans, the query, especially to a woman, is invasive. He receives my feedback with a smile.

"Have you eaten breakfast," he asks, eager to correct his mistake. Asking about food is the equivalent of "How are you?" and is not a suggestion that the two share a meal together. On more than one occasion when I've answered that I'd not eaten, the lack of follow up surprises me. No "Oh, let's go for a bite" or "Here, I have some *bibimbop* (rice with vegetables and egg in a stone bowl) I wasn't able to finish."

I do, however, invite myself along with about a dozen students for lunch and together we go to one of the student cafeterias that offers a choice of Korean and Chinese dishes. A small scuffle breaks out in front of the cashier before Yeon-sup, who greets me every morning with a broad smile, announces that he has paid for my *tan-ka-su*, a fried pork cutlet.

"Sit, sit," he urges. "I bring you." He gladly slides my tray of food in front of me at the table. When he puts his meal down, he waits for me, as is customary, the elder to take the first bite. "Is delicious," he asks.

Another harmless scuffle breaks out after lunch at the instant coffee machine where students argue over who will pay for my cup. Instant coffee costs a mere $.30. The debate has less to do with who can afford the coffee as to who warrants the honor of serving me.

I watch a few of the guys state their case, the girls looking on silently, then interrupt with a solution that has satisfied students before. Problems like who first gives the in-class presentation or which movie to watch gets readily solved by *kawi-bawi-bo*, rock, paper, scissors. They immediately divide into two groups and hands hidden behind their backs pop out like a small fireworks display. The initial round eliminates half of them. They repeat "*kawi-bawi-bo, kawi-bawi-bo,*" the draw reducing the pod to fewer and fewer until the winner drops the lucky coins into the machine.

Tall and toothy Yeon-sup designates himself my care-taker. Each

134

class at lunchtime, he escorts me down the hall and across the parking lot, translates the menu and orders. When class ends, he offers to find a student with a car to drive me home; I always decline, preferring to walk.

This sort of courtesy is common, one's well-being a shared responsibility. Every several weeks, much like a gourmand, I try a *jimgilbang,* a public bath, in a different neighborhood, in search of the perfect marinade of bubbles, heat, and sweat to tenderize my body. Each features a specialty of baths and rooms not available at other sites. Some baths come with jets directed at your legs, back, neck or head with varying degrees of water pressure. Other baths are infused with jasmine, cucumber, or persimmon, depending on the day of the week. Small rooms constructed of wood or stone have temperatures ranging from very hot to icy burn or emit pine, wormwood, sage or an herbal mix. My latest favorite is the heated salt room where tiny white granules coat the stones on the wall, the floor, and once you've dipped your hand into the bucket, on yourself. The day I salted myself for the first time, a woman grabbed a handful of granules to smear on my back, the place I was unable to season on my own, then handed me a glass of iced, green tea. After I shower, yet another woman approaches me at my locker to remove strands of hair matted to my bare back.

When my two-week term with Yeon-sup ends, he wants to extend his service. "Class want to have pizza party with you." Rarely do I turn down such invitations. "I email you with times." The email arrives with apologies. Between work and class schedules, the students can't agree upon a time. "Okay with only some from class?"

Eight of us crowd around a table at Mr. Pizza for two pies, one loaded with chunks of pumpkin and mushrooms, the other with clams and the chewy suction cupped arms of octopi curled upward, distinctively unvegetable-like. Yeon-sup makes it a point to sit beside me. "More drink," he asks. "What you need, I get." Between bites, all take turns pulling out their cell phones to snap pictures.

We all walk back to campus and stop at a corner, I heading back to my apartment, the group to return to the Engineering School. For goodbyes, rather than bow, I offer to give a hug, what's become my signature gesture. As if noting an irresistible sale on t-shirts with an American logo, Yeon-sup announces that hugs are available, finger held high like a megaphone. Everyone lines up, the last one taking care not to fall off the curb into the street. When it's Yeon-sup's turn, he wants to know if we can stay in touch by email. "Will you be my first foreign friend? I never had foreign friend before."

I can't recall when I've been someone's first, but around here, I am often someone's FFD, First Foreigner for a Daeguian, sometimes by the busload. One afternoon on campus while I strolled with Josette, a Canadian colleague and welcome female peer, a group of about forty middle school girls with white shirts and plaid navy skirts bolt out the doors from the *hanhak-chon* toward their waiting bus. When they spot us, they all suddenly change direction with the uniformity of a school of fish, their eyes gleaming as they charge down the steps toward us. "Have a nice day today?" says one. "Weather is good," says another. "You are so beautiful", "So pleasant to see you." Days and hours of English study come to fruition in this, their inaugural encounter. It was impossible to respond to each and every one of them. We smile, wave, and push our way through the giggling crowd, our celebrity ending with them boarding the bus.

My celebrity is recognized, too, at Daesongsa Temple, a short distance outside of Daegu, as I bend down outside one of the Buddha halls to view hundreds of small stone piles a few inches high, each stack a beacon transmitting someone's wish. How many represent parents wanting good grades and entry into a prestigious college for their child? How many are constructed by besotted lovers welcoming the affectionate eye of their beloved? How many piles topple over from a hungry squirrel or the careless hands of fellow wishers? A tap on the shoulder interrupts my musing. "Can you take picture," asks a plump teenage boy.

"Yes," I say.

But he doesn't want it of him alone; he wants it with me. "I never see foreigner before. You my first." He doesn't ask my name or want to know anything about me. His sole intent is visual proof of close

136

proximity to a foreigner. We stand side by side below a sycamore tree where he stretches his arm away from us to point his camera and shoot.

I imagine him bringing the evidence of his FFD into class to share with his classmates. "Were you scared," asks one.

"A little."

"Look at her hair! It bends!" says another.

"Curls. Those are called curls."

"Whatever."

For the rest of the week, his photo wins him prestige, classmates offering him their miso soup or the kiwi candy in their pocket. In class, they eye him with envy as they open their English books to look at the strange roman letters.

Celebrity does not come with the same perks when it comes to Membership Training, commonly referred to as MT. At the start of the semester, freshman are encouraged to attend their department's MT and, depending on the department, the same holds true for faculty. MT's are overnight stays at a resort with planned activities intended for student bonding. Expect sporting events, I'm told, and alcohol, which has effective bonding chemicals, especially when consumed in large quantities.

My western colleagues grumble about our required attendance, but this being my first MT, I withhold judgement. Three buses of students transport us—the Korean teachers all go in their cars—first to a movie site where we walk around abandoned streets with banks, shops, government offices, a field with artillery, faded signs, and a telephone booth, the book inside dated 1996. Other than us visitors peering through windows into empty rooms and climbing on rusting tanks, the town is eerily vacant as if a cataclysmic event vaporized its inhabitants.

From there we go to the resort at Hapcheon, a collection of buildings sandwiched between a mountain and the imposing wall of a dam. My colleagues and I find our mushrooms—yes, I said mushrooms—small, two-storied rounded dwellings with mud sides and rounded tile roofs which seem to have sprouted up from along the poorly paved, steep driveway. The wood door of each mushroom opens

137

to a room with a refrigerator, table, and a ladder which leads up to a windowless room with an *andol*. I, as sole female, get my own mushroom, but visit my colleagues already sprawled out upstairs in their fungal dwelling, successfully bonding, drinking beer and waiting for the main afternoon's activities.

About an hour later, we meet with students in a field in the shadow of the dam where a dodge ball game is underway. A student calls me onto his team and instructs me to hold onto the belt loop of another student and not get hit by the ball. Neither he nor anyone else tells me that if I avoid the ball yet let go of the belt loop, my partner and I are considered out. My feet dodge the trajectory of the ball once, twice, but as the third ball races toward us, my partner heads one direction, I another, and my hand lets go of the flimsy material. Off to the sidelines we go. No one puts me on the next game, volleyball, an exclusion that suits me just fine.

From here, teams race to complete a series of tasks which upon completion receives a score. My jump rope skills, unused since grade school, return readily. My feet spring up just as the twine approaches and land when it's safe before they spring up again. Not once do they pin the rope to the ground, a feat which prompts claps and smiles from my teammates. I'm among the fastest to race to the top of the steps and across a field with breath to spare which prompts more accolades from my team. But my abilities come to a glaring halt with the next task: reading tongue-twisters, in Korean, of course.

"No read Korean," asks a frowning student, the rest of them gathering around. After a few concerned looks, the student leader comes to my aid with what he must believe is a brilliant idea: "You sing."

All eyes turn glaringly toward me, the determining factor who holds the key to whether we proceed with a good score to the next challenge or not. In any other situation, I likely would have declined, modesty silencing me. Yet their stares and hopeful faces leave me with little choice. A refusal would hurt my team's chance of winning, so I begin to sing the first few lines of Don McLean's "American Pie," well remembered from a hitchhiking trek across Europe after college when a trucker asked me to sing the song into his CB radio.

Once I finish the initial stanza, all clap, I'm relieved, and we're awarded our points. From there we have more climbing and our next challenge, yes, reading more Korean. "Sing another song," urges the team leader. Had I grown up in *noribang* culture, my repertoire might have been extensive enough to seek out every stage, street corner, or MT to share my voice and readily fulfill even the hint of a request. But my collection of lyrics numbers no more than the first few lines of several songs, insufficient to warrant a decent score. The students gaze at me hard and breathless as if it is my kick that determines whether we win the World Cup. I don't want to let them down and be the team player who drags them into misery, yet I fear my flimsy memory will do just that. I recall a few phrases from songs, barely an entire stanza, but nothing that soars between the goal posts. It's then I realize who my audience is. Will they know if I flub the words? With new confidence, I choose the Beatle's "Let it Be" and improvise after the "the night is cloudy." When I get to the refrain, a few students sing along, then a few more, others tapping their feet and clapping to the music. Our team is awarded the highest score yet.

I walk a gravel path back to my mushroom, the sun casting my shadow in front of me. I'm laughing for the first time in months, at my song, and how one person's ignorance becomes another's triumph. The evening activity centers on dinner with, of course, drinking. My western colleagues are looking for someone to drive us back to Daegu so they can drink apart from their students. I feel sufficiently bonded and poke my head into nearby mushrooms to find a student or Korean faculty willing to return us to campus. I am, yet again, ready for the solitude of my apartment.

Whichever Way It's Supposed to Be

I wake up and turn in my bed. Do I eat breakfast, check email, or go straight to my yoga and meditation practices? These are the easy decisions. In the confines of my apartment, life is more or less controllable. I press buttons to turn on lights, pull a string to open the blinds, step over the ridge that separates the bathroom from the hall, twist the gas knob repeatedly, the gas never turning on with one twist, to heat water for coffee. All of these actions are familiar, predictable. It's another story once I leave the sanctuary of my private space.

After several months here, I still don't understand this culture full of seeming contradictions. It would help to speak the language, but my chronic handicap prevents me from engaging in more conversations. Too often, I skirt situations, the silent outsider watching for cues in hope of an opening to enter through without stepping on another's toes.

Hard not to do so, by mistake.

At yesterday's department meeting, the new chair of the department addressed freshmen and faculty from a podium at the front of the room. In Korean, of course. When others applauded, I applauded. When others listened, I similarly perked my ears. When the dean spoke, there was more applause and I, of course, joined in, one hand meeting the other, a familiar enough gesture yet done on this occasion for unknown reasons. Did he announce a pizza party? A reduction in tuition? When he finished talking, he hands the microphone back to the chair for more untranslated words. She eyes me in the front row of the lecture room and without warning hands me the microphone. I get up from my seat with the metal instrument and look out at the eighty or so students and fellow faculty. What am I supposed to do? No one explained what's expected. I assume I'm to talk, but about what? Samsung's new rechargeable batteries? The ongoing dispute between Korea and Japan over ownership of the small island, Dokdo? From the tone already set, my guess is to choose something to spur applause.

I stand to the side of the podium and lean slightly against it, one hand comfortably in my pocket. I introduce myself.

140

"Hi. I'm Professor Pallant from Virginia in the United States. I'm the woman in the department. Welcome, all of you, to the new semester. I look forward to speaking with you—in English." All applaud.

I could break into dance or recite a poem, but don't push my luck. I pass the microphone back to the department chair. Later, Juno, master of Korean etiquette, informs me about my faux pas.

"What did I do," I ask innocently.

"You leaned on the podium. And you put hand in your pocket. Professors don't do that. Not correct behavior. But no worries, the students thought you were cool."

Ignorant foreigners such as myself are forgiven our blunders. Somewhere on campus, an administrative assistant is likely keeping a tally sheet of my misdemeanors, how I've poured my own drink (a younger person pours it for you), how I've looked my superior in the eye (you're supposed to look down), how I didn't pay for a student's lunch (the invitee always pays). No pink slip has arrived in my mailbox, so my wrongdoings likely warrant no more than a dishonorable mention and furrowed brows among faculty and administrators behind closed doors.

Other situations, although more unsettling, provide a clearer path.

Usually by Sunday morning, I text Can to inquire about tango lessons. A few weeks ago, he wrote back that his wife Pala is "very, very sick" and he couldn't attend lessons. There's been an outbreak of colds and stomach viruses, and I assume she's stuck in bed with one of these. Two weeks later, I ask again about lessons and learn that Pala is in the hospital with stomach cancer.

During our last get-together, she complained about stomach pains, a diminished appetite, and bloating. The doctor she visited offered no remedy. When the pain persisted, she consulted a second doctor who discovered cancer growing outside her stomach wall which had already spread to her intestines and ovaries. As soon as I heard the news, I left the park where I was reading a book beneath plum trees and went straight to the hospital.

Another patient, lying immobile on her side, shares the room with Pala whose bed nears the window. Pala's sister pours me a glass of grape juice. I sit on the bed across from Pala seated in white and blue hospital pajamas.

"I won't be taking my class in Seoul," she says, dazed from two days of anti-cancer medicine. "I cancelled it."

A mutual friend informed me that the second doctor thought Pala had three months to live, her cancer aggressive, inoperable. I don't know what details the doctor shared with her and don't raise the possibility of death. "For now," I add.

While looking at her soft, clear face, her eyes somewhat glossy, I realize I know too little about Pala who is 31, met Can at Salsita, and has been married for three years. I want to know, in particular, about her religious beliefs, her thoughts about life and death, but as recent friends, we haven't broached these topics. I want to comfort her yet don't know what to do. For once, language cannot be blamed for my difficulty. The communication gap results not from cultural differences, but a chasm in experience. An hour ago I bounded down, then up the subways steps after relaxing beneath trees while Pala struggles to moisten her lips with a few licks, a typically undemanding gesture that prompts a wince and a labored sigh. I take hold of her hands, gaze into her eyes while looking for appropriate words or actions, then close mine, and begin to meditate. Immediately bright white light surrounds us, a field of energy gently charged by my vigor and the fresh air from the park. "That feels really good," she says. "So peaceful." I don't tell her my inner eye sees a thick, dark brown patch on her lower torso that fills me with gloom.

My eyes reopen to land on her bloated belly which gives the appearance of an expectant mother in her final trimester. Yet it's water, not a growing fetus collecting within, about a gallon already drained to reduce the bloating. Nauseated, weak, and dizzy, she complains about a parched throat, but even a sip of water churns her stomach.

She glances out the window, at something I can't see. "I want to go for a walk," she says.

"Let's go," I say, eager to escort her.

With difficulty, she slides out of bed, shuffles to the corner cabinet to remove coat and shoes, and slips them on unhurriedly as if their weight cumbersome and the fabric fragile. I offer my arm which she takes as we pass the nursing station for the elevator to the first floor. A small crowd waits in line at the coffee counter offering the usual fare: cappuccino, espresso, green tea, sweet potato latte. We pass an enclosed rock garden, light coming in through a glass opening in the ceiling. We exit through sliding doors for a small landscaped area outside with bonsai trees and well pruned shrubs, none yet in bloom. We walk among these organic shapes, away from the sterility of the hospital with its syringes, cotton swabs, and machines monitoring liquids and vital signs. I imagine us walking in the park, wind lifting her hair, us throwing down a blanket for a picnic. As if hearing my vision, she smiles haltingly, the muscles required for this simple action taxing her already diminished strength.

Back home, I have led or participated in healing circles. Friends gather to meditate, chant, place hands on, dance, talk, essentially to carry out whatever the moment calls for to restore a friend's well-being. My circle of friends here is small, yet I want to extend the same offer, determined to find a few sympathetic souls to support the endeavor if, that is, she considers the practice agreeable and not too strange.

With her pain constant and death as close as the folded tissue in her pocket, I can't afford to deliberate about offending her. Time and hesitation is a luxury of the healthy. Sometimes any action is better than no action. When we return to her room, I tell her about the prayer circle. "Would you like me to organize one? Likely I can get my American friends to join in."

She smiles like before, slowly, genuinely, all the confirmation I need.

She slips under the cover, our little excursion having exhausted her, and I watch her fall asleep. It's midday. Several blocks away, Seomseong Street Market bustles with shoppers examining dried and recently captured fish, cabbages, seaweed, kiwis, mandarins, spices, and a few stalls away, socks, athletic clothes, towels, and housewares, many of which are placed into bags to haul home. Pala's sister and I stand like sentinels watching each breath, looking for some sort of sign and ready

143

to pull up the blanket were it to slip off her shoulders or to massage a hand if requested. Can, who I hadn't seen in several weeks, comes in, bends over to kiss his wife's cheek, and looks at us. No one speaks.

Sometimes the absence of words in whatever language speaks more clearly than any sound from the throat.

About two weeks later, I meet him at his office for espresso, Chicho once again resting his head on my foot. We immediately discuss Pala. She's moved to a third hospital, about three hours away. They've been arguing. Her approach to the cancer is to "attack" the cancer cells with whatever medical means available. Her focus is too negative, he believes. I'm not sure if his criticism is an excuse to protect himself from the gravity of her condition. She finds nothing to appreciate, he says, not her friends who visit, nor her family. "I sad," he admits as tears fall. "I promise when we marry I make her happy. I agree what she wants." Her preference now means they do not talk as much as he'd like nor, with the distance from his office, is he able to see her often enough. His falling tears prompts my tears in sympathy for his loss and a ready reminder of my own grief.

"Not happy. No Pala and not dancing either," he says between tears. Just two months ago, we spent nearly an hour at his computer viewing photo after photo of their wedding and honeymoon. His affection for her was obvious. With each picture, he commented, "So lovely" or "Very lovely," that one word incapable of overuse.

Since her diagnosis, he's stayed away from Salsita because he doesn't consider it fair that he enjoys himself while she suffers. Soyoung, the Presbyterian minister who I've not seen in months, is in a similar place. Her eighty-three year old mother was hit by a car while crossing the street and suffered multiple broken bones. When not teaching or delivering a sermon, Soyoung stays at her mother's bedside. Yet months of dutiful attendance have eroded her joy. The few times we've spoken by phone, her voice sags, vitality missing, the car that smashed her mother's bones also having flattened any joyful remnant. I don't want Can similarly shattered. Is he a better or worse supporter if he temporarily relieves his sorrow? I want, at least, to give him an option

144

and invite him to my evening contact improvisation group. Since first witnessing his agile body grace the tango floor, I've imagined him similarly nimble in this improvisational American dance. He surprises me by agreeing to attend.

With shoes off and keys and other items removed from his pockets, I offer basic instruction: "At all times, maintain a point of contact. Stay in touch with your partner." As I explain further, it's apparent that he understands the idea; he quickly extends his weight into mine, our bodies rolling, twisting, and pivoting against each other. With most beginners, my centeredness reinforcing theirs, I take great care to not upset the balance of my partner who awkwardly maneuvers the unfamiliar terrain of our bodies. But Can needs no help. He stands and bends firmly on his own. Even when I take risks, wrapping myself around his torso, my feet lifted off the floor, he holds me and himself securely. Soon enough we're taking turns dangling from each other's hips and shoulders, pulling and pressing, immersed in the dance like long-term partners, not a couple fumbling through the first dance. Though the dance winds him and a few times he stretches out fully on the floor to recover his breath, soon enough he plows into me like a child at play, eager to discover new kinetic possibilities.

Afterwards, we go to my favorite bar for a Black Russian. Morrison's, which I frequent for its British and American music, is named after the lead singer of The Doors and is reminiscent of a place from San Francisco's Haight Ashbury, circa 1970. The windowless fifth floor bar is full of small couches, graffitied walls, plastic toys, guitars, and record album covers strewn about on shelves. When The Smiths come on, I pull out my air guitar (with bendable neck which allows me to switch playing it with my right and left hand). Can joins in on air drums and together we jam until the song's end. About an hour later, the usual repertoire of music makes a surprising hemispheric shift. Daria joins us at our table, but not before telling the owner about Can and my devotion to tango. The first pluck of strings from Argentine master Astor Piazolla rouses Can. He offers his hand to request we dance.

It's a rare occasion that I turn down an invitation to dance and tonight is not one of them. I take his hand and let him escort me to the small open space near a dimly lit refrigerator full of beer. The owner rushes out from behind the bar and hastily shoves tables and chairs aside to make more room. Despite his generous effort, the size of the space is far from ideal. Adapting as best as possible, Can and I squeeze between tables, twirling and lunging close to the shelves, the refrigerator, our legs inches away from an electrical outlet. Unsurprisingly, I knock over a guitar, and a few plastic figurines balanced on its body tumble to the floor. Yet none of this matters—not to Can and me nor to the owner who urges we continue and plays more tango music. Near chairs usually reserved for tipsy patrons, Can and I glide within our confined area, our connection undisturbed by any accidental redecorating.

As an aficionado of dance, contact improvisation or tango, any space is sufficient for me. Step into the dance and I float without hesitation on the eddies of life. Dance generally delights every nerve of my being, but doing so with a skilled partner increases the pleasure tenfold. A dark, cavernous bar transforms into a grand dance hall. A body enmeshed in the darkness of sorrow finds bloom, a reminder that tomorrow holds the possibility of color, light, and celebration.

When we both finally sit down to resume our drinks and nibble on popcorn the waitress delivers, I'm aware that the usual excuses used to push life off until tomorrow—when the room is larger, when we're more skilled or less tired, when we're away from the eyes of judgmental strangers, when we're wealthier or healthier or happier—such thinking clutters the mind and clogs the natural flow of expression. When the excuses drop away and we welcome the rhythm of the dance floor, even something as devastating as the loss of a spouse leads to new breath.

As if on cue, we both lift our drinks. "*Gom-bae*," I say in surrender to the inevitability of change.

"Cheers," replies Can.

Our outing took place on Monday. A few days later, on Friday, Can calls, his voice halting, broken. Pala died that morning.

Energy Upgrades or Talk No Talk

An apple a day may keep the doctor away, but it may depend on who gives the apples. In my case, the gift of the box of apples from the doctor placed me in the role of eater. Likely, my daily consumption has kept a cold and flu away, but the locally grown fruit hasn't succeeded in keeping him away. He refuses to allow his wife's threats to stop my treatment.

After several weeks of no communication, he phones. "How your energy? How your sleep? What you eat? Finish apple yet?"

Eating all the apples, excluding a few shriveled in the refrigerator and a few dozen handed out to neighbors, will take over nearly three months to complete.

Not only did he gift me apples, but subsequent weeks generated a bag of walnuts, ginseng tea, a bottle of organic sesame seed oil, a facial with massage, all intended to strengthen my body type according to Chinese medicine. He invites me back to the clinic for treatment, but his wife's fury has ruined my ability to take comfort in doing so. Talking on the phone feels safe and he reassures me that receivers pressed to our ears is okay. Gladly he continues my treatment, much reduced—no needles and cracks—verbal only, and resumes my lessons on Korean culture. "You excellent student," he says repeatedly, welcoming my many questions. "You fast learn."

He explains the body using the metaphor of a candle. Our physical body is the wax of the candle. This is *jung*, which also refers to hormones and plays an essential role in the body's functioning. The fire produced by the candle is our *ki*. The light that emanates from the candle, *shin*, is our spirit. In the west, each part is considered separate. As a result, we choose which doctor to visit based on our ailment; an incessant cough prompts an appointment with a physician whereas depression delivers us to the door of a psychologist. In the Korean way of thinking, *jung ki shin* are not separate but interdependent, a coalescence. Mind links to body linked to spirit linked to mind. Hard to refer to one without implying the others. An acupuncturist will treat the cough as readily as

147

the depression.

When the doctor uses the word "mind," he's referring to the heart, the site where emotion and thought pulse together. For him, there can be no flame without a candle, no *shin* without the fire. Insert a needle and its tip pierces the skin and reaches the light of one's flame.

He tells stories about Korean history. I'm particularly taken with Dangun, the first king of the country. Ms. Kim spoke of him as well and set up her retreat center to be as close to his place of birth in the North as possible. Depending on the source, this famous creation story is either myth or fact. My telling with minor embellishments follows:

Once upon a time, say about 5000 years ago, give or take a few days, there was a heavenly prince called Hwang-un. Although living in heaven had its merits, allowing him to roam the universe freely, he really wants to walk on land and bathe in streams. One day he leaves his cloud and asks his father, Ruler of Heaven, for permission to pursue his dream of living on earth. Good dad that he is, Ruler of Heaven agrees, confident that his son will be a magnificent generator of happiness. On a stormless day, a day likely without any soccer matches anywhere in the world, Hwang-un lands beneath a sandalwood tree in the rugged Taebaek Mountains of Korea. There, for the first time ever, like any other creature with a body, he smells plants, touches stones, listens to birds, tastes berries, and watches the sun rise and set. Yet he knows he cannot manage the earth by himself and enlists help from three key ministers, Chancellor of Rain, Chancellor of Wind, and Chancellor of Cloud. These ministers, in turn, seek assistance from about 300 officials who oversee agriculture, medicine, and morality.

One day, Hwang-un meets a bear and a tiger. These furry creatures are less than happy with their lot as animals and desire to become human. Hwang-un explains that if they stay in a cave for 300 days eating only garlic and mugwort, their wishes will be granted. Both herbs have medicinal value, garlic good for digestion and killing unwelcome bacteria, mugwort highly effective at cleansing blood, creating hallucinations, and providing astral travel. The four-legged ones know nothing about these effects but they trust Hwang-un to remedy their unhappiness. After twenty days, Tiger grows bored and clambers out of the cave back into the fresh air and sunlight and is not seen nor heard from again. Bear, however, persists, and on the hundredth day, Hwang-un rewards Bear's efforts by turning her into a woman. Hwang-un eventually marries her and together they birth a son. That son, Dangun, rules Korea for 1500 years and upon death becomes a mountain spirit. Archeologists have supposedly found his bones.

The doctor and I discuss less fanciful ideas, too, like Buddhist non-attachment, Confucian harmony, and the work of people like Jung and Levi-Strauss. Always our conversation returns to Chinese medicine, the body in general, mine in particular.

My moods are yo-yoing, an indicator, according to him, that his treatment is having an effect, my energy moving, not stagnant or blocked. My *shin* is glowing brightly—yes, he, too, uses that word—but not constantly because of my curved spine. Within several hours, one moment walking up the mountain to my office, later passing the amphitheater to the cafeteria, I feel ease, then drained or sad, nothing identifiable prompting the swing, although sometimes, a silly commercial about hand cream or cell phones is enough to provoke a mood shift.

"Feeling's wave not strong," he explains, a symptom of my still weak lung pulse. "Up, down, up, down. Your treatment must continue."

So finally, one day, about six weeks after my last visit, I allow him, due in part to a few back spasms, to convince me to return to the clinic for a new mouthpiece, a spinal adjustment, and needles.

"No worry," he says when I enter his office, his head downward as he writes notes about his previous patient.

When he closes his notebook and looks up, it is the eyes of two friends meeting, not just a doctor and patient. Here is a welcoming presence, a Korean who is not a student or someone seeking me out to improve his English. His hair is shorter than last time and his slender body more thin, though I question my memory for the perceived weight change. I'm sure our mutual smiles intensify the glow of my *shin*. Although he emphasized on the phone how satisfied he is to have his spirit connect to mine, this American is not content to hover solely in the clouds, regardless of the proximity of Ruler of Heaven. I welcome landing below a sandalwood tree or, in this case, his clinic, a concrete location that engages eye and ear. It is good to see him, to join the voice on the phone to a face. We hug, arms wrapping around each other like a sweater, our *ki* in fluid exchange.

The sequence of the treatment is familiar enough: opening my mouth for the silver strips, finger strength testing, cracking my neck, and inserting the needles. On the acupuncture table, once again, my body stirs, streams of energy coursing through my body. My waxen self softens, shaping and reshaping. One moment, heat fills me, then coolness, audible thoughts dissolving into murmurs before merging with the beat of my heart and rhythm of my breath.

After the requisite twenty minutes on the table, the nurse switches off the heat lamp and removes the needles. I sit up, my feet dangling from the table, and carefully lower my more pliable body to the hard floor. I return to the waiting room groggy, unable to focus on the plants or wall hangings, and sit down on one of the plastic chairs. Since my arrival, the room has filled with a dozen or so patients, none having made an appointment as is customary in the States, the Korean system contributing to an empty waiting room one hour, the next one possibly packed. I wait to be welcomed back into his office to retrieve my mouthpiece.

Somewhere within the stupor of my wait, I notice a woman standing near the shoe shelf waving toward me. When it becomes apparent that it is me whose attention she wants, I get up and follow her into the hall.

Once away from the patients, she yells, "I Han wife! I Han wife!"

What she said afterwards I don't know. Between my post-needle stupor and her speaking Korean, I hear an explosion of noise twisting forth from her mouth like a bombed bridge whose metal has buckled and is crashing into a mangled pile on the ground. Her glare and shrill voice lead to only one conclusion; she is upset. Very. She pulls out her cell phone, dials, speaks briefly, then shoves it into my hand. On the other end is the chair of my department.

"Why are you there?"

I explain about my spasms.

"Why not go somewhere else?"

"Where?"

No response.

It's hard for me to be articulate in that hallway with my *ki* in acupunctural swirl, every nerve seared by a woman awash in hate. Air enters my throat, yet my palate, jaw, and tongue refuse to cooperate. Any attempt to formulate language, English or otherwise, falls mute from my lips. Eventually to my chair I manage to say something to the effect that the Korean faculty have not been accommodating. "It's hard to figure out this country alone. I need help from someone. Some sober departmental support would be great."

What I didn't say is what nearly every other foreign faculty member has shared with me; we are regularly slighted, sought after for our English skills and the opportunities we provide Koreans to improve their professional position, yet once the classes are taught and a text is translated into English, beyond the lines of grammar and well pronounced words, there's little or no interest in us. We're rarely invited to functions and are told, never asked what we might like. We're envied for our language ability and lidded eyes, but otherwise unwelcome and disrespected, out of sight and mind in the foreigner's ghetto. Not only is the doctor's treatment helpful to my ailment, but I count him among my few friends. We've established a reciprocity and otherworldliness that surpasses my usual understanding which has me more than a little intrigued.

Before I hand the phone back, my chair offers to find me another doctor, an offer I doubt will materialize.

The wife gestures wildly in an uncontrolled blaze of emotion. "Leave! You leave!" she screams. I tell her that her husband is a gentleman, that he's given me hope for a straightened spine, and his treatments refresh me and reduce my pain, but with her minimal English and my abysmally scant Korean, it doesn't matter if I'm warning her about a tornado swirling toward the building at 100 miles per hour or trying to sell her plastic dinner plates at a fraction of their advertised cost. She'd come to the same furious result, guilty by reason of foreignness, jealousy, and denial about her own unhappiness. I go back into the clinic, retrieve my bag and promptly depart, the positive impact of the treatment undercut by the wife's wrath.

When the doctor calls a few days later, he wants to know why I left the clinic abruptly.

"Your wife..."

"What about my wife?"

He explains that she came to the clinic because she locked her keys in her car and needed the spare he keeps in his desk. Apparently, she never mentioned our encounter in the hall to him, neither while she was at the clinic nor afterwards at home. My telling him is how he finds out.

"She said nothing?" I say in disbelief.

I discover how little they talk—about anything. When he returns home from work, he eats dinner, reads, chops wood for the *andol*, watches a movie or goes straight to bed. She may be in the house. Or not. Either way, talk or shared activity between them is minimal or nonexistent. They don't go out to dinner, a movie, or talk about their day. He drives her to the car mechanic if she needs a ride. She picks him up from the train station if it's late at night. He gives her money to pay bills. She weeds the garden. Their joined lives suggests something more akin to housemates who share a roof, cutlery, a driveway, but little else.

"Don't worry," he offers, a familiar refrain I've come to distrust. "Her anger already gone. No problem talk on phone."

I'm not so sure.

What, I wonder upon our hanging up, is the point of their marriage? Is my dialog with him worth pursuing?

I already know his answer.

A Great Passage

If there's one Korean lesson I'm failing miserably, it's the one about ancestors. Both Ms. Kim and the doctor, like many Koreans, treat as fact that spirits of the deceased roam the world. Few of us can detect when these spectral entities are sitting beside us at the computer or watching us toss rice into a pot on the stove. It's rare individuals like Ms. Kim who sees these spirits and communicates their messages in a way the rest of us can hear.

My western upbringing comes to a lurching stop upon the mention of the unbodied. When it comes to the afterlife of a corpse, I realize to what degree I'm a spiritual cynic—my *yung dae*, the spot on my back, obviously still blocked. A body buried or cremated turns to dust. End of story. Unless blown by wind, dust is about as inanimate as it comes. Many Koreans explain there's a part of the body that gets absorbed back into the earth but another part that hangs around. Depending on the quality of the person's life and manner of death, his spirit either stays around to help or to hex us. Failing the TOEFL exam may be the work of an ancestor with a vendetta. A chance meeting with a stranger at the market that leads to marriage might have been arranged by one of our happier deceased relatives. To help the departed find a peaceful resting place and not raise their ire against those of us still alive, Koreans perform elaborate funerary rites and yearly rituals with offerings of food and money intended to appease whatever bad feelings may remain. The doctor has urged me to make offerings to the spirits of my relatives killed by Nazis to help them find peace and to enlist their support, but the *shtetl* where they lived no longer exists, every last Jew exterminated, their homes burned, the town renamed. Visiting their resting ground, as was attempted by one of my cousins, is a geographic impossibility.

Perhaps I'm judging myself a bit too harshly, my cynicism not thorough, because if there's a knock at the window, I'll pull aside the drapes to look. I may, or may not, blame the wind.

One night before going to bed, I check my email and find a message from my soon-to-be ex-husband with "Sad News" in the subject line. I know immediately what it's about, Java my beloved cat who I left in his care and with whom I share a telepathic connection. In the last few days, I'd been receiving unusually unclear messages from her. Ever since her adoption as a grown cat from a vet, she and I communicated in words, meows, and silence. Regardless of the distance between us and whether I went away for a week or longer, I could hear her frightened meows along with her wanting to know the time of my return. "Soon," I would say assuredly while imagining myself stroking her long black fur, stopping only upon hearing her comforted purr.

When anyone entered the house, she bolted up the stairs for one of her hideaways, usually under the bed or beneath the couch in my office. I received altogether different treatment. Upon my return from teaching or dropping off a package at the post office, she'd run to the door to greet me with lengthy meows and then follow me around the house as I grabbed an orange from the kitchen, sat down in the living room or changed my mind for the back porch. Regularly she positioned herself nearby on my desk top or on a chair while I wrote or read.

Every night we had a ritual. I'd tell her I was headed to bed and she'd hop onto the mattress as I left for the bathroom to brush my teeth. Once I got under the blanket, she'd sit nearby to watch my lids lower. Once I fell asleep or a few moments before, convinced I was safely tucked in, she would walk to the bottom of the bed and curl up for sleep. The ritual would repeat if I awoke in the middle of the night and left the bed to pee.

I regularly defended her from the second cat, Zuni, who joined our household a few years later. Found abandoned in a field when he fit into the palm of a hand, he grew into a sizeable tomcat who delighted in swatting, scratching, and using any and every opportunity to shove her around. The spot on the couch where she slept he wanted. The window sill where she watched squirrels he wanted. He bullied his way to her food bowl, her chair, her tree, her table, all territory eventually becoming his.

Leaving her behind was among my hardest farewells. Days before boarding the plane, I sat on the stairwell beside her and patted her nonstop while explaining as best as possible about my overseas move and promise to return. She was my home, my family, the reason I would return to the house. Which is why when the email announcing her sudden, unexpected death arrived, guilt at my failure to protect her and the all too familiar pain of loss ripped me apart, the final loving tie to my house, my home, gone.

I tried to reread the email but it was too late, the words all a blur, the hum of the computer fan quieted. The black chair which moments ago seated a teacher now held a weight. The weight pushed the chair away from the desk, got up to walk to the sliding door, then the sink, the bed, the door, the bed again. Each traversal emptied the weight further until a shell of a woman lifted the phone and dialed. "Daria," says a voice, "can you come over?"

We sit on the bed. "How old was she," Daria asks. "You were very close, I can tell," she comments as she places my hand in hers. It's about 11pm. We talk for the next few hours, the dark embracing tales about beloved pets, lost loves, and the homelessness we feel from living so far away from family and friends.

"Do you want water, juice, or tea?" I finally offer though am unsure whether my shaking body has strength enough to get off the bed.

"I'll get some for us both," she says finding a bottle of carrot juice in the refrigerator. During those hours when the two of us should have been asleep dreaming, it occurs to me that I may be wrong about neglecting to protect Java. Perhaps it was she worrying about me, and death enabled her to join me.

After brushing my teeth in preparation for sleep, I slip under the blanket and believe I hear dainty paws leap onto the bed and make their way toward my pillow. It seems that if I could focus my eyes better, I would see her green eyes and pink nose poking out from within the fluff of her black fur. Putting my cynicism aside for the moment, I let the vision of her on the bed continue and watch as she curls her warm body, belly up against my torso, eager for my petting. Then, as Ms. Kim did with spirits that visited her at her retreat center during the *kut*, I ask questions, namely why Java is here in Korea with me. Her reply stuns

155

me; she tells me I have to embrace my Jewish background.

In fifth grade, I developed a crush on Joey. He lived next to the farm around the bend from my house and rode the bus with me to school. He usually sat several seats away, close enough for me to stare without being seen. No one knew about my affection for Joey, himself included. One day in the hallway, he stopped me on my way to math class and shoved a folded paper into my hand. My heart fluttered at the thought that he may share my crush. I unfolded his penciled note as if opening a gift. It contained the image of a few grave stones, one including my name in bold letters. Below it read: *Death to the Jew!*

Other cruel notes followed, then anonymously spray painted swastikas on the windows of the synagogue that my family attended, which several months later was destroyed by an arsonist. These incidents, along with learning a few years later how Nazis fatally shot my great grandparents and their children, several boys and girls, outside their home, left me with an acute sense of the danger in being Jewish. Best, I realized, to keep this incendiary information private.

Over the years, I attended services at the synagogue, participated in family Seders, and studied kabbalistic texts, but for the most part, I shared my background with a safe select few. Java was urging me to a coming out, to be more publically spiritual and untie a stranglehold of fear.

This reluctant shaman who did not prepare herself through dancing, drumming, or singing might have attempted to discount the incident with Java as hooey, if it weren't for the email that arrived the following morning from a colleague in the States. He recommended me for a university position as a creative writing professor. A Jewish foundation funds the position with the stipulation that the applicant be Jewish. Would I be interested in applying to teach at the school and work with the Jewish community? Rare to be solicited for a job, rarer yet a Judaic post.

In Isaac Bashevis Singer's short story, "Gimpel the Fool," a simple bread maker becomes the butt of the townspeople's jokes. He believes whatever lies they tell, that a cow flew over the roof and laid brass eggs,

156

a rabbi gave birth to a calf, the Messiah arrived. He seeks the truth and goodness in each tale and repeatedly says, "Everything is possible, as it is written in the Wisdom of the Father. I've just forgotten how." He marries a wife who cheats on him and he unknowingly raises the other man's children as his own, yet by the story's end, he realizes that there are no lies; what doesn't happen by day takes place in dreams.

Perhaps I'd forgotten the words or never read the Wisdom Book, but when a synchronicity like this strikes, only the chronically and fatally foolish ignore it. Were my ancestors in cahoots with my cat and a few key Koreans? Had they met in one of the many spirit houses built on the side of mountains to discuss my fate? Regardless of the answers, I knew I had to apply for the job and felt my chances of getting the position were strong.

A few days later, a colleague drops by my apartment to discuss a class. After a few minutes, he begins to sneeze.

"A cold?" I say, offering a tissue.

"No, I don't think so. Feels more like an allergy. Like I have with dogs. Cats too."

When he leaves, I check my bedding and the shirt draped on the chair for signs of fur. Nothing. Dander is, of course, not easily visible. As are spirits.

Samul nori and Soju

"You may find it interesting," she shares with me in the hallway after class, knowing my interest in dance, "but don't expect much. We're not professional," says my grad student, A-yung, who invites me to watch her perform a traditional dance, part of a harvest festival to be held at Duryu Park in the heart of Daegu. This festival of dance, music, and theater rooted in shamanism beckons bountiful crops. Daria along with Chardin, a friend from my contact improvisation and Zen group in Richmond who is visiting for several weeks, go with me. Before coming to Korea, Chardin hiked the Appalachian Trail by himself. Both of us aimless drifters, we kept in touch through letters while we roamed separate regions of the globe. With part of his journey completed, he decided to join me on mine.

Wood barricades close the park's tree-lined roads to cars. We quickly learn it's safer to walk on or as close to the sidewalk as possible, away from roller skating children whose mobilized feet throw off their balance, their bodies in race to collide with any unalert pedestrian. Swift pedaling, skilled bicyclists whir past us while pairs of lovers and a father with his daughter riding slowly in tandem punctuate their cycling with periodic gasps.

We head to a small stone bridge that doubles as a fountain and leads to a tiny island with a small Buddhist temple. On hot days, jets lining both railings of the bridge shoot arcs of water, a wet welcome to sweaty visitors. Today the water is turned off, inviting many visitors to amble onto the bridge dry with bags of rice to feed thousands of perch below. They compete for the grains hitting the water's surface, their mouths popping open like gum chewing adolescents pushing and slapping their scaly neighbors.

We double back to follow the path around the pond to a wooded area along one of the closed roads. On raised platforms, men sit cross-legged, their arms folded, playing *ba-duk*, a type of Korean chess, their concentration so intense that it seems mind power alone could slide the round black and white game pieces across the board. No one notices us passing. It's an entirely different story, however, for a small group of elderly men and women reveling in drinking *soju*. As we approach, their smiles broaden and they raise their bottles in anthem to their newly-arrived guests. One man grabs my hand and twirls me around. Another approaches Chardin and chuckles while stroking Chardin's long sideburns, facial hair a genetic rarity among Koreans. Daria is offered a glass of *soju*. Were we not so intent on getting to the performance, we might have prolonged our jovial welcome. I bow in appreciation before we move on and pass yet another group in *soju* jubilance, several men shaking their hips, their arms lifted above their heads, their hands fluttering to loud music from a radio positioned on the seat of a motorcycle.

The festival began in the morning, yet we arrive midday, in time for the end of a mask dance, a large crowd having formed a circle in the middle of the street. Mask dances, a combination of music, drama, and dance, rose in popularity during the Chosun Period. Then as now, performers wear simple costumes with wooden masks painted with exaggerated expressions of persons, animals, and spirits intended to parody daily life, much antagonism aimed at the privileged class.

A farmer with a ragged shirt, a maiden with bright red circles for cheeks, and a Confucian dignitary with a long black thin sprout of a beard stand slightly bent in the center of the circle. The farmer keeps trying to clutch the woman's hips. She pushes him away coyly, looking over her shoulder repeatedly to fan his interest. The dignitary pushes the man into a pile of straw who then tosses strands of the dried grass into the dignitary's face.

An unmasked elderly man wobbling among the performers catches my attention. Obviously drunk, he careens among them as if a part of the play and comments on their antics with a screech or guffaw. No performer asks him to leave nor do any spectators shoot him a disdainful look. Even when A-yung and her troupe all stunningly dressed in white raise and lower their shoulders, spreading their arms like herons, common Korean dance moves, he remains on stage in blissful oblivion, occasionally mimicking the performers.

A-yung's troupe dances with meditative deliberateness, a type of tai chi, each movement precise, unhurried, their energy rising and lowering gently, a single fluid gesture done in unison. The angle of their heads and twist of their torsos are steady and contained, nature outside the body intended to reflect nature inside—if it's fair to make such a division. Koreans would likely not separate the outside of the body from its interior. A few thousand years of Buddhism and Chinese medicine is so pervasive here that even those in recent years who have embraced Christianity see unity. Nature within, nature without. All is One, a continuum of forms, separation distinguishable only through the import of western words.

The next act is the percussive beats and accompanying moves of *samul nori*. A group of twenty people hit one of four types of drums, flat or hour-glass shaped, each differing in size. Representing cloud, thunder, wind, and rain, the combined sounds are meant to balance yin with yang. Drummers wear yellow and blue silk pants and distinctive hats unlike anything I've ever seen from a milliner. From the center of their hats sprouts a white ribbon several feet long. Performers crane and rotate their necks around and around, their ribbons sailing upward to write a script in the air, feet moving to the beat of the drums.

By now, the wobbly man, whose performance cues come not from artistic direction but the spirits of *soju*, is joined by a few other standing-challenged audience members in similar states of inebriation. Only when one of them cuts into the dance line are they pushed aside by a blue eye-shadowed, slender onlooker whose sizeable Adam's apple suggests a man despite his—or her—wearing a dress.

With twenty drummers vibrating my body, it's hard to remain still on the curb, my feet tapping the concrete. I accept a glass of *soju* from the man beside me and share it with Chardin who has yet to experience this popular alcohol regularly mixed with beer. When the group parades out of the circle, I consider leaving, but A-yung appears beside me on the curb to thank me for watching before insisting we stay, the best yet to come. All day long, various *samul nori* groups have been performing, she explains, and all will drum together for a finale.

Sure enough, one group after another enters the circle, dozens upon dozens of performers, head ribbons swirling in the air, a bonfire of ethereal white flames. A few wear high hats covered in paper flowers with a sizeable blossom rising up and bobbing above the others. The ensemble performs a simple routine like a marching band at the half-time of a football game, everyone turning and skipping in perfect unity, one line merging then separating from the next. But it's not the choreography that impresses me, whether a hand or elbow lifts just so, but the resonance of the drums, the strikes upon their skins penetrating my own. The polyphony of so many drums pulsates, then passes

160

through my skin like water through a strainer. Each wave of sound presses into and massages me to the bone. I am defenseless, at the vibratory mercy of the pulse. I could walk away and flee the assault, but my heart beat is happy to synchronize with the rhythm of the drums, a solo beater who after a long solitary sojourn has stumbled upon kin. Head to toe in tremor, I am the drum—many drums—the ceremony outside generating an extravaganza of quivers and thumps within.

The drumming transforms the street. More and more drinkers as well as sober onlookers abandon their passive role as spectators, abandoning, too, their usual reserve. They step off their perch on the sidewalk and shuffle into the center of the circle to dance. A performer pulls Daria by the arm into the merriment and urges her to move. Soon, the same happens to me, except my invitation comes with being handed a drum.

Oh, glory. Me and a drum. A bit like a boy and his dog. I hit the drum skin and raise the instrument up, down, and away from me as I witnessed performers doing throughout the afternoon. There's something about generating loud, rhythmic noise that appeals to my reflective, quiet poetic side. Call it my flip-side, an often-neglected part of me getting noticed. Call it my unabashed or bold self. A drum insists itself upon its listeners. Its rapt vibration strikes against ears, an onslaught of sound demanding it be heard whereas my poems graze and invite, a sinuous vocal path that always allows readers the option of refusing to listen. Every now and then, there's nothing more satisfying than a good hit of insistence.

As my drum engages with the crowd, an elderly man shimmies over, hands held high. He circles around me with an unrestrained smile and gyrating hips, motion that seems to break through a final levee of restraint for other men, then women to do the same, some brushing against my arm or back with Mardi Gras glee. The spectacle prompts several photographers to snap pictures. Daria, now bestowing a bobbing flower hat, comes over, too. She bobs, I strike, she bobs again, I strike, our synching inspiring several gleeful spins. More photographers, amateurs and professionals, buzz around us with their small and large telephoto lenses unable to resist our nectar.

By now, a tide of spectators, young and old, have rolled into the circle, leaving no more than a few folks watching. Dancing has erupted everywhere, on the pavement and the grass, near food carts and behind souvenir stands. It's hard to find anyone who is stationary, the drumming's steady thunder pushing away the evil spirits who might disrupt the harvest—or, I imagine, pushing away locusts or any type of pestilence or obstacle to growth. Every time it appears the drumming may end, another round ensues, the energy building further and further.

In past years, a few of my dance performances ended with the audience getting up from their seats to join me on stage, but rarely has it happened with this degree of open-armed, fleet-footed exuberance. Here, there is no restraint, no self-consciousness. Stranger greets stranger in word and movement. A hand grabs another hand, a hip joins sides with another hip. Any prohibition against public motion and expression has been spirited away, the moment fertile with possibility.

If there's a highlight to my time in Korea, this may be it. Watching people burst into dance in the middle of the street, all senses engaged, limbs and muscle in full play, tossing aside whatever frustration, disappointment, or struggle to participate joyously in life's rhythms fulfills me like little else. Ancient practice collides with the present. Circulating oxygen and the steady pump of blood delivers an unmistakable visceral reminder of how change takes place continuously within and beyond the skin. An inhale follows an exhale like the moon's rise follows the setting of the sun.

It's dark when we finally leave. Rather than head directly to the subway, we climb one of the wooded hills in the park, unsure of where we're going. "This way," I say, not really caring if we find the subway entrance immediately or wander for a while.

"Up, only up," says Chardin leading the way, his shoes displacing some of the dirt beneath him, we three foreign wayfarers pounding our rhythm upon the earth.

I want the joy of the day to continue. I know better. Change and I are intimate partners.

162

Secrets and Shame, an Ax and an Emperor

On the way to Insadong in Seoul to find a restaurant, I am distracted by several life-size puppets draped over a metal fence and resting on the sidewalk with flush faces, oversized eyes, neon colored hair, and bodies swathed in simple cloth. I am drawn to them like a child to a doll. As if to awake them from their paper mache stupor, I poke my face into theirs. They, of course, don't stir, but a puppeteer comes over and I compliment his artistry.

"Not only mine," he says in perfect English. "All of ours." He points to a group of people in the square adjacent to the sidewalk.

The purpose of the show is for more than entertainment. "Mixed race children," he replies. He, in his 40's, explains that his Korean mother married a Canadian. When he was born, she found it dangerous to live in Korea with a mixed-race child. "Her life was threatened. Mine, too." They moved to Canada. The other puppeteers, similarly mixed race, grew up in Canada or the U.S. and returned to the country of their birth to raise awareness about the reprehensible attitude toward such children and their parents.

At least in Seoul, there's an attempt to go public and challenge the shames of the culture. For the most part, Daeguians hide their disgraces. What doesn't fit the social norms doesn't get discussed. Look away, case closed. There is an exception however, a place in the city where no argument with such realities takes place. For students flirting with the liberty to reveal their secrets, my office and classroom have become a refuge.

When Ji-sa visited my office, I knew there was something more than her wanting to discuss a grade and bring me a can of ice tea. Students frequently deposit coffee, tea, or juice on my desk during class breaks and after class. Whether it's a gift or bribe isn't clear. Either way I welcome the gesture and, if it's not heavily sugared, usually I drink it. I explain my reason for giving her partial instead of full credit on her vocabulary exam, but her glum, downcast gaze leads me to question her further. "Is there another vocabulary word you want to discuss?"

She had another lexicon in mind, one having to do with family. "My mother unhappy so I unhappy."

"Yes," I say, following but not understanding her leap away from definitions of "bankruptcy" and "aptitude."

"I want to help but don't know how." Her fingers ruffle the edges of her quiz, ripping it in places, the clean borders of paper now rough, the fibers loosed. She looks at me, one of those glances that speaks volumes, yet for better or worse, I can't hear what her eyes say other than to guess that she's disturbed.

"My sister one day disappear."

"Disappear," I ask.

When she was six, her four-year old sister was abducted from the playground outside their apartment building. The young girl had enough smarts to press the red button to alert the security guard to report a suspicious character, but the guard never arrived. By the time her mom went to reclaim her, the playground was empty.

"We not talk about it. Forbidden. Mother will suicide if mentioned. Blame herself. Mother always to blame."

I can't imagine losing a child. I've lost car keys—misplaced them really. They eventually turn up, discovered slipped between the couch cushions or in a pocket of my pants already folded and put away in the dresser drawer. I can't imagine losing a child or sister, a stranger responsible for the heinous act.

"She never showed up?"

"Sometimes I wish me be taken."

I'm considering what more to say, but she's tucking the quiz into her notebook and pushing out her chair. "I quiet in class. I sorry. Often I shy."

And that was it. She walked out the door, and there was no further mention about the sister whose story cannot be told. I watched her more closely in class as she unzipped her pencil case or tucked her cell phone into her bag and encouraged her to participate in conversation, but shyness—or loss or fear—kept her mouth closed.

On the day we discuss blended families and gay marriage in my

American Culture class, So-moon corners me in the hall near the elevator and slouches against the wall. No tea or juice this time, only, "What do foreigners think about gays?"

"I can't speak for all foreigners, only myself," I reply.

"My friend, we get along well," she begins, pausing when the elevator door opens and a student walks out. "Good friend. But last week she told me she lesbian. Should I end our friendship?"

"You like her?"

"Yes."

"You get along?"

"Yes."

"I have several lesbian friends..." That's all I needed to say. She cuts me off, then announces she can't be late to class, thanking me in words and a smile before she disappears down the hall.

Another day, another knock, this one taking place about a week after a class discussion on the qualities of an ideal spouse, a topic chosen by the students. Most of the girls agree that a man's finances is his most important quality; the boys want a girl with a good personality. Students tell me that couples only live together once married and until then, live with their parents. But not always. After Jena gives me plum juice using both hands, a more polite gesture than a one-handed gift, I offer her a chair at my conference table where she shares information about herself not revealed during class. For almost a year, she's been living with her boyfriend in a one-bedroom apartment. Neither her parents nor any of her friends know.

"What happens when your parents visit?"

"I shove his stuff in closet."

I can't imagine the effort that goes into regularly stuffing and unstuffing the closet with his beer bottles, shoes, underwear, magazines, or any other mannish possession lying on the table or a shelf that provides evidence of cohabiting with me. What happens if someone drops by unannounced or an item meant for the closet gets overlooked?

"Where'd that baseball trophy come from?" says imaginary Friend A.

"Oh, that?" I reply. "I, um, I collect them. They're so... heavy, metal, sleek. It's my latest indulgence. I love baseball, don't you?"

"I don't remember you liking baseball."

"Oh, you know how it is. A touch of home here in Korea is welcome. Hey, want some *kimchi*?" I say to change the subject. "I just got a new batch."

Or Mom visits and comments about the cool temperature and needs a sweater from, where else, the closet.

"I'll get it," she says, wanting to be helpful. "I'm already in your room."

"No! Don't! I'll get it! I mean, I want you to have a warm and fitted one, something that complements your hair. It's in one of the drawers. You won't be able to find it."

I'm incapable of lying. My upbringing coincided with tales about George Washington and his cherry tree. I can keep other's secrets, but fail at keeping my own. Ask and I shall tell. Friends have told me that I sometimes reveal more information than is wanted. The funny thing about telling the truth is that it's often disbelieved especially if, as happens frequently, I smile nervously, an idiosyncrasy my listener assumes is a cover up, not an indication of discomfort.

Herein lies a huge difference between Americans and Koreans. The lore of George and his ax are part of most Americans' upbringing. Soon after we stopped drooling, balanced ourselves by grabbing hold of Dad's leg, and spoke our first words, we're taught to tell the truth, nothing but. "Did you pull your sister's hair?" "Whose dirty plate is this?" "Did you take the car?" Yes, mine, yes! I did it! All of it! Whether to parents, teachers, spouses, our boss, or the clerk at the grocery store, we're encouraged not to lie, neither the small, inconsequential ones nor ones registering high on the Richter scale.

Koreans value harmony above truth-telling. They go out of their way to "save face," dignity and reputation highly prized, especially if it impacts a group. To disrupt harmony with bad news or a difficult truth is considered more dishonorable and uncultured than concealing it. Obviously, what students reveal to the entire class differs from what they share with me through one-on-one exchanges. During conversation class when I ask how many of their parents are divorced, two hands go up, but as I move around the room and stop at their desks, new details emerge.

For fourteen years, Du-ho's parents have been divorced, but only he and his sister know. His dad lives in an apartment on one side of the city, his mom in a house on the other. They appear together at weddings and other ceremonies, arriving in the same car and sitting together with family, yet out of the public eye, they refuse to talk on the phone or have anything to do with each other. Du-ho often acts as the go-between, arranging who drives which car and when.

"No one else knows?" I respond.

"My father and my mother each see someone else," shares another student.

"They live apart?"

"No. Separate rooms. Same house."

"Why don't they get separate homes? Divorce?" I say naively. He gives me a look that speaks volumes which by now, I'm learning to hear.

The following day in class, I tell them that divorce in Korea is more common than I thought. To inform them about my homeland, I add, "Americans divorce all the time. The latest figures I've read are that 52% of married couples terminate their love." I say nothing about my own contribution to the statistic or that I'm increasingly wondering why anyone marries, given the poor odds about it lasting "through sickness and death." The myth of the white knight scooping up the damsel in promise of domestic bliss suffered its final gasps several months ago.

Then, with American brashness, I say, "How many of your dads have a girlfriend? Five hands in a class of twenty-three go up. I do the math, figure that a few others are reluctant to share the information. Even for this number challenged professor, the imbalance in the figures tilts toward a hush-hush of reality. "Can someone explain?"

Jin-hae rolls her eyes. "Korean men are *that way*," she says bluntly.

I want to find a copy of the pamphlet that my students read about me. "All secrets deposited here. Safe haven. Price: plum juice or

167

unsweetened tea." I have sipped my way into hearing about abortions, cigarette smoking (okay for men, not women), pot smoking (while he was in the Philippines), and considerations of suicide. Students regard me a risk-free repository for secrets otherwise unspeakable.

Public shaming, the loss of face, carries significant consequences. There's no need to throw a punch if you can mar a reputation.

Today ex-president Roh Moo-hyun, beloved for his support of human rights and opposition to authoritarian rule, committed suicide. He was walking with his security guard on the mountain ridge behind his home. When the guard turned his back, the beleaguered leader tossed himself off a cliff. He left a note detailing his reasons. "It has been so tough," the suicide note said. "I caused so much trouble to many people."

He was upset with an aggressive investigation into funds received, a charge of alleged bribery. Of late, he's been hounded by a special prosecuting committee, his wife and two children also under investigation. A charge of bribery for a man who built his presidency on financial transparency and cleaning up corruption tarnishes his reputation. By tossing himself off the cliff, his face and that of his family is "saved." Ending his life puts a stop to the investigation. "I have no face to show to the people," he said to a special jury a month prior to his death.

What value is the truth? If the emperor is happy with his new clothes, do you tell him that he is naked?

The doctor's wife wants to destroy my reputation by spreading stories about me on campus, distressing, for sure, yet I believe in the power of truth. The doctor tells me that our phone calls contribute to him curing more and more patients and increases his family's wealth. I watch the emperor's coach pass and listen to stories people feel at liberty to share with me. In my pocket, I finger a needle and thread for pants, shirt, and coat, silk lined, of course. On a moment's notice, I will set all on a table and start sewing.

Roh's suicide is spurring other suicides. Editorials in the newspaper blast the media for paying so much attention to his manner of death.

Each day I read about a student upset about grades or an elder who can't pay bills having tossed himself off a balcony or onto the tracks of an approaching train.

I'm looking at my students differently, wondering about their tipping point. I walk into class aware that something I say could be the statement that determines whether they choose life or death. At Salsita, I say nothing when my partner, a few months away from completing law school and graduating with honors, answers his phone and lies to his mother, telling her he is at home studying, not dancing tango, this social dance not widely accepted by older generations. At what point does pain become too much? When does the drive to live succumb to the shame of one's circumstances? When do the mores of a country or the remarks of a family or spouse become the very weapon you use upon yourself? Here I hide my "disgrace" and nurse my pain in private, but what gave me the impetus to transform my pain not into bitterness or death, but into something more life supporting?

Sitting on my bed, my back against the wall, I jot down these questions in a notebook designated to my musings. I stop after the last question and slide off the mattress to prepare myself a cup of green tea.

Hidden Paradises

There are many reasons to be grateful for Children's Day, a holiday founded by children's writer Pang Chong-hwan in 1923. Intended initially to instill national pride, it has evolved into a day when parents indulge their offspring by taking them to amusement parks or movies, going on picnics, essentially finding a way to delight them. This year, Children's Day coincides by a few days with Buddha's Birthday, occurring on the eighth day of the lunar calendar. He turns about 2573, most scholars disagreeing about the precise date of his birth. Around the country, many businesses are closed and the university has followed suit. The usual two-day weekend has expanded into five.

I've needed time off. This semester, I'm teaching six classes. Too many. Four days a week, classes start at 9:00am and on three nights, go until 9:30pm. Many Saturdays, I'm encouraged—some colleagues say required— to participate in the planned extracurricular activities with students and faculty, all of which cuts into needed down time for hiking, reading, or doing as little as possible unbound to a schedule. I thank Pang Chong-hwan and Buddha.

It's spring. On campus, lilacs and lavender bushes, wisteria, and cherry, magnolia, and plum trees have exploded into an orgy of color and scent. For the last intoxicating week, I walk to class torn between going inside to teach and pressing my proboscis into blossoms. A suggestion of hiking appeals to Chardin, Daria, and me even though it's also the season of yellow dust. Yellow dust, to an unschooled observer like myself, looks like pollen; its yellow powder coats cars, sidewalks, and any outdoor surface, and makes eyes tear and throats itch. Therein the similarities end.

Yellow dust, *hwangsa*, fine particles of soil, are little storms of clouds that blow in from China's Gobi Desert and are downright dangerous when inhaled, unavoidable, unless sealing oneself inside a specially constructed room. In recent years, these little storms have grown in size and toxicity, the result of increasing desertification and the wind's ability to pick up sulfur, lead, arsenic, and a cocktail of other metallic carcinogens spewed in abundance from China's environmentally unregulated factories. Its neighbors to the east in Korea and Japan suffer from severe asthma, and on the worst of days, when the government issues warnings that citizens stay indoors, death. Periodically I check the particle count: 200 is considered unhealthy and anything over 300 is hazardous. Imagine the alarm in April 2006 when levels in Seoul reached 500 (some newspapers reported it as higher). On the day of our hike, the level squeaks by at a mere 125, supposedly safe as long as we drink a lot of water and by day's end, wash thoroughly, especially the face. Many Koreans opt for soft cloth face masks that filter out some of the pollutants.

We decide to travel to a nearby park for a short hike up its highest mountain, Mt. Apsan, 3000 ft. At the base of the park is an anti-communist museum dedicated to the Korean War. If there's time, we may go inside to check out the photographs of atrocities and read the stories of horrors perpetrated by the North, but mumbles from Chardin and Daria about going in suggest I may have to do so myself later. Is this the way to celebrate a birthday? We begin our ascent, Chardin several yards ahead of us, barefoot, a preference developed during his Maine to Georgia Appalachian hike. Shoes stay on for Daria and me.

"No books!" chimes Daria, her green eyes almost the same shade as recently emerged leaves.

"No students!" I say to echo her rejoicing in the opportunity to leave campus and step gladly into the forest, a reminder of what's important, a dirt path and muscles exerting the effort to climb, a brief reprieve from our usual responsibilities.

Every mountain houses at least one Buddhist temple and Apsan Mountain with three is no exception. After walking briefly, we're drawn to the colored lanterns lining a path to Daesongsa Temple. For Buddha's Birthday, people purchase lanterns and make a wish that gets written on a piece of paper which hangs from the bottom of the lantern like a tongue licking the wind. This day more so than others, wishes supposedly have greater chance at realization. Thousands of candy blue, pink, green, purple, and yellow orbs sweeten the path and form a canopy over the main courtyard of the temple grounds. It's morning, yet by midday, people will pack the sanctuary in welcome of a free meal and the good luck that comes with the visit. Several women are cutting mounds of cabbage and carrots behind an outdoor kitchen with large cooking pits. Chardin and Daria squat and grab several felt-tip pens to fill in thinly drawn black and white Buddha figures on a large cardboard paper leaning against a stage.

I wander over to lotus flowers in full bloom floating in stone pots and am joined by a monk who asks, "American." My response prompts a slight bow before he informs me about the day's events. Before he finishes however, his attention is diverted by the arrival of two men in suits. "Sorry, I must attend," he says, bowing once more. His brown robe sails with him as he slips between aisles of chairs in the courtyard to greet them. Then all three walk towards me, one offering me his hand in greeting. This gesture and his ease with English lead me to assume he's familiar with western customs. Somewhat.

"I am governor of this province," he starts, then inquires about my stay in Korea. I tell him about my teaching and he shares that he attended a university in Massachusetts. An entire conversation ensues beneath a sky of lanterns, small talk, all well and good. All the while, he has not let go of my hand, his palm pressing closer and closer against mine, our two countries bonding, my history marking itself by this, my longest handshake ever. I don't mind the diplomacy with its faux pas. I am, after all, an admitted podium leaner, and likely guilty of a much longer list of offences. Eventually our hands pull apart, and we continue with our separate mission, mine involving a hike to the peak.

The trail we've chosen leads to a tram, should we choose an aloft way down, but en route we find a restaurant perched on the mountain side. Since none of us packed adequately for lunch—one energy bar, a bag of nuts, and two bottles of water—we venture up the few uneven stone steps and through a screen door that shuts sharply behind us.

Three walls of restaurant windows suggest an ideal location with a panoramic view of temples, trees, and the city below, a potent combination of sacred and verdant beauty, nature harmonizing with humanity. But ripped vinyl chairs, missing linoleum floor tiles, and broken window screens spoil the vision, the heyday of this place long past. I slide open the window at our table to let in air and a few inches of view. Two patrons, a couple, share the restaurant with us, along with the owner, a burly woman who is also the cook, and her brother who is busy talking with her.

He, slender and angular, shouts to us jovially from across the room. His manner gets me wondering if he's tipsy or profoundly gracious, the latter typical of many Koreans of his generation when they encounter someone they believe is American. He saunters over to our table, fascinated by Daria's "blonde" hair (she would describe it as brown), and curious about her studying Korean.

"Why you choose this country? Other country also interesting."

"No," replies Daria, "Korea has a rich history. It's very interesting to me."

He asks additional questions, his body inching his way flirtatiously toward her. When he turns his attention to me, his stance shifts, as often happens when my high status is revealed. "Oh, a professor," he declares standing straighter, his hand removed from the table. "Love America. Best place." About seventy-five years old, he's worked for the U.S. Army since the Korean War. "Many good friends. I know Philadelphia, Texas, Georgia, Washington D.C. They treat me well. My life good."

When we first entered the restaurant, Daria asked the cook if one of my favorite dishes, *pajeon*, a green onion pancake, was on the menu. She was told no, but now through the miracle of amity—as well as status and blonde hair—he yells across the room and insists his sister make it for us. After a brief wait, she places on the table the food we ordered, along with rice cakes which we didn't order, and he waves from his table to inform us he's paying for our lunch.

The following day, Daria stays behind in Daegu for work translating a Korean text into Russian, and Chardin and I bus an hour to Gyeongju. Once the capitol of the Silla Kingdom, Gyeongju contains a palace, hundreds of royal tombs, several pagodas, fortress ruins, temples, and a number of parks. UNESCO has selected it as one of the ten most important ancient cultural cities in the world. The excursion launches my first extended tour since arriving in Korea. I welcome Chardin's company.

We rent bicycles to maneuver this car and bus choked museum city that attracts thousands of tourists daily. Swarms of people clog the sidewalks and spill into the streets as we head to the king's tombs which date back to 57 B.C. From a distance, we survey a tomb, a 30 foot earthen mound, then pedal to the kite flying park. Chardin's bike is equipped with a bell attached to the handlebars which he rings like Moses commanding the sea of humanity part, areas of sidewalk quickly clearing for our bikes to pass.

No one minds our bold navigation. When families turn and see westerners as the source of the ringing, a son or daughter shouts, "Where from?" or "Have a good day!" Whether we're on our bikes or walking the grounds, young and old alike wave, say hello, or approach us to chat. We're luckless movie stars whose celebrity is recognized by others, yet we cannot recall the roles or names of our movies as if due to a bout of amnesia. Our polite fans make no specific references to them either.

As designated map reader, Chardin is an ideal travel partner. We take turns deciding upon a destination, he charts the route, and when necessary, I ask a passerby for help. By afternoon, I'm convinced he can't have come all the way from the U.S. without seeing Bulguksa, one of three beloved jewel temples of the country. Having visited the temple a few months back, I was originally disinclined to return, especially after hearing that countless Koreans regardless of religious affiliation will sojourn there, unwilling to ignore a chance to invest in their luck, eager to pack any available space to worship with their favorite *Bodhisattva*. As a teenager, I welcomed the push and prod of a crowd. My devotion then was directed at rock music, the wiry or laid back electric guitars my salvation. Its pulse propelled me to purchase record albums weekly, my reverence extended to staying in long lines if need be to acquire a ticket to witness my idol live. Like everyone else attending these concerts, I pushed my way to a spot as close to the stage as possible, friends and I squeezing in and rubbing against the skin and sweat of strangers, their bodies bobbing alongside my own. But age erodes tolerance, and these days I prefer an ample cushion of space around me and many fewer bobs, however well synched to music.

I've been fortunate to have seen another of the temple jewels: Haensa. The lure for Buddhist pilgrims around the world is its Tripitaka, 80,000 wood carved blocks of Buddhist scripture created with moveable metal type from the 13th century, 200 years before Gutenberg invented his press. Four windowless buildings constructed with open slats to maximize airflow preserve the blocks for antiquity, eyed only by monks, scholars, and, of course, spirits.

Yet when else might I get to celebrate Buddha's birthday in Asia? I want to see the spectacle of lit lanterns at night and am willing to be jostled by a crowd. Okay, but only briefly. The map shows the temple an inch from our current location, Chardin wants to bike, yet I recall a colleague warning me not to trust local cartography. Our bicycles are functional, the seats less than optimal, their springs uneven and covers frayed in places. Rather than risk a sore that we'll pay for later, I suggest we take a bus.

It hasn't rained more than a few minutes in all the months I've been here, but as we await the bus, the size and density of an approaching cloud suggests the arrival of a new season. We run into a convenience store to buy umbrellas in case my amateur forecast is correct. When we return to the bus stop, the doctor calls.

"Where are?" he asks.

"Gyeongju. At a bus stop."

I tell him about our tour. "How is your condition?" he says, his customary question along with wanting to know my energy level and the food I've consumed.

"You?"

"Fine. I fine." This is his pat reply. For more details, I've learned to ask again, often more than three times, before hearing about the number of patients seen that day, what he ate for lunch, if he's tired, and what he's thinking. But his response this time stuns me.

"Confused." Long pause. "Wife tried to kill me last night."

"What! How? Why? Are you okay?" I'm stammering. Chardin looks up from his book.

"With kitchen knife. Drunken and came after me."

"Why?"

"I don't know."

"Did you call the police?"

Silence.

He has perfected this sort of non-reply, a response Koreans seem to give if they'd rather withhold information, believe it disappoints, or doesn't contribute to increasing harmony. I prefer the response "Can't" or "Wouldn't work" or "When I finish my soup." The writer in me, or perhaps the American, wants a grunt, a syllable, a verbal reply, anything really, but not silence.

"How about a psychiatrist?" She's got a temper, as I well know, but supposedly it's never escalated to this.

Again silence. Then, "Threatened her sister, too. Wife tell me to leave, not return. She left house, spend night away."

"What are you going to do?"

"I don't know."

"Will you go home tonight?"

"I don't know. What I do?"

I'm not used to uncertainty from him. Usually he's a fount of surety, whether espousing on the customs of his fellow countrymen or explaining the difference between yin and yang. Strongly yanged by the violence of his admission, I blurt out, "Chardin and I are headed to Bulguksa. Join us." I don't expect him to accept the offer. Since I stopped going to the clinic, we've met for lunch, talked on the phone, but go weeks without any communication, except, of course, telepathically.

"Where meet?"

I'm surprised by the acceptance. "The ticket building at the entrance."

My predictive acumen proves correct—nothing like looking at the sky. A heavy drizzle intensifies into sheets of rain as the bus arrives. Visibility out its windows is minimal. Car lights deflect off the glass to create headache-inducing hallucinogenic blurs. Repeatedly I wipe moisture from the window to no avail. Moist phantasms insist on limiting sight to immediate surroundings within the bus, not anything out the window like geography or commerce or an unfortunate pedestrian caught by the elements.

When we reach the temple parking lot, the rain has let up and we take the winding path to the main gate where we wait beneath our umbrellas. Beneath his, the doctor arrives, a profile in the dark. I'm glad to see him unharmed. "Not too wet?"

"Rain good," he replies, beaming a smile. "Visit temple and rain on

Buddha's Birthday increase luck."

The rain has already delivered my good luck; the crowds have fled to their cars, leaving the temple grounds with a trickle of visitors. Mist surrounds the buildings, cloaks trees, the earth emanating vapor. Lanterns illuminate the main path and reflect splashes of color in puddles. A symmetrical stairway that leads to the Buddha realm, the main building, is closed, but on this night of soft vaporous lines, it seems any entrance would deliver us from *samsara*, the perpetual wanderings, misgivings and fortunes of existence. We enter through a side gate a short distance from the main path where it's dark and dreamlike, nearly impossible to distinguish a window from a door or one person from another. Forms slowly emerge from the mist, then disappear again as if receding into the hereafter.

The levity of the doctor's voice and easy stride don't strike me as a man whose life has been imperiled. With great pride and grace, he leads us around, explaining when the Japanese burned which buildings, the date a building was rebuilt, a story about his last visit. He resorts to silence at the golden statues of venerated Shakyamuni Buddha and the celestial Amitabha Buddha to let us hear our own thoughts and any whispers which may come from these honored figures.

Chardin and I previously discussed taking a late-night bus back to Daegu or staying at a hotel or a *jimjilbang*, one of the public bath houses where women and men sleep side by side on the floor. The doctor's presence supplies a new option, driving us back. When he hears about our choices, he urges us to stay to see Seokguram. This stone cave hermitage at the top of the mountain is a must-see, he tells us, especially at dawn. Then the first rays of light reflect off the Buddha inside the grotto Indiana Jones-like to prevent invaders, specifically the Japanese, from taking the country.

"You stay," he insists. "I join?"

Thus begins the travail of looking for a vacancy during Gyeongju's most popular weekend of the year. We drive to one *jimjilbang* after another, one hotel then another, ask one taxi driver then another. Each stop, recommendation, and direction leads to the same result: no available bed or floor in the entire city. After about the tenth stop, Chardin and I dipping in and out of sleep, I'm ready to return to Daegu, but the doctor suggests we drive out of town.

Nearly three hours after leaving the temple, we find a hotel about forty-five miles from Seokguram which means if we're to see it at dawn, we get only three hours of sleep. Three hours of sleep destroys my functionality. Commonplace objects like chairs and countertops become moving targets that jut out unexpectedly into my hip or shin. Otherwise simple tasks like purchasing a bottle of water or boiling an egg inflate into a gargantuan project with multi-tiered planning and usually bungled results. I vote for sleep. Chardin can go either way, and the doctor supports my decision. After five luxurious hours of shut eye, we skip breakfast, save for instant coffee in the room, and set off on our pilgrimage to Seokguram.

Many sojourns have their obstacles, pestilence, locusts and such; we hit ours halfway up the winding mountainous road. What might have been a fifteen-minute drive from the base of the mountain to the top lengthens into ninety restless minutes of bumper to bumper traffic, idle cars endlessly inching upward, a few impatient—or ambitious— passengers abandoning their vehicles to huff it to the top on foot. Increasingly hungry and impatient, I'm questioning whether or not to continue, yet the doctor insists we do.

When we finally park, we shuffle our way onto yet another line that leads to the arched entry to the inner chamber, the entire structure built in 751 A.D. Inside stands a twelve-foot high Buddha that shimmers within the soft light of a rotunda. Immediately I understand how ascending the mountain trail from Bulguksa was intended as a sojourn to nirvana. The depth of serenity radiating from the Buddha's smooth face, slightly upturned lips, and chiseled lines of his body seems capable of turning the most tenacious demons, negative thoughts and pain into melting sweetened butter.

A few second glimpse is not enough for me. I want to stay, to meditate on one of the *zabutons*, the cushions near the foot of the statue. I want to turn the heat on my own rancid thoughts and hear the screams of my demons weaken to no more than a murmur. I want the lingering pain of my loss to burn off and leave only the cool of memory. I step away from the line, apart from the shuffling crowd, and close my eyes, infusing myself with the energy of the room. I inhale deeply, enough to fill my belly, energy rising up and down my spine, then moving outward to the rest of my body. Inner attention both witness and participant, muscles relax, breath partnering with energy to tango, waltz, improvise, surrender, and settle. With my breath slowed, useless thoughts, energy, and emotion exfoliate. When my eyes eventually open, a profound peace arrives. My entire being is purring.

I exit through the side archway to a line of people continuing down stone steps, others meandering chaotically en route to the toilet, a cliff edge, or in loud chase of a running child. No longer agitated by the crowd or hunger, I step away from the grotto, my footfalls no heavier than clouds barely touching the earth. A soft halo of light surrounds every tree, rock and person. Buffered by my newborn ease, I look around for Chardin and the doctor and then float alongside them back to the car through the afternoon and into the night when eventually my head lands gently upon the pillow.

The sojourn continues the next day without the doctor. Minji joins Chardin and me for a trip to Toyeoung City to take a ferry to Somae-mul Island. Daria would like to go, but she hasn't finished some translating work. By the time we arrive, the last ferry has departed, leaving us to figure out what to do with the rest of the day.

We take a taxi to a lacquer museum which houses colorfully designed room panels, furniture, jewelry, and other decorations for home and body, but it's only a few small rooms and we find ourselves with the same dilemma as before, figuring out what to do with our time. Minji suggests visiting Yonghwa Temple. Chardin and I have wanted to do a templestay, but every temple I phoned days earlier explained the impossibility of doing so on this birthday crowded weekend. Only one place welcomed us, but with a caveat, staying three months, longer than either of us wanted.

As a child, I used to play in the Connecticut woods. A few thousand acres of undeveloped land adjacent to the family home beckoned me to hang out with trees and twigs, beetles and bees, neighborhood friends joining me for long walks along rolling hills, across streams, and up small cliffs. The dense woods leading to Yonghwa similarly beckon, and I have an inkling, despite contrary evidence, that we'll be staying.

Once at Yonghwasa, which in English translates as "future paradise," I tell Minji about my desire, not for a complete weekend templestay with 108 bows, the construction of paper lanterns, a brief talk, and too little meditation time, but something more informal. Although the courtyards are empty of people, pairs of shoes neatly arranged outside building doors suggest occupants. Chardin and I enter one of the halls. Paintings and gold statues of various *Bodhisattvas* populate every inch of wall. I am drawn once again to meditate and retrieve a cushion from a corner of the room. Like yesterday at Seokguram, my breath deepens and slows, cells and hormones recalibrating, subtle shifts which feel like a shawl wrapping itself around my heart. Wave after wave of compassion begins to emanate from my heart like a beacon. I choose to direct them and initiate my own version of *metta bhavana*, an ancient loving kindness practice. I pray for a peaceful resolve for the doctor and his wife's dispute. I pray for the well-being of my friends and family in the U.S. I pray for my students and others I've come to know here. I pray that my heartache subsides and pray, too—this part difficult—for the two who contributed to the anguish that set into motion my departure to Korea. Each thought rides on the tail of a breath until dissolving in the pauses between the inhale and the exhale. Every cell of my being seems to stir in the sweet, spacious air of the temple, my body vibrating in attunement with 1500 years-worth of meditators, the boundaries of my body softening, becoming more porous.

When Chardin and I emerge from the hall, Minji informs us that we've been invited to stay the night, dinner served in an hour. She leads us to our room where we pull out our bed rolls from a closet and rest briefly before heading to our private dining room. There a woman serves us dish after dish of leftovers from the afternoon's birthday feast.

Once we empty our rice bowls, we cross the grounds for tea and conversation with a monk. Shaven head and brown robed, he bows as we enter his small room and motions for us to join him at a table with a tea kettle and cups. He pours water into our cups, into a pinch of tea, then drains them of liquid, before refilling our cups, a by now familiar ceremony.

"Welcome to Yonghwasa," he begins. He explains that the temple focuses on the Middle Way, the Tenfold Path of Buddhism, which aims to establish equanimity, a midpoint between indulgence and denial. The site for Yonghwasa, chosen for its location on a middle mountain on a middle island, enhances the teachings of the temple.

"What brings you here?" he says to me.

I can think of two ways to answer such a question, particularly from a Zen monk. What brings me here, as in this lifetime? I would tell him about my perceived purpose, my place in the scheme of humanity, my writing and dance, and expound on various philosophies about qualities of life. He speaks English well enough to understand me. Or I could be more direct, immediate: this moment, this moment only. My gut pushes for simple: "We were headed to an island but missed the last ferry."

"I feel your practice," he says to me as if hearing my unvoiced words. He turns to Minji and Chardin. "Do you also meditate?"

After a further exchange, he then asks if I have any questions. I want to know how long he's resided at Yonghwasa and what he did before coming here.

"Used to live in Seoul, but was never happy with my job. I knew there had to be more to living and I found it. Here is quiet, focus, less stress, all manageable. Life makes more sense."

He smooths his robe, lifts the kettle to refill our cups, then asks me if there were only one question to ask him, what is my question.

My response comes quickly. I blurt, "Who am I?" I might have added why.

"Oh!" he squeals. "That is the central question of Korean Zen. Who is self? What is self? Who are you? Do you know who you are?"

He wants me to answer the last question. I leave simple behind,

181

brain weariness unable to form any other response. "Now?" I begin. "Certainly I'm not who I was yesterday or a year ago. Now a temple sitter and tea drinker in conversation with you."

"And tomorrow?"

"I don't know." I'm enjoying our volley.

"Your spirit Korean!" he exclaims, palms coming together, echoing the doctor's conclusion months earlier.

I've not asked his name and do so now, rather than have to return later when it may be less convenient.

"Hidden Monk," he replies.

"Yours?"

I grab the first name that pops into mind, one inspired by the temple's name. "Paradise." Minji introduces herself as Green Tea, Chardin as Barefoot Hiker.

At 5 am, when the temple bell rings to call those to the main hall to meditate, I remain asleep under the blanket of my bed roll. Chardin ambles out of bed and slides opens the rice screen door. When he returns about an hour later at the start of dawn, Minji and I have dressed, our bed rolls folded and returned to the closet. We slip quietly away from the temple to catch a bus to the ferry.

I want to glimpse this peninsula from afar, from the South Sea, and view its craggy, uninhabitable cliffs. I want the water's currents jostling the boat to challenge my balance. I want distance, perspective, to be far away from the illusory security of the mainland. Something tells me though, I'm already seeing it, the ferry ride just a ride on a ferry.

DMZ

No trip to Korea is complete without a visit to the DMZ. I've been calling the reputable American run USO (United Service Organizations) to book a tour of the region, but two weeks of phoning has yielded no return calls to my messages.

Call it a morbid curiosity to want to visit the DMZ, but it strikes me as bizarre, although not without precedent, that two countries once one go to war, divide, and split families apart. Within the 151 mile long, 2.5 mile wide area, no one is allowed to walk, build, hunt, or fly over the land. Fishers can't boat the waters either.

After three years of fighting, the Korean War ended with a truce, not quite an end to the skirmish, communists to the north, democrats to the south, but at least the guns stopped firing. Both sides continue to war with words and incendiary acts like assassination attempts, tunnels, and abductions. Since 1957, the two Koreas continue to compete to prove one ideology superior over the other.

The North was founded by "Dear Leader" Kim Il-sung, a similar name of endearment passed on to his son and successor Kim Jong-il in 1994. To refer to either Kim in a way other than Dear Leader or to mar the current leader's picture which hangs on a wall in every citizen's home gets you arrested and thrown into a labor camp. Kim Jong-il publicly despises the West, despite a love of western comforts like cognac, movies, and swimming pools (with a wave machine). He contends that his southern neighbor is a puppet government of Americans who are a trigger away from invading the North. Severe sacrifices of time, work, and quality of life are expected of each citizen who believes every word of Kim's propaganda. Tuning into a radio or television station from outside the country for entertainment or news lands you in a gulag, so most N. Koreans remain ignorant to alternative points of view.

It's apparent who has lost the race. Since the 90's, N. Koreans have suffered mass starvation as a result of poor agriculture policies, drought, and a government that funnels its resources to its military and ignores the needs and wise counsel of its people. S. Korea, initially behind in the race, surpassed its northern neighbors in the 80's when it embraced industrialization which grew the economy and contributes to a comfortable quality of life for its people.

The relationship between the two countries is a strained one. S. Koreans living near the border do so at their peril, particularly those who make their living from the water. N. Koreans have a habit of plucking fishermen who stray close to northern waters. (They've also abducted film producers and actors.) Northerners board the boats of Southerners and hoist them away to the interior of the country, to parts unknown, cut off from communication with the rest of the world. Rumor has it that the government tries to convert them into spies. Meanwhile, horrified family members who have found their father's or uncle's abandoned boats adrift initially asked and now demand help from the S. Korean government who refuses to acknowledge the politically explosive occurrence. "Likely fell off the boat from a heart attack" or "Ran away to China with a mistress" are among several excuses offered before the clerk hangs up the phone. There are stern looks and hushes, too, from neighbors who have escaped the mishap, despite as many as 200 people disappearing.

Japan lost its citizens to abductions, too, but its insistence that N. Korea return its people has brought many back into the tearful arms of relatives along with an apology for the "mistake." Several others, including a thirteen-year old girl, still unaccounted for, remain missing.

Chardin reserves three spaces for Daria, himself, and me on a tour bus run by a S. Korean company. There's a dress code: no faded jeans, t-shirts with slogans, or flip-flops. Photographs are allowed but only in specified areas. We'll be told where those areas are; violators will be swiftly removed from the bus. Before the Berlin Wall fell, I walked on both the east and west side of the imposing concrete blockade and cringed at the sight of armed men, their rifles alert to my presence. When guns are involved, I don't take chances. Not only is the DMZ the most heavily guarded border in the world, its soldiers are told to shoot with even a slight provocation. Last year a tourist was shot dead by the North when she "strayed" off a path in a resort area. I dress carefully in dark blue jeans, a light orange sweater, and closed sandals.

A van picks us up from a hotel in Seoul and delivers us to another hotel less than a mile away where a man in polyester pants and a button-down shirt checks our passports. The three of us and other foreign tourists board a tour bus for a forty-five minute ride out of town. As we approach the region, we drive under a few small bridges which double as bunkers designed to explode readily and drop concrete, rebar, and combustible material onto the road to slow down any northern invaders. As we approach the military base, Camp Bonfas, for another passport check, this one by an armed guard, we pass field after field of the country's most important crop, ginseng, over 5000 tons harvested annually. In dirt rows between plants, farmers in straw hats squat and pluck leaves; I imagine their hats fitted with night vision goggles, the controls for an unmanned, robotic aerial vehicle tucked in their pocket, a hand grenade dangling beside a water bottle at their waist.

A modest price permits entry to the edge of the DMZ where visitors peer through binoculars to the other side and see "Peace Village," a.k.a "Propaganda Village." The North claims two hundred families live an ideal collectivist lifestyle in luxury villas with childcare, state of the art hospitals, and other amenities duplicated nowhere else in the country. The buildings are pristine and the landscaping immaculate, yet no people have ever been spotted on the streets, except for an occasional landscaper. High powered telescopes reveal the interior of the buildings missing furniture, walls, and occupants.

Tourists can also visit the Joint Security Area building where soldiers from one country eye with an eagle's attentiveness those on the other side. Years ago, there was an ongoing competition over which side's soldiers blink less, fewer blinks indicating national superiority, so now all wear sun glasses to conceal the inadvertent lowering of the lid. The North's soldiers scrutinize each other as well, in case one gets a hair brain idea to defect, doing so resulting in an immediate gun blast to the chest.

Tours go to one of four tunnels found between 1974 and 1990 built by the N. Koreans to invade the South. The North claims the tunnels were dug for mining operations only and points to the blackened walls as proof, yet numerous geologists determined the black not as coal, but a thin veneer of paint. Our tour begins with Tunnel 3, about 1800 yards long, designed to move about 30,000 troops every hour. We deposit our camera and other belongings in a locker, snap on a yellow safety helmet, and begin our descent toward communist granite.

I'm glad for my helmet. The tunnel is about 7 feet wide and an inconsistent 6 feet high, so within minutes, I hit my head on the ceiling once, then twice, and from the sound of it, others are knocking their heads, too. As I go deeper, 82 yards below ground, the air cools and water drips from the walls. The tunnel ends with a boarded up opening and a sign in English that reads, "No further entry permitted. Turn around." As if we have a choice!

The next stop on the tour is an easy walk across the parking lot to a building where we're to watch a video about the history of the DMZ. "History" is a misnomer. It's more a case of southern propaganda. The film depicts a young girl walking along the edge of the DMZ crying. Three years of war is summarized in about 40 seconds, followed by an animation of rabbits, deer, green lawns, and water fountains, the young girl skipping happily as the speaker announces that "The DMZ is no longer a partition. It is our home, a symbol of peace." The families of the 600,000 Korean and 27,000 American soldiers who died there as well as the separated families who have not seen each other in decades might not agree. Then there's the little unmentioned detail of the 700 active land mines. Somehow an image of land mines doesn't readily come to my mind when I think about peace.

From here, we board the bus and are supposed to go to the observation tower to peer onto the other side. It's then our guide delivers unwelcome information. The Prince of Belgium is currently touring the tower and the military is keeping tour buses away. But no worry, we're told, we can go to Dorasan Train Station. As one who uses subways several days a week and the train station about once a month, visiting a train station, even one whose rails leads to the North, holds no appeal. In the large steel and glass modern building, empty of frantic travelers rushing to catch a train, tourists and several armed guards wander about in geopolitical limbo. There's a souvenir shop and a place to get a stamped train ticket that indicates heading North, but we're warned not to stamp our passport which would cause great trouble with immigration upon leaving S. Korea. I ask a clerk to stamp a page in my notebook instead.

We board the bus again for a larger souvenir area, this one complete with amusement park, several lunch stands, and a large cafeteria where we grab a bite. Once we begin our return trip to Seoul, our bus comes to a lurching halt within yards of our little tourist mecca. Several passengers bolt awake from sleep. Explosives? An unannounced search by a guard? A spy among us? The tour guide grabs the mic, then instructs us to look out the window. Nibbling its way along the roadside is a deer, its fur rough with bald patches, likely from disease. In a country that decades ago devoured every critter it could find, wildlife sightings are a rarity.

Deer are not a rarity where I've lived. Instead they're a controversy, an ideology, rarely an object of wonderment. They're considered four-legged vermin who destroy gardens, vehicles, and carry disease-ridden ticks. They're also victims, their population proliferating, in competition for the same woods and fields as people, many of their natural predators like wolves and bobcats killed or pushed off the land.

It's easy to condemn a country as starkly and brutally totalitarian as N. Korea and point to the successes of another regime. What is it about us that we feel compelled to drag others into our beliefs and if refused, we install barbed wire and armed guards, willing to war in words and weaponry?

I look out the window, roused by the guide's excitement over the deer.

Or I don't look. I flip open a magazine instead.

Or I take a few photos of fellow passengers peering out the window with an aim to publish the picture.

Or a tourist a few seats away leaps up from her seat excitedly, suffers a heart attack, and I and others rush to her aid.

Or I yell at the driver for stomping on the brakes, my neck lurching forward almost smacking the seat back.

Or I miss seeing the animal entirely, my gaze too high or low or left. I must believe others have seen what I have not.

Or I don't believe them. Perhaps it was a goat.

An endless stream of possibilities emerge as they can from any experience. Yet we regularly seize our initial experience of seeing or touching or listening and institute them into a collection of ideas that can trap us, knowingly or not, to consequent goals, expectations, and actions. This tendency we have is *sunyata*, the Buddhist notion of emptiness which recognizes that no thing possesses an inherent or enduring quality until mind or culture colors it. We perceive what we expect, consciously or not, and overlook the rest.

"Do not attach," says the doctor during an earlier phone conversation on Buddhism. "Not to feelings, not to circumstance, not to love, not to fear. Like the wind. Koreans aim to be like wind."

I look out the window. Light catches my eye. A smudge on the glass reveals grass unevenly cut, each blade seemingly merging with the ones beside it to create a green carpet. I slip off my shoes to sit in lotus position and try to fall asleep.

Tango Returns

It's been a while since I've tangoed. Can continues to mourn Pala and hasn't returned to the place where their love took root and blossomed. His absence has meant no Salsita for me either. He was my centerpiece, my eye continually following him as he adorned the floor with each partner, his leg sliding easily between his partners, his torso bent forward as if with amorous intent. As my teacher, he guided my misplaced hand into its rightful place on his arm or demonstrated again, sometimes again and again, about keeping my knees together while swinging my foot backward for a *goncho*, *saceda, cerrado*, Spanish words whose meanings I easily understood but couldn't embody with his grace. His absence left an empty space on the floor and in my enthusiasm.

Minji, now my assistant, expresses interest in going. Juno found a girlfriend, a Korean girl, and since then, he shows up to my office infrequently. Even while he worked for me, he regularly littered the table with his candy wrappers and empty soda cans which never found their way to the trash unless I tossed them. Minji took it upon herself to empty the trash and clean the room. Now my official assistant, she continues to clean, but she's also acquired a coffee maker and regularly stocks my shelves with tea, coffee and cookies. She revels in every chore and opportunity to serve me, pouting in the doorway if I say there's nothing for her to do for me.

She grabs a ginseng candy from the tin beside the napkins on my bookshelf. "I want to see what tango like." Whether she's serving me or herself little matters. A few days later, we board the subway together.

"There may only be several people in attendance," I say, watching the passenger across from me touch up her makeup in the reflection of her cell phone. "It's been so long, I may not know anyone." I prepare her—and me—for what to expect. "Maybe one man will ask me to dance, or a few. I never know."

She fears being asked to dance. "I not want to dance, Professor. Only watch."

"If a guy asks, just say, Thanks, no."

She blushes and lets out a breath of relief.

I, too, am a bit nervous. It's one thing to enter a room of people and maneuver the awkward territory of small talk, but if after months you've learned little Korean, you at best resort to a wave, smile, nod, or if ambitious, a fumbled, barely remembered phrase. "*Man-na sau pan gop-simnida*," Nice to meet you. Or "*Chung mal chile-choo she-ne-yo*," You dance very well. My listener smiles, I hope, because a resemblance of my intention has been communicated, my attempt to break through the language barrier a success.

As we climb the stairwell, voices from the second-floor restaurant where Can, I, and others frequent between lessons and open dancing compel me to poke my head into the doorway. A group sits on the floor around a table eating dinner, and a man I've not danced with before waves to us. The gesture increases my ease.

Salsita is surprisingly packed. People crowd the bar, every couch and stool occupied with *tangueras* in slitted skirts and *tangueros* in dress shirts or snug-fitted tees. Others lean against the walls and mirrors. I wonder if we've stumbled into a show. The bartender welcomes us with a broad grin as I hand him our money.

Minji sits beside me on a couch where I replace my sandals with tango shoes. Within minutes, the photographer Dae-ook rushes over. I hadn't seen him since dinner at his apartment with his wife, two children, Can, and Pala, a dinner to be the last meal Pala ever cooked. He gives me a large embrace, takes my hand, and speaks rapidly and at length. Minji translates. "Glad to see me. Thanks for my support of Pala and Can. Very helpful. Join his tango class next week. Six more weeks left to the session. Free."

"I leave in five."

"Leave?" he says in English, either unsure of his pronunciation or astonished to hear that I was offered and accepted a position at the University of Tulsa.

"Home I return. U.S. New job." I've adopted a habit of speaking mostly in single syllables outside of class, my English sounding more and more Konglish, my sentences clipped, grammar skewed.

He falls silent, then announces he wants to throw me a party. I look to Minji. "Tell him I agree." I turn to him. "Okay." This he understands.

He pulls me up from the couch and leads me onto the floor, my first dance of the evening, the month, longer. The straps of my shoes have stretched since last wear and increase my difficulty in grounding with the floor and leaning trustfully against him. Whereas Can dances with supple wonder, Da-ook stands with rapt precision, his body and mine brought into a quick, crisp focus, much like his photography which decorates the walls in his apartment. We tune briefly as my foot lifts in preparation.

By now, I shouldn't be amazed at how immediately delight arrives once my body begins its glide around the floor. Whenever I step into the hold of a partner, one hand in clasp, the other clutching an upper arm, it's as if my body is navigating intimate space, breath, and heat for the first time, my smile as uncontainable as a child's. The freedom in moving through space intoxicates and sobers me. We sail around the floor, my elbow pert as I follow his lead.

He escorts me back to the couch after only one dance because others are pushing furniture to one side of the room, a sign that something other than dancing is about to take place. Everyone finds a chair, arm of a chair, or out of the way place to stand and settle in as spectators. Da-ook walks to the center of the room and begins talking, again at length and with great speed. "New tango manager," interprets Minji leaning into me whispering. But there's more to what he's said, much more. Groups of five to fifteen people take turns crossing the room to one of the mirrored walls. One by one, they bow, give their name, and say something about themselves.

"I don't know any of them," I say to Minji about the first group. "Them either," I say about the next group.

When all groups introduce themselves, Da-ook returns to the center and opens his mouth about to talk. But before any sounds emerge, the onlookers begin to chant like fans at a football game. Eventually my ear tunes to their words: "the foreigner, the foreigner, the foreigner."

"Oh, Professor, that's you," Minji says excitedly. There could be no other. I, of course, stick out like a slice of apple pie on a plate of *kimchi*. "They want you to introduce yourself."

I, a group of one, cross the room, bow, a coterie of Korean eyes peering at me. There is much I want to say beyond my name. I wave to Minji, urging her to join me and translate. She rounds her shoulders, reluctant to take my side.

I introduce myself, me, solo American, Cheryl, living in Daegu, not tangoing for a few months, how wonderful to begin again. Great to see so many people enjoying themselves. I turn toward Minji to translate. Blah blah blah improvisation blah blah blah English blah blah blah Virginia blah blah blah Oklahoma. The few words I understand I didn't say. We bow together and when we sit back down, I ask for an explanation.

"I say you are my professor and I very sad that you leaving." I forgive her for favoring her expression over mine. She already does enough for me.

Dae-ook comes over and explains to Minji how tango men ask

191

women to dance, sometimes with their eyes, sometimes with words. Cheryl, he says, is a challenge. Not only is she a professor but she speaks English. The men are afraid of her. He urges them to have courage and tries to convince them about how nice I am. Once he finishes his explanation of tango custom and my precarious place in their society, he puts out his hand and invites Minji onto the dance floor. Immediately she scoots back on the couch, shields her chest with a cushion, and slinks down. "No! No!" she says with increasing volume while slouching further, a response whose intensity baffles me.

I get in a few more dances before we head downstairs for the subway. Once on the street, I thank her for getting me to come back to the club.

She turns to me, her eyes bright. "This weekend, I say to God, why you make my life unhappy? You want me to be sad always? But tonight, watching tango, I see another world. I happy." Then she grabs hold of my arm for the duration of the walk.

The following week, Hero wants to see this other world, too. A student from my composition class, he answered a question correctly for a department sponsored contest and won a pair of movie tickets because of information I provided one afternoon. During our mid-class break, he says he wants to take me. I squirm, trying to hide my discomfort, uninterested in what seems like a date, but then assume his intention more innocent and accept. He claps his hands and grins while pushing his glasses up the ridge of his nose. "I tell class. Ask if they want to go, too!" He positions himself at my podium to address his classmates.

A week later, only red dyed hair Sang Hwi accompanies Hero and me. At twenty-eight, both having completed their requisite two years of military service, I am struck, as is the case with the majority of my students, by their seeming naivete, behaviors I typically attribute to grade or middle school students. They slap each other on the back, playfully push and nudge with their hands or elbow, and delight in each other's comments. Their physical comfort leads me to think they're long-time friends, but they tell me as we walk three abreast that they've never gone out together before.

192

We sit in the last row at the cinema to watch a mystery thriller and afterwards dine at an Indian restaurant. "Too spicy," asks Hero.

"Is good," replies Sang Hwi.

We pay the bill and as I'm rummaging through my bag for my subway card to return back to my apartment, Hero requests another activity together.

"What?" asks Sang Hwi of Hero as we stroll past shops for cosmetics, jeans, and sun glasses.

Hero answers in Korean and Sang Hwi nods vigorously in agreement. "Oh, sorry Professor," says Hero, now ready to translate, "I say I want picture of us."

I'm expecting him to pull out his cell phone and us to squeeze together on the sidewalk within aim of his phone's lens, but he has another idea in mind.

A few blocks away is a brightly lit store with aisle upon aisle of photobooths, an entire colony of them, all imported from Japan. The exterior of each booth is painted in dazzling bright colors, cute animated figures, and glittery bold letters. "Which you want," asks Hero as he points dizzily from one to another. I walk past the booths, unable to see much difference between sparkly hoola-hoops and smiley faced butterflies with polka-dotted bees. Periodically a curtain pulls back and giggling girls and boys exit. I imagine someone is about to offer me blue cotton candy, pink cupcakes, and invite me to a game of Pin the Tail on the Donkey. I consider escaping this pubescent psychodelia, but don't want to disappoint my companions.

"Whichever you choose is fine with me," I offer.

Hero chooses one with monkeys dangling from moons and pigs riding asteroids, and in we go. Once our coins are deposited, we continually reposition ourselves on two levels of benches, squeezing in close, pressing our slanting heads together, lifting a leg or arm in front, to the side, or across each other. We're laughing and yanking each other's hair, blocking another's sight with our hands, limbs in a twist, and I'm saying words in Korean that no one understands, and we're eight or twelve years old, all of us playmates buzzing on sugar from

193

eating a tray load of cupcakes, a bag of licorice, and several flavors of lollipops.

When we use up our allotted shots, we reconvene at a nearby booth and the guys press buttons in a decorating frenzy. Ziz-zags, stars, diamonds, hearts, squiggles, hexagons, and every imaginable cartoonish doodle appear on a screen and they laugh nonstop while superimposing these shapes upon our image. The machine spits out our images from a slot and we view the results, unerasable evidence of degeneration, our bubbly trio caught in poses like the flashy posters or CD covers of teen bands at the height of their fame.

Already an accomplice, it's no surprise that Hero wants to join Minji and me at tango. He meets us downtown outside a subway stop. We chat for the first few blocks before street and sidewalk construction forces us into a single file. Every several yards poses a new set of challenges, uneven gravel, a bonded felt walkway, toppled plastic cones, men with drills kicking up dust. I aim for flat surfaces wherever possible. Suddenly, it's a Gene Kelly moment, but instead of rain and umbrellas, I'm kicking up dirt and hopping up onto the thin ledge in front of a restaurant or onto a bench at a bus stop with arms stretched wide for fullest dramatic effect.

"Professor!" exclaims Hero to Minji. "She not behave like professor!"

"Yes," confirms Minji, "she like child."

I turn around to look at them and Minji is smiling knowingly. This time, she gives me an approving thumbs up.

Good Deeds and Other Threats

I receive a text message on my phone from the doctor's wife. "Yae son of Beach killd you." I'm not familiar with the beach spirit, Yae-son, whom she's conjured, get busy with classes, later realizing the actual ill intent of her mangled words.

Two days pass and the messages continue, every few hours a new one, in broken English, in Korean that Daria translates, some as voice mails. All threaten me with death. I don't know what has prompted her latest round of wrath and mention it to a colleague. "Ignore it. Korean wives do that from time to time. Need to vent somehow. Nothing serious."

Depends on how you define serious.

I've taken to turning my phone off but once back on, a handful of electronic daggers await me.

Lily calls to tell me the wife called her wanting help in arranging a secret meeting with me, the wife to surprise me with her presence. "She sounded very strange on the phone. I didn't like her voice or manner. I told her no."

"Good. Because she's been calling to say she wants to kill me."

Depends, I guess, on how you define kill. I don't know if she's content to spit fire across cellular frequencies and sear me with her words or if she'll chuck the phone for a more lethal instrument deliverable in person. Getting drunk may determine the potency of her vitriol.

"She's crazy. She's done something like this before at Salsita," says Lily. "She's not happy. I'm sorry she's doing this to you."

I ask another colleague for advice. "Ignore it," he offers, before adding. "What is she saying?"

"Other than wishing me dead, I don't know. I'm not translating every message."

We solicit help from a graduate student who works in the main office. He scrolls down through my messages and leaps up from his chair gasping. "Go to police!"

"What do they say," asks my colleague.

"Too terrible to repeat."

My colleague invites me into his office where he shares stories about how poorly the police treat foreigners. "So what do I do?" I say, not appreciating the vulnerability of my minority status. It's getting harder and harder to concentrate on planning classes. I'm forgetting books in my apartment, forgetting words in class, forgetting what I walked to buy at the market. Each time the phone vibrates or rings, my back stiffens and the contents of my stomach roil, intruders encroaching upon my usual calm.

"Call the doctor. Does he know she's doing this?"

"She out of control," the doctor explains. "Won't listen to me or anyone else."

Great, I think. "Many of the messages come from your phone."

"My phone?" He knows she confiscated his phone, but didn't realize how she was using it.

"She signs her messages from you." One message tried to get me to visit the clinic. Aside from my not having been to the clinic in months, her misspells gave her away, her pattern of errors unlike the doctor's.

"Do you recognize these numbers?" I rattle off numbers of callers from the last few days. He recognizes them as from his daughter and his sister-in-law. Apparently, she took their phones, too.

I tell him about going to the police. "Good idea," he says.

I find out where the nearest police station is, but realize I need a translator to go with me. The people I most trust are all foreigners, yet I'm unsure whether their help lessens or increases my trouble.

I call one of my Korean colleagues. "Ignore it," she insists. "It's nothing." Again, I'm told her response is typical of a woman in a failed marriage.

It's hard to ignore this type of nothing. I can ignore the nothing of a sprinkle of rain, the nothing of a loud ticking watch, the nothing of hair that falls into my eyes. I can ignore the nothing of a student clicking his pen, falling asleep in class, a paper turned in late. I can skillfully ignore a whole cluster of nothings. But when voluminous words poisoned by hate and bitterness greet me day after day first thing in the morning and stop only when I turn off my phone for the night, this sort of nothing is impossible to ignore.

I am locking my office door, asking whoever knocks to identify themselves. I am peering around the corner of the hall and inside the classroom before going in. I cautiously open the door into the restroom and look under the stalls for shoes that don't appear to be those of a professor. I've become preoccupied with my safety, feeling more and more helpless, the pitied character in a news story whose tale of suffering upsets me, but with whom, after turning the page and going for a walk, I usually can leave her or his woe behind. That buffer falls apart now. The page does not turn. It is my phone ringing and vibrating. It is my phone with bold type and multiple exclamation points. It is my mind obsessing about if or when she'll follow through on her threats.

Then, on the morning that I'm determined to find an appropriate translator and go to the police, my phone is oddly quiet. Has the storm blown over the mountain to the sea?

A day later, a Sunday, the clouds reform and darken. She crosses the line into total impropriety by threatening to harm my students.

First thing Monday morning, I meet with the chair of my department to enlist her help.

"This situation is not good," she says stating the obvious. "She phoned me, too. I don't want information about this getting out. It's best that no one at school knows." I rest my hands on my legs, sit back, not sure where she's headed, unsure if I can count on her for support. She continues, "I want this to go away."

Go away. The phrase echoes, then repeats. Go away. How do I make it go away? Deny the story? Deny the entire story? I never met the doctor. I do not dance tango. My spine is not curved. I am not a writer. I am not a professor. I am a traveler with the misfortune of being a woman from nowhere in particular. Just like that, erase my history, my perspective, even that I exist. Erased of a past, I feel suddenly free and realize then that if the doctor and I were to meet again, I may not withhold the full expression of my feelings for him.

But then I return to the impossibility of my erasure and blurt out what's become my recent mantra, "But what can I do?"

"To be frank with you, I don't know." She pushes a stack of books aside and leans across the table. "What would you do if you were at home?"

"Call the police. Or a women's shelter."

197

"A women's shelter? We don't have anything like that." She falls silent. "Hmm, let me make a phone call."

I await the translation, the clear path toward resolution, the words that will close the curtain to this scene and dissipate my tension.

"She doesn't know either," she says hanging up on the unnamed caller.

"I'd like to go to the police," I voice up. "But I need help. I need someone to go with me to translate."

"Your assistant," she suggests.

I can't imagine happy-go-lucky Juno or docile Minji as beneficial advocates. Wouldn't the status that comes with their age prevent them from challenging the police, if necessary, and speaking up for me? "I prefer it if you went with me. If you could," I add.

She offers disapproval, Korean style; she doesn't say anything. Then, "Perhaps I should try talking to her husband."

"Do that," I urge, "and tell him about my going to the police." Once he's on the phone, she makes several hesitant ughs and ohs, polite, gentle sounds that don't match the more emphatic ones I would have chosen.

When she terminates the call, she shares with me that he agreed to call his wife to request she stop. If the calls continue, I should go to the police. He'll get back to us later.

Later. This word refers to a succession of nows, perhaps minutes, hours, even a few months worth of them. In his case, I expect later to mean a day or two. I'm also expecting, given their tumultuous history, that his request either goes unheeded or fuels her anger. Later, to my surprise, takes place much sooner and with equally surprising results. He calls back after a few minutes to say that his wife has agreed to stop calling.

And just like that, my phone reclaims its previous peaceful purpose. Calls come from students and friends asking to meet for lunch, coffee, usual casual requests, friendly voices, benign messages, my fingers happily punching keys to text a response. When I walk through the hallway, the light seems to have brightened, and the stress in my back and stomach has already moved on.

But change, as I well know, is constant. Nothing remains the same, or not for long. Marriage, fear, peace, all eventually morph into something else, hoped for or not, tangible or phantasmic. Sometimes the change takes a form unlike anything you might imagine.

Consider missiles. Long range ones. Consider jet propulsion, projectiles made with metals like titanium and magnesium and mounted with explosive warheads, nuclear ones. Consider deadly munitions capable of reaching Daegu or Japan or Russia or the U.S. Consider yourself a target. Typically, these sorts of images reside neither in the forefront nor the hinterlands of my imagination. Until now, that is.

N. Korea decided it will no longer honor its truce with the South. It needs to vent, to get a few missiles off its nationalistic chest. Is this saber rattling or something more dangerous, question the news writers. Other than the media, no one in class, at the coffee shop, at Salsita, or on the subway are talking about this unnerving development. Is this an example of Korean complacency, their customary non-reply to an unpleasantry, or is it an instance of my American paranoia?

One morning as I dress for class, several fighter jets fly over my apartment building. There's an airbase nearby so the roar is not so unusual. About an hour later, while I walk up the hill to class, more jets streak across the sky—less common. I search for justification, fear seeking a coat tail of reason. It's another test run, the previous one failed; a pilot didn't fly in unison or was mistakenly ejected. My nerves recently patched from the wife's attacks are fraying again.

In class, the threads loosen further; I'm standing behind the podium teaching when a thunderous boom shakes the building. I stop talking. I look out the frosted windows, unable to see anything other than shadows. I look at the students. Their eyes are fixed on me, but I can't tell if they're afraid or waiting for me to tell them to turn the page. No one says a thing. No one moves. I'm convinced a bomb has fallen and a band-aid of denial is keeping them calm in their seats. Yet when no one runs down the hall screaming and no noxious fumes slip in through the window to burn skin and eyes and vaporize my students and our books, I conclude that all is safe—for now—and I turn their attention to the exercises at the end of the chapter.

In the days that follow, the menacing rhetoric from the North escalates, this belligerent nation now fully replacing frightful fantasies of the wife. Unlike the wife, however, the Dear Leader's military makes good on his threats. A missile, supposedly carrying only satellite equipment, is launched from a base on the east coast, fragments landing benignly in the sea near Japan. A few days later, another missile is launched. Then another. More follow. The media features experts arguing over how to interpret the North's actions. A show of might and unity intended to rally the people to obey Kim Jung Un, the son expected to assume the post of Dear Leader's post? A muscle flexing tantrum aimed at getting respect from the west? What about the health of the elusive Kim Jung-il? Is he still alive? The hair and shoes and bend of finger in every photo of him is scrutinized for clues of health and authenticity.

Meanwhile, riots are flaring up in Seoul, citizens angry over how President Lee Myung-bak pursued the investigation into the bribery allegations of ex-president Roh. Lee is prohibiting any public displays of mourning. No one is allowed to convene in Seoul Square, a small grassy plot of land in the city's center that in the late 1980's became the symbol of democracy and freedom of assembly. The president cites the official reason for the prohibition as wanting to deter traffic congestion, but citizens see through his flimsy lie. Police buses are parked bumper to bumper around the square and heavily armed guards stand shoulder to shoulder in the area to keep out any sniffling, crouching, flower laying trespassers who might, just might, display not grief but anger.

I bring up the events in my graduate class. Students glare at me like deer caught in a car's headlight. A few move their chairs, the legs scraping the floor. A few others look around the room to see who might speak up.

"I'm nervous," admits one finally.

"Me, too," says another, one by one, their voices faltering in admission of concern. We talk about the perils and benefits of reunification. On the down side is economic stress, the South needing to share its wealth, amenities, jobs, and government support. The North's extreme poverty would slow or halt the South's steady rise. On the up side, family members would finally be able to share a meal and visit ancestral graves. A suffering people would find relief.

Talk returns to the launching of missiles. The North has played this sort of game before, explains one, but not to this degree. This time, the threat is more menacing, the stakes higher. Yet no one is alarmed enough to do anything. Their hands remain folded on their desk and all face forward with as much aplomb as ever. No one comments on the police presence at Seoul Square, so I don't press the issue and hide my surprise by pretending to pencil notes into my book.

I'm hoping that the luck generated from the massive crowds who visited Bulkugsa, Sekorum, and the hundreds of other temples around the country on Buddha's birthday has traction now, that the wishes of a few million people is potent enough to keep missiles in their bays. But it may be that the luck supply is already depleted, every sack empty, or the rain kept too many people away and, therefore, too little luck was generated. Or perhaps it's how you define luck and where you place the beginning and end of a story.

Worried friends and family from home, less willing to see what side turns up in the roll of the dice, are emailing. "Just leave," says one. "Pack up and return to the States."

The idea holds appeal, but classes haven't ended. "So you break your contract," pleads another, "you'll be alive." If war were to break out, an idea a few of my students have begun to entertain, leaving behind so many people I care about provides me with little comfort.

My departure is scheduled to take place in a few weeks, after grades are turned in and the appeals period ends. I begin to prepare. I walk across campus to transfer money and close my bank account.

Whenever a customer enters the bank, a guard at the door yells in Korean. I've never asked what he's shouting, something like "Greetings Customer!" or "Order up!" Tellers perched in booths ready their fingers for handing out change, explaining an overdraft charge, or calculating

interest rates of a CD. I grab a number from a machine that assigns me to a window, although there's only one teller with decent English skills and every teller I get passes me on to him. He sits behind a desk, dimples punctuating his constant smile, a courtesy that comes at a price. As the youngest and most recently hired worker, therefore, with the lowest status at the branch, he is expected to work longer hours than everyone else. Six days a week, he is the first to enter the bank and the last to leave, often staying as long as fourteen hours. He gets blamed for anything that goes wrong, a malfunctioning ATM machine or a customer unhappy with the lack of *won* accumulating in his account. So intense is his stress, the left side of his face stopped moving and registering sensation. Each morning before coming to work, he receives acupuncture to restore motion and feeling.

I pull my chair in close to his desk and ask, "How's your cheek."

He tears up. "That so very nice of you," he says. "Nobody ask how I am."

My hand is poised to troll through my bag for my ID but holds still, preferring to pursue this more immediate transaction. There is time enough for him to pull out the requisite forms for me to fill out, the necessary stamps and copying of my passport. Right now, it's his flesh that concerns me, that tender, pliant membrane that distinguishes him from all others and helps connect him with computers, people, and the world nearby.

"There is time," I tell him.

There is time, I tell myself.

Reaching Toward the Present

We put on our shoes, I lock the door behind us, the contact improvisation students and I heading up the stairs out the main door into the evening. We linger under the lights in the courtyard outside the gym, our bags slung over our shoulder. Last week Daria suggested we get *patbingsu* and the group of us crossed the street arm in arm to dip our spoons into this shaved ice, bean, and fruit treat. Tonight no one suggests a cafe nor does anyone rush away. Everyone knows I'm leaving in a few weeks and won't return next semester. When someone brings up my departure, one or a few of them tear up. "You come back, dance with us again," insists Hee-jon."I miss you already."

"Maybe I return," I say. In all honesty, I don't know what's possible. Other than immediate events and measurable hours on a watch, time and schedules have abstracted, as tangible as a neutron emitting an electron. In a year or two, maybe my fingers will seek a crevice as my legs push me higher up a cliff or maybe I'll be pedaling my bicycle through the streets. In what state or country any of this takes place, I don't know.

Before coming to Korea, I was committed to a house, a husband, a routine, but now my feet set out roots groundward while additional roots turn skyward like a tillandsia plant that thrives on the air and absorbs nutrients from whatever mist or insect happens by. I am moving again, this time to a job in Oklahoma. Like my draw to Korea, something unnameable calls me to this forty-sixth state to join the Union, perhaps a person or a prairie or an opportunity to engage with beauty and breath.

"Anything is possible," I say to Minji who is crying freely. "Maybe you'll visit me in the U.S. or I'll come back," I say, an established global nomad. It's odd not to firm a plan or provide the latitude and longitude of where I'll be living. In another year, I may be crossing an ocean or hemisphere or state yet again.

With each passing dance class, we linger longer and longer in a loose huddle. We lean into each other, arms draped or twined with the person next to us, our limbs at ease to explore new ways to move and fit together, the lessons from class extending into this more casual setting. The guard has developed a habit of joining us after each class, no longer to rant, but hovering a few feet away, his knees bent as if ready to dance should any of us pull him in. He and a fellow guard stand with us and welcome the opportunity to get a photo taken with me.

As Soojeon initiates a hug, there's the rumble of a motorcycle. Can pulls up beneath the covered walkway, turns off the ignition, legs straddling his bike, and removes his helmet.

"Professor return to U.S.," announces Soojeon.

"I know," he responds. "Salsita miss you." But Can, not one to linger in long goodbyes, arrived with a mission. "Take ride?" he says to me.

I secure my bag, climb on, and wrap my arms around his torso. There's nowhere he or I need or want to go nor do we discuss a destination. I press against him as he turns up the hill to the chapel, the moon peering out from behind the mountain. We reach the parking lot at the top and he immediately turns back down the road, crossing the campus to the east, then north, then west, past the library, the administrative building, and student commons, both of us happy to ride, synching our bodies to motion, his hair tickling my face, my hands clasping his belly, air flowing easily over our skin.

A few nights later in my apartment, Daria and I cook a meal which couples familiar western ingredients with unfamiliar Asian ones and only approximates a Russian or American dish. The butter is not quite buttery and the crust of the bread too soft. The ginger, seaweed, mushrooms, bean sprouts, zucchini and tofu tossed into a skillet don't quite rise to Korean cuisine either. We make do, delighting in the creamy treasure claimed from the refrigerator, our homesick mouths welcoming each lovingly cut sliver of brie recently discovered at a market that caters to westerners.

In a few days, she leaves for Russia by ship. I've asked her to reconsider her plan, a two-day trip skirting N. Korea. I don't want any "test" missiles hitting her boat intentionally or mistakenly. After we wash dishes, I accompany her to Morrison's Bar to return a book borrowed from the owner and bring up my request again.

"If it's my time to go, then it's my time," she responds, her arm around my waist as we walk past a building with a hand cranked cement mixer on the sidewalk. "I'm not worried. I want to go the slow way home." Once the ship deposits her on Russian soil, she'll board a train for a fifteen-day trek across her homeland's plains and pine thickets to arrive at her parents' house. A flight would place her safely in their arms in fourteen hours.

People in pre- or post-alcohol euphoria crowd the street to Morrison's. Talk is loud, interspersed by spitting, usually after the toss of a cigarette. A car squeezes around a tight corner with several parked cars and misses hitting us by inches.

The hall outside the bar is dimly lit, the entrance a solid, windowless door. There's a small sign on the first floor near the building's entrance, but like so many establishments around the city, you wouldn't know it existed unless someone gave you precise directions with landmarks, building description, and the number of flights to climb. She pushes open the door, the eyes of a poster of Jim Morrison following us in.

"Hey Boss," she says, using the expected Korean address, she his junior and former employee, never even learning his name. He walks out from behind the counter to give her a hug. When he learns that I, too, am leaving the country, he insists on giving me a gift. He wanders around the bar, pausing to eye various specimens of his collection. He returns with an orange lacquered egg constellated with cubic zirconium standing on gold legs.

He says something to me in Korean which Daria translates. "He says you deserve an elegant piece because of your grace. He wants you to always remember him and to return anytime. His home at Morrison's is your home."

Over the next few weeks, many students request we meet for coffee, lunch, or dinner for a farewell. A few call only days later to get together again, as if the previous meeting didn't occur or only a second goodbye suffices. Yena, who has not brought up the shaman ceremony since we attended, says, "This time we walk, Professor. We must take photo."

Minji and I talk almost daily. After inserting the key in my office door and discovering it unlocked, I find her at the table studying for finals, drafting a letter for a job, or waiting for me, just in case she's needed. "Professor want coffee? Need sesame oil?" She lists a series of items, hoping, it seems, that one may prolong my stay. I accept her offer to drive me to the airport.

On the second to last morning, the doctor calls. The new clinic opened with great fanfare two weeks ago. "I very sad you not attend," he says. There was, of course, no way I would consider going and he knew it. But now, twenty or so hours before I board my plane, he insists I see the new space. "Without your help, I have no clinic. Because of you, I happy man. You must visit." I'm still unsure, beyond listening and asking questions, what I did to help birth his dream. Foolishly or not, I agree to visit the clinic.

We meet in the brass and marble lobby of the building and ride the elevator to the twelfth floor. I'm nervous, my breath shallow, my ears cued to sound, any sound, my eyes alert to sudden movement. I know he would never trick me but I can't trust his wife to not find out about our meeting, eager to leap out from the emergency stairwell or from behind a door, weapon in hand.

He unlocks the clinic door and turns on the lights. Small individual pools of circulating water have replaced plastic chairs. Waiting patients can dip their feet or sit nearby at a table for tea. Everywhere is bamboo, wood, and numerous potted plants. He shows me the view from his office which overlooks the busy intersection floors below. "Here I meditate," he says as we walk into an adjacent, corner room with two walls of windows. Several paintings in bubble wrap await placement on a wall and lean against a book shelf.

Each room is a soft shade of green, more lively than his previous clinic dragged down by a drab white. "Good color," I say.

"Remind me of Cheryl's smile," he replies. "Every room is you. You like?" he says with the pride of a tenant who recently signed papers.

"It's beautiful. I know your patients will be happy. Their health will return more quickly."

He points to a large picture on the wall, his parents sitting side by side on a couch looking directly out, the backdrop a hazy screen from a professional's studio. "They with me, too."

I don't want to stay long and suggest we leave. He locks the door behind us and we pause in the hallway. He begins telling me a story from the Choseon period: A few hundred years ago, a princess from the Koguryo Kingdom journeyed south with her father across many mountains to the Silla Kingdom to attend a ceremony. After many days of walking, her porters lowered her palanquin at a palace and she stepped out in all her silken finery. Immediately, her eyes met those of a prince. At dinner, they sat close, talk and an unbroken gaze igniting a tinder of love. The prince marveled at her voice and demeanor and the princess cherished his quiet strength. They retreated to their separate quarters for the night, the flame of their love growing. Their love could only burn so far however. Their parents had already chosen spouses and the smitten pair were keen to obey their parent's wishes. On the day the porters pulled closed the curtain on her palanquin to head back north, their eyes met a last time. Neither stepped into the other's kingdom ever again, although every day for the rest of their lives, they connected in spirit, the presence of each other alive in their respective palaces.

"You and me spirit connect," he says concluding the story. "Always when I meditate, I think of you. I with you in mind." Then he stands up straighter and bows. Deeply. "You my forever friend. My love for you like wind." One of those winds carries him closer toward me and we kiss.

My feet are angled toward the elevator, one step in Korea, the other eager for American soil, yet the warm press of our lips sets into motion a dream of having kissed many times before, years, decades, longer. In an eon of a moment, I am floating on the ocean hearing the ringing of temple bells, I am traipsing across a field carrying a sack of rice, and I am sitting on the floor with chopsticks plucking mackerel. Or maybe it's him carrying the rice and separating the bones from the fish's flesh. Or it's corn or wheat in the sack and I or he is a seed carried by a breeze. In the stillness of the hallway, we are dancing tango in glide with the music of our blood and breath yet our feet do not move nor our fingers braid and the elevator door opens awaiting in emptiness. I am myself and not myself, glad that our lips touch, the membrane around my heart in quiver, sad, very sad, to depart this dream.

Who are these people who have entered my life, these people

whom I now leave? Will I see any of them again? Which promises of staying in contact hold up over the miles and years?

Do any commitments last?

Missiles fly across the sea. Moony got married, a few of my students engaged. Men throw themselves off cliffs and in front of subways. Students sit in my classes and at the table in my office. Can has taken up golf. Chardin found a job with the forestry service in California. Soyoung the minister continues to sit by her mother's bedside. I read the resume of the woman who is to be my replacement next semester. The spotty cell phone coverage in my apartment still requires calls get answered on the porch or in the hall. I haven't learned more than several phrases of Korean and *Hangul* remains as remote an alphabet as ever.

Two suitcases flew across the Pacific with me and these same two bags refilled return. A quilt and a few dozen books have already been sent. I tuck a few snacks into zippers of my backpack for the lengthy plane ride.

Epilogue

After a nineteen-hour drive divided into three days, I pull into the garage in Tulsa and fumble around for the keys to enter the brick house that is to be my new home. I hesitate to use the word "home." In time, I hope, my new dwelling will provide comfort. Fifteen hundred square feet will house my clothing and books. A queen-sized bed will provide a needed surface for rest, and a kitchen with ample cabinets awaits its fill of pasta, lentils, nuts, and bread. Already a small stack of mail has arrived. I thumb through the stack and pull out a bill for hooking up electricity and an ad for a Chickasaw powwow featuring people with names like Impichchaachaaha and Tahdooahnippah. Both are in English, the letters gloriously readable.

I have returned to the U.S. but I may never return completely. I am not the same person I was a year ago. Nor a moment ago. I am continually arriving, watching thought, watching feeling, seeing arise what I believe is mine, then watching as it departs.

Now inhale. Exhale. Inhale again.

Before my trip to the Midwest, I stopped in Richmond to the house that one day I hope to move back into. Friends and I gathered at an art gallery to hear a band perform in benefit for two women fighting breast cancer. Halfway through the show, the drummer left his drums to join those of us on the floor dancing. Sticks in the air, he squatted beside one woman, then a man, in kinetic play to the music, the crowd absorbing him like a pool of water encountering a droplet. His seat in the band now empty, I vacate my spot on the floor, grab the pair of drum sticks on the snare and with loose wrists, play air percussion. At some point, the fieriness of the music draws my sticks closer to the surface of one drum and I strike it, then hit one and another, the cymbals too, my repeated strikes accenting the rhythms helping to drive a beat. Fellow musicians glance at their impromptu band member and play on without interruption.

After carrying in a few boxes from the car, I sit on the carpeted floor in the living room. Five large windows, a fireplace, and an archway that leads to the dining room wall me off from other rooms and my neighbors. I turn on music, tango fused with African overlays. A woman's sultry voice rises up like smoke. I slap my thighs and the floor in accompaniment. After so many hours of driving, it's good to be in one place and engage muscles previously restrained by driving. The music stirs my sluggish self to get up and move about the room, feel the breeze slipping in through the window, and notice the orange glow from the setting sun. I stretch arms, legs, and torso in invitation of breath and space. When the music cuts off, I return to the floor, lie flat, and energy rises up my spine and materializes as syllables land upon my tongue. I chant, "Sha-bu-jew, Sha-bu-jew." Sounds vibrate me to the bone, a *niggun*, the Hebrew word for a spirit language or song beyond words, mouth movements connecting to something primordial, a yearning along with its satisfaction, a coalescence of an ever-shifting identity. At some point, I fall asleep because the next thing I know the room is dark and there is no movement or music except for the chirp of crickets hidden in the grass and flower beds outside my window.

I am alone. Exquisitely.

About the Author

Cheryl Pallant is a poet, dancer, and healer who has authored several books. She teaches dance and writing at University of Richmond.

96534864R00131

Made in the USA
Columbia, SC
01 June 2018